Harvard English Studies 4

Uses of Literature

HARVARD ENGLISH STUDIES 4

Uses of Literature

Edited by Monroe Engel

Harvard University Press, Cambridge, Massachusetts 1973

Publication of this volume has been aided by a grant from the Hyder
Edward Rollins Fund
Library of Congress Catalog Card Number 73–82627
Printed in the United States of America

Editorial Note

We know that the life of a literary work depends on readers whose existence it confirms or (the more valuable possibility) augments. This formulation and variants of it are both embarrassingly obvious and embarrassingly easy to forget, and anyone who is engaged in literary studies is peculiarly subject to both embarrassments.

When contributions were solicited for this volume, its working title was "The Uses of Literature in the United States," and the intent of the title, it was explained, was "to have this assumption exemplified rather than discussed or debated." The volume differs from its predecessors in this series in having neither the immediate thematic unity *of Veins of Humor* nor the historical unity of *Twentieth-Century Literature in Retrospect*. Its coherence is rather that of a periodical with reasonably defined and delimited interests.

The essays that now make up the volume are grouped in three sections, as considerations of theory, practice, and teaching. The net is wide, but the catch has common characteristics. All the essays move, explicitly or implicitly, from the concrete particularity of the historical and cultural situation in which we find ourselves; and each, some more and some less overtly, suggests that the vitality of the literary enterprise is related to usability, its capacity to strengthen or alter our options. So among the critical essays in Section Two, for example, two are concerned with American attitudes toward war, one surveys a contemporary American novelist's use of history, one considers women as a special audience for fiction. The theoretical essays in Section One seem necessarily, I think, to originate less concretely in our present problematic climate until we fasten particularly and in juxtaposition on their subjects: habit, originality, religious perspectives on literature. The cogency of an essay on the resistance of literary studies to significant self-examination will be apparent to anyone who has followed the professional polemics of the past several years at all — and should be of particular interest to anyone who feels that neither the crudity of the attack nor self-interest justifies the narrowness of the defense.

I suppose that the thematic congruence of the essays in Section Three, having to do with the teaching of literature to students whose privilege and (consequently) previous literary experience are not large, may be more obvious than that of the other essays, but that should not operate to isolate them. One of the several possible subjects originally suggested as appropriate for this volume was "the teaching of literature to the culturally disadvantaged." A prospective contributor, who has happily become an actual contributor, contended that this was a false category, that everyone was culturally disadvantaged. Whatever disposition I had at the time to hear this as a piety (correction is rarely welcome), I have since savored its wisdom frequently. The responses to literature of students in the SEEK program at the City University of New York or at a community college in western Massachusetts are not, I think, different in kind from the responses of students at more selective universities though they are frequently extreme. But this extremity can be translated to use rather than repudiated by anyone committed to the importance of literature and not simply to its propagation.

The themes and convictions common to some numbers of these essays are both more substantial and more comfortably or even honestly stressed in the collective than in discrete essays. The modulation from the original working title to the present title is intended to make clear the editor's understanding that the volume is representative but scarcely comprehensive.

M. E.

The fifth volume in this series, *Studies in Chaucer and Medieval English Literature,* will be edited by Larry D. Benson; the sixth, *The Worlds of Victorian Fiction,* by Jerome H. Buckley.

Contents

ONE

PHILIP FISHER

The Failure of Habit

Habit, necessity, the eyes of others. To these three the French
captain in *Lord Jim* credits what cannot even be called his
heroism. He stood for twelve hours on the deck of a ship that
might at any moment sink under him, and, unlike Jim, he did not
leap or panic. This same habit, so essential to the captain's victory, had been identified in a famous passage by Pater as the root
of our evasion of life: "To burn always with this hard, gem-like
flame, to maintain this ecstasy, is success in life. In a sense it
might even be said that our failure is to form habits. For, after all,
habit is relative to a stereotyped world, and meantime it is only
the roughness of the eye that makes any two persons, things, situations look alike."[1]

Pater had made perception, not action, the center of the self.
His is a paradigm of pleasure; the captain's, one of work. Time is
bound and even blurred in the repetitions of work, but the famous
moments of which Pater speaks are islands, self-contained, remote
from one another. Within this atomized time, the time of sensations, the intense colors, the curious odors of which Pater so often
speaks excite, satisfy, and then exhaust the mind, vanishing, hope-

1. Walter Pater, *The Renaissance* (New York: Macmillian, 1900),
p. 158.

3

fully before they cloy. The most brilliant of colors saturates the eye in a matter of seconds. Pater begins from attention, from a lively awareness, whereas it is difficult to call Conrad's captain a hero precisely because his act omits the consciousness that, for Jim, makes both heroism and its double, cowardice, possible. Unlike Jim, unlike Pater, the captain has no "experience." He seems absent during the hours he stands, inattentive to the danger of death, forgetful both of himself and his situation. He manages to eat his lunch calmly. The habit to which he owes his triumph is a kind of automated moral life, a momentum of action, an accumulated reserve assembled deliberately through the discipline of everyday life, able to contain emergencies almost by a simple process of addition. Created when reason is active, the reservoir of habit extends control into moments of extinguished or, as in Jim's case, dangerous consciousness.

Since habit works automatically, it is a form of moral unconscious, the partner of the reasoned choice, debate, and conscious act that make up the pattern of moral attention. George Eliot wrote that her interest was in the numerous small acts of indulgence or denial that pattern the will, determining its form in advance of the rare moments of crisis. In moral vocabulary, good and evil become variants of strength and weakness. Her languid, weak-willed characters are, in the telling metaphor of the period, those who have never mastered themselves.

The defense of habit speaks almost equally of efficiency and anxiety. Beneath work lies the habit structure that efficiently simplifies both acts and awareness, but in the moral life habit betrays an anxiety in the face of the unexpected, the future, the emergency in which panic and haste will distort reasoning. Even more, it is an anxiety about the sudden revelation of the true self. In *Lord Jim* the French captain's summary begins, "Man is born a coward. It would be too easy otherwise. But habit, necessity, the eyes of others . . ."[2] The control that habit extends reaches out to events and inside to the feared natural self. From the other side, the attack on habit pictures again and again the disease of boredom, banality, the stunned condition of a man within this simplified world; literally, within an inhabited world. The poetry

2. Joseph Conrad, *Lord Jim* (London: J. M. Dent, 1923), p. 147.

of aestheticism begins with those experiences where habit fails. In *To the Lighthouse* Virginia Woolf describes this moment: "It was a way things had sometimes, she thought, lingering for a moment and looking at the long glittering windows and the plume of blue smoke: they became unreal. So coming back from a journey or after an illness, before habits had spun themselves across the surface, one felt the same unreality, which was so startling; felt something emerge. Life was most vivid then."[3]

In *A Portrait of the Artist as a Young Man* each of Stephen's impulses in turn degrades into habit, what begins as an experience of deliverance hardens into a new form of bondage; sex turns to the sordid routine visits to the prostitutes; the religious experience of communion to the habits of prayer, observance, empty ritual; even the freedom offered by the prize money declines to family bookkeeping. But in structure the book defeats habit with experience, each chapter ends with a new ecstasy, a new escape from that pattern into which the previous escape had frozen. The exeriences of terror in both Sartre's *Nausea* and Rilke's *Notebooks* begin, like the joy of Stephen's life, the delicate poetry in Virginia Woolf, with the cracks within the world of habit that widen to become windows onto a world of experience. These assaults on habit, combined as they are with narrative experiment, only emphasize how essential the notion of habit was to what was understood as self or character, and to what made up a narrative.

The study of psychology in the nineteenth century is in essence a study of habit. William James's classic summary of the field, *The Principles of Psychology,* begins, after a short description of the physical structure of the brain, with a major chapter on habit, and under habit James includes such phenomena as the moon's "habit" of circling the earth, man's "habit" of walking upright, as well as individual habits, such as "snuffling, putting one's hands in one's pockets, or biting one's nails." Public life described itself for James through customs and ceremonies, the social forms of habit, and each man, drunkard or worker, uses or is imprisoned within habits of life. Habit is for James almost synonymous with order; every victory over randomness is for him a variety of habit.

3. Virginia Woolf, *To the Lighthouse* (London: Hogarth Press, 1927), p. 294.

Stones fall by habit, birds build nests by habit. In structure James's chapter rises from the physical, to the social, and at last to the moral life of the individual. The unifying element is habit. The continuity of all life, in fact of all matter, is one of the deliberately emotional elements of this first section of *The Principles of Psychology,* as is the progression from physical to moral life, from description to impassioned plea. The enemy for James is not the drunkard, the gambler, but the man without habits, the man of sensibility, Paterian man, "the nerveless sentimentalist and dreamer, who spends his life in a sea of sensibility and emotion, but never does a manly concrete deed." The drunkard and the gambler because their lives are constructed out of habits, can be reconstructed, bad habits remain habits. James quotes with relish Mill's definition: "A character is a completely fashioned will." In his enthusiasm for the socially conservative force of habit, James concludes, "It is well for the world that in most of us, by the age of thirty, the character has set like plaster, and will never soften again."[4]

In the next generation of psychologists, James's ideas about habit are pushed to an extreme by Watson — and in extremity the vulgarity (James recommends a little gratuitous asceticism, a few strengthening habits as a kind of "fire insurance"), the economic bias, the totalitarian implications faintly present in James turned lurid and offensive. Simultaneously, the new Freudian psychology redefined the self in terms of its experiences, reserving for habit the image of compulsion and illness. Watson's behaviorism became the foundation of American experimental psychology. Watson seems at times a caricature of James: "Personality is the end product of our habit systems." And when he speaks of himself it is to guarantee to the reader that like the machines he deals with, he himself is only the tool of the machines beyond him. "It is part of the behaviorist's scientific job to be able to state what the human machine is good for and to render serviceable predictions about its future capacities whenever society needs such information."[5] The human machine, the habit systems, or rather the

4. William James, *The Principles of Psychology* (New York: Dover, 1950), p. 121.
5. John B. Watson, *Behaviorism* (New York: Norton, 1924), p. 271.

ones visible because they are good for something, are both variable and answerable first and last to the needs of society.

Through all discussions of habit runs the metaphor of industrial production, the relation among raw material (the self), human will, and a designed product (character) intended for a limited use. Watson's personality is the "end product" of habit, which is itself the product of the will, either one's own or that of the scientist, the educator as he was once called. Mill's phrase, a "completely fashioned will," shows that the access we have to the self through habit is to the constructed self, the manufactured self, the preformed and then performed character.

Where Mill and James see this industrialization that creates the commodity of the self as an internal, chosen, moral relationship, an act of discipline and self control, self education — what Arnold would call the route to best self — by Watson's time, the image is of the construction of selves by others. To describe habit systems, predict which ones will be needed, and then to manufacture the requisite personalities, by a process now called conditioning instead of education, this is the behaviorist's public role. The elements of the industrial process are specialized. The will resides in society, the process of production in environments created by the behaviorist, the raw material alone is in the self.

If the extension of James leads in the writings of the behaviorists to a revelation of the hidden implications of a system based on habit, the work of the new psychology, the alternative discipline begun by Freud, contains a repudiation of habit as direct as that of Pater and the modernist writers. Freud, whose formula includes transformation — where id was shall ego be, where "it" was shall "I" be — studies a specialized and exterior, manufactured self. The habit systems of patients, the rituals and stylized acts, are designed by that intruder within the self, illness. The self is not expressed, but imprisoned, the compulsions give no efficient direct access to life but interpose themselves, distort and neglect experience, impoverish without refining. In Freud the analysis of habit assumes anxiety and flight from experience, a drain of energy, never the economy of action that for James is the essence of habit.

If character is a completely fashioned will, then Bergson's exaggeration written at the turn of the century takes on the power

of prophecy: "All *character* is comic, provided we mean by character the *ready made* element in our personality. It is, if you will,
that which causes us to imitate ourselves."[6] In his *Laughter*, Bergson makes of habit the source of all comedy. Like Pater, Bergson
begins from the vitalist claim that life never repeats itself, every
moment is unique, therefore, any repetition is mechanical, a
denial of living process. In Bergson's essay all art is a temporary
lifting of the veil of habitual, utilitarian perception — that social
simplification of experience interposed between man and nature.
Habit comes out of inattention, a failure of consciousness to
accept the uniqueness of experience. It is, in short, absent-
mindedness.

> There is no pool which has not some dead leaves floating on its
> surface, no human soul upon which there do not settle habits that
> make it rigid against itself by making it rigid against others . . .
> The rigid, the ready-made, the mechanical in contrast with the
> supple, the ever-changing, and the living, absent-mindedness in
> contrast with attention, in a word, automatism in contrast with
> free activity, such are the defects that laughter singles out and
> would fain correct.[7]

The elements of Bergson's description combine to either laughter
or terror. More often in modern art the rigidity, simplification,
inattention, the pool of life covered with dead leaves of habit has
been attacked with terror than with laughter. The experiences in
Nausea, based on the failure of the world of habit to successfully
prolong the inattention of daily life, begin with the banal, the
objects of utility — chair, fork, or doorknob. "A little while ago
just as I was coming into my room, I stopped short because I felt
in my hand a cold object which held my attention through a sort
of personality. I opened my hand, looked: I was simply holding
the door-knob. This morning in the library, when the Self-Taught
Man came to say good-morning to me, it took me ten seconds to
recognize him. I saw an unknown face, barely a face. Then there
was his hand like a fat white worm in my own hand."[8] Each of

6. Henri Bergson, *Laughter,* in *Comedy,* ed. Wylie Sypher (New York:
Doubleday Anchor, 1956), p. 156.

7. *Ibid.,* p. 144.

8. Jean-Paul Sartre, *Nausea* (New York: New Directions, 1959), p. 11.

Bergson's elements is here in reverse. The chasm forms in the pause before recognition, habit, and familiarity can glide past, a pause comes into being that inattention is trusted to erase. For the habit to operate, one must never feel or experience the doorknob. Habit designs a world familiar, but never known, one in which we move from the mystery of why a switch on the wall when touched produces light, a mystery broken down through repetition not knowledge, through inattention to the goal of habit, banality. Habit, Sartre is saying in *Nausea,* is a false alternative to knowledge. The commonplace is in effect mystery turned banal. We pass from mystery to familiarity without moving through a struggle of understanding. Perception tries to know, but the momentum of habit lies in the name, the word that persists, that absent-mindedly sees repetition. Language is, in *Nausea,* the model of the simplification — a tree, any tree, some trees. In place of the common sequence of name, recognition, inattention, familiarity — the sequence that forms habit — Roquentin's sequence is a pause, sense perception, attention, and finally metaphor. Into the pause arises the dream substitute, the false name — the fat, white worm. If the word *hand* is wrong, then of course *worm* is too, but the metaphor includes a confession of arbitrariness and inadequacy. Instead of the relaxation of the name *hand* that recognizes, the metaphor introduces a second disturbance, the pause of helplessness is succeeded by the terror of arbitrary transformation.

The tactic of aiming first at language through the use of the image, then with the weapon of a reborn, crazed language doubling the attack on the inhabited psyche is the essential strategy discussed in the surrealist manifestos, but the tactic is of course a wider element of modernism, one shared by poets as different as Stevens, Eliot, and Rilke. The form of narrative invented by Rilke and Sartre could be called the gothic of everyday life. Recreating wonder and terror, recalling mystery into what is only to our less and less attentive vision banal, the gothic of everyday life stands to middle-class civilization as the earlier gothic novel did to the weakening aristocratic society, or rather to the miniature image of that society, the family. Where the earlier gothic novel reawakened the elemental forces of family life — inheritance and guilt, marriage, incest, the terrible authority of the father, the mysteries of ancestral presence and connection, the half-reality of individual death in a world of families — placing these elements within that image of the family in time, the decaying castle, the gothic of everyday life, set within that castle of middle-class individualism, the city, reanimates the terrifying and yet illuminating otherness of things, of our double connection to things as they are and things as we have diminished them in our structures of use and habit. Both gothic forms sear experience to insist on its lurid drama. Both court and yet toy with insanity, and finally, both restore a religious, even a sacramental importance to the experiences of wonder and terror.

At best the epiphanies of Joyce, the moments of perfection in Virginia Woolf, and the full experience of sex in Lawrence are "illuminations" in the basic gothic and religious sense. The definition Joyce gave of *epiphany* in *Stephen Hero* depends on a familiar world of objects of use — a clock one passes every day. The epiphany restores the clock to itself in one act of seeing, of experiencing it for the first time. The struggle between experience and habit in *A Portrait of the Artist* and *To the Lighthouse* has already been described. In *Lady Chatterley's Lover,* it is Sir Clifford who is defined by the habit structures of his life, Constance and Mellors, by their experiences. And when Sir Clifford suggests to Lady Chatterley that she take a lover, he assumes the marriage will survive because it is the form of habit in their lives, repetition in the face of which all experience seems to him superficial.

In *Sons and Lovers* the same technical distinction is made. The miner Morel is characterized through the rituals of his life, the repetitions that relate to his work, his early morning preparations, the weekly ritual of paying the men. His wife and son are defined through the unique experiences each has, through the dramatic moments of greatest intensity, consciousness, and vision.

With the repudiation of habit in modern literature it becomes rare to hear of the structures of work and repetition without self-conscious satire. In Hauptmann's famous story "Flagman Thiel," the insignificant railroad flagman prepares for work.

It took him a lot of time, as for everything he did. Each move had been regulated for years. The objects carefully spread out on the walnut dresser went into his various pockets always in the same order — knife, notebook, comb, a horse's tooth, an old watch in a case, and a small book wrapped in red paper. The last was handled with especial care. During the night it lay under Thiel's pillow, and by day was carried in his breast pocket. On a label pasted on the cover was written in Thiel's awkward and yet flourishing hand, "Savings Account of Tobias Thiel."[9]

The force of work and habit comes to define what we so aptly call "The Little Man" in the century, and the many characters like Thiel, whose life is extinguished for most of his waking moments, at last concentrate their release in some exaggerated and violent form. For Thiel it is the sexual relationship with his wife, which she from her side uses to victimize him. Finally, Thiel is an accessory to the death of the one child he loves and slaughters his wife and other child in the final investment of his saved-up life. Thiel is the little man to whom Wilhelm Reich addressed his *Listen, Little Man,* the goal of Fallada's novel *Little Man, What Now,* the pygmy man of Freudian theory, reduced fraction of the child.

The changes in psychology, in moral and aesthetic bases of character, in the importance of uniqueness and repetition, in the force of experience (single and illuminating), the many changes that I have tried to show in relation to the rejection of habit — these touch only the content and structure of narrative. Deeper yet are the forms and methods of narration whose fate is tied to the fate of habit. Two elements are essential: narrative iteration and the form of what we might call the manual. I use the word *manual* to isolate that part of any realistic novel or memoir independent of the line of action, suspense, and adventure, that part that documents how lives are lived as a means to celebrate or denounce styles of life. Half of *Moby Dick* is a manual of whaling life, the best half of *Robinson Crusoe* is a manual of solitary life. The special relationship of the novel to middle-class society depends on the ease with which the novel alone of literary forms can subordinate the pleasures of language and drama to the curiosity about modes of life that the manual provides. Thoreau's *Walden* is a manual for life in the woods, but *Madame Bovary* is equally a manual, one that exposes instead of celebrating the

9. Gerhart Hauptmann, "Flagman Thiel" in *Great German Short Novels and Stories* (New York: Modern Library, 1952), p. 340.

general mode of life it depicts in its everyday form. Proust, in addition to the journey to art, outlines a manual of civilized life. The research that came to complement imagination among realists and naturalists is the foundation for the manual within the novel.

In its familiar meaning a manual is a book of techniques, a how-to-do-it guide, and finally that is one of the uses of the manual of habitual life. Stendhal's *The Red and the Black,* Thoreau's *Walden,* Joyce's *A Portrait of the Artist as a Young Man* have a force of pattern stronger than could be described by that out-of-date phrase for the novel — a conduct book. Huysmans's manual of decadent life, *Au Rebours,* became one of the elements of Oscar Wilde's style.

Rousseau, who is the key to the romantic manual, popularized the form in his *Confessions* and *Reveries of a Solitary.* He writes to describe *"l'état habituel de mon ame."* Any manual gives the basic English of a life, its typical, repetitive, habitual acts and feelings. From a modern point of view, one of the odd qualities of *Walden* is that Thoreau has so few experiences, so few privileged moments. His concern is with habitual life. "Sometimes, in a summer morning, having taken my accustomed bath, I sat in my sunny doorway from sunrise till noon, rapt in revery, amidst the pines and hickories and sumachs, in undisturbed solitude and stillness, while the birds sang around or flitted noiseless through the house, until by the sun falling in at my west window, or the noise of some travellers wagon on the distant highway I was reminded of the lapse of time."[10] The sensations are interchangeable, the most vivid details are given as alternatives separated by *or* because it is the deep pattern that is the base. The word *sometimes* like the words *often* or *whenever* or the phrases *every morning* or *from time to time, again and again,* introduces an iterative scene. Iteration is the collective form of time, as the type is the collective form of character. Both are essential to meaning in the nineteenth-century novel and manual. Three of the four central chapters of *Walden* begin with the word *sometimes.* And, of course, Proust's novel, the greatest of all novels of habitual life, with its walks and days all collective in the mind, begins "Longtemps, je me suis couché de bonne heure. Parfois, a peine ma

10. Henry David Thoreau, *Walden* (New York: New American Library, 1960), p. 79.

bougie éteinte, mes yeux se fermaient si vite que je n'avais pas
le temps de me dire: 'je m'endors.' " The two initial words *longtemps* and *parfois* give the signature of iteration. Rousseau raised
the power of iteration by using the pseudoscene, the ideal day
which is described as though it were an experience while being in
fact a summary. His "jour typique" selects details across the collective time of memory to render the habit visible in a single
scene. The goal of this life of habits is not ecstasy, and never the
sharp contrasts of sensation and experience. Rousseau describes
it as "a simple and permanent state, which has nothing keen in
itself, but the duration of which increases the charm, to the point
of finding there the supreme felicity."[11]

In iteration, ideal days, or typical days direct us at once to the
paradigms of experience. *Madame Bovary*, registering deeply the
struggle between habit and experience, the life of Charles and the
life of Emma, shows profound use of iteration. After the initial
scene in the school, a unique "experience," the novel smothers
experience in the collective time of the marriage. The blurred
time of iteration gives way only as the novel approaches the end,
and the final days of frantic search for money and then death are
once again unique. But in iteration lies deep pattern.

> When it rained or snowed, Charles would direct his horse over the
> shortcuts. He would eat omelets at farm tables, put his hand into
> humid beds, receive full in the fact the tepid spurts of blood-letting,
> listen to the death rattles; examine the bed-pans, and tuck in a great
> deal of dirty linens; but every night he would come home to a glow-
> ing fire, the table set, the furniture arranged comfortably, and a
> charming woman, neatly dressed, smelling so fresh you wondered
> where the fragrance came from and whether it wasn't her skin
> lending the scent to her petticoats.[12]

Two ideal or false scenes contrast by smell and food, by awareness of the body in disease and in desire. The two create Charles's
double world as doctor and husband, as a man in each relating to
the body. The vivid apparently random details become sequences:
from food to excrement, opening the bed to straightening the linen
over the corpse. The doctor opens the bed, examines, treats, and

11. Jean Jacques Rousseau, *Reveries of a Solitary* (London: George
Routledge, 1927), p. 112.
12. Gustave Flaubert, *Madame Bovary* (New York: New American
Library, 1964), p. 77.

the patient dies; autopsy is performed; the corpse is covered. Yet there is no genuine patient, no time, or rather none but the collective patient of his professional failure, the time of his entire career.

Where iteration was the base of narrative — and it is in such different but central books as *Madame Bovary, Walden,* Rousseau's *Reveries,* Proust's *Remembrance of Things Past* — the narrative created from the start a technique of mediation between the unique and the universal, between experience and ideal. From iteration the writer moves naturally in three directions; he moves back to unique moments which are *examples* of the pattern; he moves to metaphor as a perception of *analogy,* a repetition of structure like that already within the iteration; and finally, he moves to summary or abstraction through *condensation,* the basis of iteration itself. The paradigms of *Walden* are profound examples of the ease of movement from the false scene, the habit scene, to the connected levels of individual experience, metaphor, and meaning.

> When my floor was dirty, I rose early, and setting all my furniture out of doors on the grass, bed and bedstead making but one budget, dashed water on the floor, and sprinkled white sand from the pond on it, and then with a broom scrubbed it clean and white . . . it was pleasant to see my whole household effects put on the grass, making a little pile like a gypsy's pack, and my three-legged table, from which I did not remove the books and pen and ink, standing amid the pines and hickories. They seemed glad to get themselves out, and as if unwilling to be brought in. I sometimes tempted to stretch an awning over them and take my seat there. It was worth the while to see the sun shine on these things, and hear the free wind blow on them; so much more interesting most familiar objects look out of doors than in the house. A bird sits on the next bough, life-everlasting grows under the table, and blackberry vines run around its legs; pine cones, chestnut burs and strawberry leaves are strewn about. It looked as if this was the way these forms came to be transferred to our furniture, to tables, chairs, bedsteads — because they once stood in their midst.[13]

Where the modern writer intends to create a manual, as Joyce does in *A Portrait of the Artist* or as Huysmans does in *A*

13. Thoreau, *Walden,* p. 80.

Rebours, he abandons the base of false scene, iteration, and habit and is forced, Marxist critics have shrewdly seen, into allegory. Both Lukács and Benjamin have described the failed allegory of modernism, an allegorical leap from the unique to the general based precisely on the lack of ordered connection rather than on its familiarity.[14] For Marxists, the middle ground between the unique moment, person, or thing and the realms of generalities beyond is occupied by types, habits, and familiar life. Because the iteration, the collective form of time, is no longer there to bridge experience and meaning, the writer creates leaps from the specific to the widest of implications. In *A Portrait of the Artist* the Christmas dinner scene is forced into an allegory of family disintegration, and social tension, religious and political barriers to a common life, and these many general truths that the scene epiphanizes have a troubling relationship to the scene itself. Epiphany is the form of connection in the absence of iteration. In *Ulysses* the opening scene's allegory of the Irish situation is embarrassing, even comic. It is so because epiphany is arbitrary and personal, a matter of perception that takes this moment to symbolize the deep structure. Iteration is never arbitrary because the deepest structures are those that recur most often.

Where the collective of time is iteration, that of character is type, which is similarly joined to habit, utility, and role. The sociologist Peter Berger has called "significant others" the parallel lives that form an aura of connection out from the individual. The group of commuters taking the same train every morning from the same town form parallel lives. United by habit patterns, dress and mood, the commuters are in fact strangers to one another. Like the members of a crew on one of Conrad's ships, they do not experience one another, or rather, they are not the content of each other's experience, but its form. The consciousness of each commuter can fasten on the newspaper memories of the morning, anticipations of the coming day at work, but the fact that he is alongside others in structurally identical lives legitimatizes his life, even though the others never interest him enough to become his experience. But as each one moves through his day alongside

14. Georg Lukács, *Realism in Our Time* (New York: Harper & Row, 1971), p. 44.

a changing group of parallel companions, he is surrounded by a group that mediates his personal existence and that distant "other" so often called up in modern literature. For Bloom, for Dedalus, for Kafka's K., for the essential modern character, there is never the mediation of significant others. Such parallel lives we know only as dehumanization, the generalized self is seen as an erased self.

> Along the row of seated women, painted fans were fluttering, bou-quets half concealed smiling faces, and gold stoppered perfume bottles were being turned in half-opened hands whose tight white gloves revealed the shape of the fingernails and hugged the wrists. Lace trimming, diamond brooches, and bracelets with lockets trembled on bodices; sparkled on breasts, jingled on bare arms. The hairdos securely arranged and twisted at the napes were crowned with clusters or bunches of forget-me-nots, jasmine, pomegranate blossoms, wheat ears or cornflowers. The mothers, sitting quietly in their places wore red turbans and frowning expressions.[15]

The daughters, dressed for the dance, the mothers anxious and grim nearby, have all been erased by fashion and role. They "wear" both hats and moods.

In his famous essay "The Metropolis and Mental Life," Simmel has shown that the mental life of the city, abandoning the base of habit, creates the need simultaneously for unique stimulating experiences and for a unique, even bizarre, character. Rapidity, extreme contrast from moment to moment, and the quantity of events and surprises create a mental life in need of shock, and of instant presentation. The characters of Dickens are in Simmel's perception the first examples of the metropolitan self. Similarly, the theories of Pater and Joyce, the notions of experience and epiphany, are urban psychic structures. Even the growing impor-tance of the idea of awareness or consciousness is for Simmel related to the city. "Lasting impressions, impressions which differ only slightly from one another, impressions which take a regular and habitual course and show regular and habitual contrasts — all these use up, so to speak, less consciousness than does the rapid crowding of changing images, the sharp discontinuity in the

15. Flaubert, *Madame Bovary*, p. 68.

grasp of a single glance, and the unexpectedness of on-rushing impressions. These are the psychological conditions which the metropolis creates."[16] In a paradox Simmel carefully explains, the man in the city is both more detached and more alert, more absent and more attentive. He becomes conscious of his world, he himself becomes as a self, a consciousness, a Leopold Bloom. Habitual life is not conscious life, nor is role; to become aware of either is to become suddenly embarrassed or helpless. Conrad often studied the dangers of consciousness. The quality of intellect that "processes" the environment is what Simmel sees as the insulation between the deeper, now buried life and the rapid, continuous, surface experience. Written twenty years before *Ulysses,* Simmel's essay remains an act of prophetic criticism.

The image of production is essential in every description of habit. Through habit character is manufactured. Iteration and the ideal scene are similar constructs based on natural experience. Manuals like those of Thoreau, Rousseau, and Huysmans describe the construction of ways of life. These forms all use the authentic past tense, each begins not with experience, but with that product of experience, memory. Memory like dream is a construct, a reconstruction of events, and it is as often collective as individual. Through its stress on the present as a product of the past, the iterative narrative creates a futureless man, one whose present acts are dynamically set between the habits of the past and the circumstances of the present. One element of the pessimism and elegiac tone of this literature is its lack of future moods: Charles Bovary never plans, anticipates or expects, apparently he never looks forward in the morning to the noon. His life is something he performs. Habits are adjusted to new circumstances. The event designs itself against the momentum that would seemingly allow the past to repeat forever. Rousseau's ideal days are always the days of his lost past. Proust's title combines the elements of loss and past and reconstruction that identify the world of habit. Significantly, one of the few unique experiences described by Rousseau in his *Reveries of a Solitary* is a momentary loss of self. Knocked down unexpectedly by a large dog, he lay on the ground. What is a richly described modern experience, filled with

16. Georg Simmel, *The Sociology of Georg Simmel,* translated and edited by Kurt Wolff (Glencoe, Illinois: Free Press, 1950), p. 410.

sensation, presence, and an almost perfect joy, Rousseau can only call a loss of self, because it is a loss of memory and connection.

> The night was coming on. I perceived the sky, some stars, and a little grass. The first sensation was a delicious moment. I did not feel anything except through them. I was born in that instant to life, and it seemed to me that I filled with my light existence all the objects which I perceived. Entirely given up to the present moment, I did not remember anything. I had no distinct notion of my individuality, not the least idea of what had happened to me. I did not know who I was nor where I was; I felt neither evil, nor fear, nor trouble. I saw my blood flowing as I might have looked at a brooklet, without dreaming even that this blood in any way belonged to me. I felt in the whole of my being a ravishing calm, to which, each time I think of it, I find nothing comparable in the whole action of known pleasures.[17]

The moment outside his memories is a moment of absence from his constructed self. Because the experience is unconnected, because it is unique, it is for Rousseau a small preview of death. His blood flows from him as he passively looks on.

Outside memory and habit the past is no longer the decisive form of time. The journal form used by Sartre, Rilke, and in part by Joyce; the novel of the single day or of the present time found in Woolf, Joyce, and many later French novelists — these forms accept perception and sensation. When sensation is freed from the past and from our insistence on seeing it as a repetition or variation of the past, the margin that grows in value is that between the present and the future. Sartre's is a philosophy of the present and the future, of freedom, projecting forward in time, waiting, expecting. The novel of perception is attuned to those almost future experiences of surprise, shock, the thrill of the unexpected. In Sartre the weight of obligation or role, the momentum of the past, and our cowardice in attempting to capture the future before experiencing it characterize bad faith. What occurs on the margin of the present and future is experience in the very special, revolutionary modern sense of the word, and experience relocates that center of the self once understood as the margin of the present and the past — the margin called habit.

17. Rousseau, *Reveries of a Solitary,* p. 48.

ALLEN GROSSMAN

Criticism, Consciousness, and the Sources of Life: Some Tasks for English Studies

"Criticism"

I wish to lay before you some problems which preoccupy me as a teacher of English. The first (perhaps the most general) has to do with the meaning of criticism in literary studies. Much of the virulence of the current attack on academic literacy is justified, if not caused, by the inveterate inability of literary studies to take its own nature as a subject of rational attention. The inner disposition of the literary person is to regard his enterprise as permanently and by its nature exempt from indictment among the forces which are hostile to human life, provided only that its practitioners remain disinterested and its practice correct. The unwavering concern of the literary professional with, on the one hand, the external enemy or alien alliance (the philistine), and, on the other, the internal enemy or deformed practitioner (the dunce) has left him with a sense of unquestionable innocence. Thus, art, and particularly literary art, has become the latest, perhaps, because of the epigonal status assigned it by theorists of secularism, the last, certainly the least pregnable of Western canonicities. This state of affairs accords with the general disposition in culture to view the most fundamental inquiries (for example, molecular biology) as if it were their deformed and not their perfected state that made the greatest difference. But the issue lies not between correctness and deformation, or between creation and destruction, but between this whole complex of closely related terms and their dialectical opposite, which is consciousness, choice, criticism. If after the perfected state of a discipline (the most admirable and completely evolved instances of a kind) has been discriminated, the enterprise of critical attentiveness comes to an end, then the real consequences of labor and admiration will remain unconscious — and the outcome of judgment will be the abrogation of choice.

Whether the result of the insertion of literature (or any basic inquiry) in a truly dialectical critical frame would be to choose for or against it in view of the human good, the possibility of so choosing has not been enhanced in literary studies by the assignment to the word *criticism* of a heterogeneous bundle of weak or limited senses.[1] Hence, the expression literary criticism, while serving as a term of reference to all that can be done in the presence of literature, is insufficient to include what devoted men of letters must do and indeed do do. The strategy whereby the names of other disciplines are predicated upon criticism, as in psychoanalytic criticism or Marxian criticism, or by which an intent is predicated, as in practical criticism or judicial criticism, or a disciplinary politics, as in new criticism, calls attention to the difficulty of thinking freely in the presence of art which is a consequence of the failure, for statable reasons, of the development in the descent of the word *criticism* from Bentley, Dryden, Pope, Arnold, and Richards of a strong sense, such as in philosophy, for example, it acquired in the works of Kant. In addition, the alliance of the literary object with the central and unalterable terms of human worth, such as creativity, divinity, immortality, unity, rationality, and emotion has contributed to the disposition of its professionals to ascribe to it in the most general form the status of canonicity, the status of an object which does not take

1. There is a fairly extensive account of the word *criticism* in René Wellek, "The Term and Concept of Literary Criticism," *Concepts of Criticism* (New Haven: Yale University Press, 1963).

itself as a subject of rational concern. We observe, for example, that English departments in America are divided functionally between the teaching of writing and the teaching of literature. The assumption that the same persons charged with the transmission of literature should also be charged with the facilitation of literacy implies that not merely literature, but *this* literature, and the basic terms not merely of civility, but even of consciousness itself, entail and predict one another. We see teachers and students around us who cannot affirm, dispense with, or change the literary education which they have received, because the literary fact is mythologized and hence largely unknown in its relations and consequences. In the absence of a meaning for criticism which can undertake the negation of all these alliances, it is difficult to be free and choosing in the presence of the artistic form of words.[2]

Poetry itself is of course the strong root from which modern criticism was separated in the time of Bentley and Pope. The function of terms of decorum, such as *correctness,* was to prohibit descriptions of experience inconsistent with the normal functioning of consciousness in a known place possible to life. The separation of poetics and criticism determined the scope of the latter science. Its purpose was to control experiment with the fundamental coordinates of perception as represented in literary structures, but to permit on its own terms what Barfield calls the archaistic element, the substantial *prisca virtus,* to startle consciousness toward evolution but not to appall. This substantial reciprocity of poetry and criticism (to the extent that it remained intact in the nineteenth century) was in effect destroyed in the modern period (the period which saw the rise of the English department) by the acceptance in the academy of the dominant poets as the dominant critical group (Eliot, for example) just at the moment when poetic structure was most radically concerned with the reconstitution of the fundamental coordinates of conscious life. The "legitimation" of experimentation, by casting institutional sanction over art itself, prepared the separation of

2. I use the word *negation* throughout this article in a sense resembling that of Leszek Kolakowski, "But negation is not the opposite of construction — it is only the opposite of affirming existing conditions." See "The Concept of the Left," in *Toward a Marxist Humanism* (New York: Grove Press, 1969), p. 68.

the artistic interpretation of experience and the management of the ordinary crises of consciousness that every teacher of literature at the present time must painfully have observed. The alignment of the university and the social sponsors of art with the avant-garde at what was in effect the first possible moment in the history of English studies (modern art was so notoriously well suited to academic treatment) led to the cooptation of poetic knowledge and the evolution of the current post modern situation in which art and criticism have lost all vital interconnection. In addition, the institutionalization of the avant-garde trapped literature in the poorly understood and heteronomously determined dialectic of the teacher-student relationship. The university is now the world of literature, and the great poems, ancient and modern, are the folklore of that world. Consequently, the two abstractly separable questions of the nature of literature, on the one hand, and the bad management of it by the institutions to which it has been committed, on the other, have become inextricably involved. And the notion of criticism, which derives its significance and limits from its inclusion within the sanctions of art, requires reconsideration, since neither in its eighteenth-century form nor in its modern devolution is it adequate to the problems that, in my view, both startle and appall consciousness.

An illustration of these matters can be drawn from the situation in contemporary poetry. The structures of poetry in English at this present make at least two kinds of statements, the features of which will be well known to the readers of this paper. On the one hand, the open structures of some writers specify that by contrast to the poetry of closure ("the poetry of the beginning and the poetry of the end," in Lawrence's phrase),[3] there is or must be a poetry of aperture in the prosodies of which poetry ceases to be coimplicated with the past. Since the present is radically dangerous and includes the possibility of final violence, the business of poetry is not with the continuity of past and future but with the present as free, newly discriminated and therefore innocent, human energy. The future must be unlike the past, and therefore poetry as a cause and consequence of causes must be disjunct from tradi-

3. D. H. Lawrence, "Poetry of the Present," *The Complete Poems of D. H. Lawrence,* ed. Vivian de Sola Pinto and F. Warren Roberts (New York: The Viking Press, 1971), p. 181.

tional accounts of experience that in their very perfections are of one nature with the human violence which characterizes history. On the other hand, the traditional poet insists that human nature and social consciousness are identical with closed prosodic structures which are the mimetic correlative in words of rational and civil identity. Aperture advocates participation; closure seeks to provide the conditions of the social communicability of selves. From the point of view of the traditional poet the destiny of poetry is with the personal, and the personal is obtained in a chain of conscious acknowledgments across time and across the space between persons. Hence, it is structure of a certain kind which is anthropogenetic, civil recognition and not energy which is redemptive. By contrast to the poet of closure, the poet of aperture exacts of his art, to put the matter in its ideal generality, experiment with continuity, relationship, and recognition of a kind precisely as fundamental as those threats to human safety which arise from the general culture, for example from nuclearism. Now the point of my illustration is that this conflict, between closure and aperture, exactly to the extent that it is *really in* contemporary poetry, represents a much more fundamental questioning of the nature of culture interior to the culture itself than similar disputes in the past that it resembles, such as that between quantitative and accentual prosodies or in general between ancients and moderns. Much of the ease with which modernist poetry and its inseparable criticism became legitimate derived from the fact that it became as it reached the universities still another debate about dunces and philistines. If the modernist debate within poetry was really a debate about correctness, the postmodern debate is with the missed business of modernism, the question of what structures of consciousness are consistent with the continuity of human life. There is, therefore, one urgent sense in which English studies cannot consider the present state of the art, one that flows from the fact that the foundations of the art itself are in question, the perfected form of the thing in both the specific (closure) and the more general notion of perfection. For that reason, if for no other, the social nature of the institution becomes of dominant concern. Only its social nature, in a broad sense its political organization, is left to talk about. English studies as an institution becomes in itself an example of the absence of vital reciprocity between art and

the social order, that is to say, of the absence of criticism. Literature, in the best of situations, has no necessary institutional form,
unlike, let us say, religion (the church) or law (the courts). In the
stronger sense of the word *critical* for which I search, it should be
possible to experience voluntarily the finitude of literary meaning
and value. Even *unendlichkeit* ought to be knowable in terms of
alternatives, an occasion of choosing. Not merely the meaning of
best in the phrase "the best that can be thought" but also the
meaning of *can*. English studies being a very recent experiment, it
is reasonable to inquire whether the experiment should be
continued.

Institutions

The counterdevelopment to the change in the social sponsorship
of literature recorded in Johnson's letter to the Earl of Chester-
field was the legitimation of English studies in the universities, and
particularly of modern literature in the national language. In evidence of the fact that this counterdevelopment evolved its own
dialectic of liberation, one need only submit Stephen Potter's *The
Muse in Chains* (1937), E. M. W. Tillyard's *The Muse Unchained* (1958), and Graham Hough's balanced *The Dream and
the Task* (1963), derived from a set of talks called "The Muse
and Her Chains." In Johnson's sentence, "The Shepherd of Virgil
grew at last acquainted with love, and found him a native of the
rocks." The contrast between the first official English paper set
for matriculation in London University in 1839, the first honors
English papers set at Oxford in 1896, and the papers set for the
English tripos in 1936 (all cited by Potter) shows the gradual
acceptance of the aesthetic and moral concerns of literature in the
mother tongue as part of the truth that institutions can test for and
verify. The future desiderated by Potter in 1937 has also come to
pass: "Entirely changed, also, will be the attitude towards contemporary writers. One of the most dangerous characteristics of
Ang. Lit. has been from the first a neglect or implied discouragement of the study of modern writers."[4] The assignment of academic status to ever deeper ranges of interior freedom, sentiment,

4. Stephen Potter, *The Muse in Chains: A Study in Education* (London: Jonathan Cape, 1937), p. 264.

style, judgment, has supplied what Potter called with reference to English studies "the missing subject," the phenomenal subject of experience. As Trilling remarked in 1965, "We seem to have arrived at the future." By what grace did we become acquainted with love?

The acceptance of modern letters in the mother tongue as a university subject runs fairly parallel, as is obvious, with the liberalization of the polity in England and America and particularly with the emancipation of women, so far as it occurred. Where the university could not ignore a class or group, it was inclined to offer it a pathway to academic legitimacy that satisfied claims upon status but excluded from the means of rule.[5] In addition, the Masoretic relentlessness with which in its early stages English studies gripped both the language ("How many letters of the English alphabet may, for the purposes of spelling, be regarded as superfluous?")[6] and the text calls attention to the intensity of the motive to keep hold of the canon and make it mean what it always meant and not some other troubling thing. The struggle for control over the meaning of words which underlies much philology and text criticism and which continues at the heart of the hermeneutic controversy (note, for example, E. D. Hirsch's distinction between meaning and significance)[7] has a very complex bearing on critical and pedagogic styles. The dominant privatistic ethicalism of the New Criticism[8] and much rhetorical and structuralist theory place the reader in an aesthetic space where meaning and really knowing (which leads to power in one's situation) are mutually exclusive, as in any true poetic they must not be. Modernism itself in the persons of Yeats, Eliot, and Joyce promulgated the notion of literature as a place where consciousness and status but not freedom was to be obtained and enhanced the

5. Kipling's fine story "Regulus" (1908) reminds us of the role of Latin in the training of army officers in the period of the first advancement of the modern subject. "Those were the days when Army examiners gave thousands of marks for Latin."

6. Potter, *Muse in Chains,* p. 267.

7. E. D. Hirsch, *Validity in Interpretation* (New Haven: Yale University Press, 1966), pp. 139ff.

8. See on this matter Richard Ohmann, "Teaching and Studying Literature at the End of Ideology," *The Politics of Literature: Dissenting Essays on the Teaching of English* (New York: Pantheon Books, 1972), pp. 130–159.

tendency of English studies to become a sort of *Weibestaitsch,* a strategy for dealing with the demands of the third estate (both the third estate of sentiment and of social history) — a fact which should be borne in mind by proponents of particularisms too willing to give up the inherent power of their negations to the aesthetic frames of the institution.

Seen from the point of view of this present English studies was an early episode in the process of the incorporation in the expanded university of an ever increasing number of the functions of the natural community. This quasi-aesthetic process of the replication as departments of the various social functions of moral life including literature, religion, sexuality as coeducation, and politics tends to subject these functions to the necessary terms of institutional life, such as toleration and pluralism, which become when translated into interpretive rules disabling restrictions upon meaning analogous to aesthetic categories. The first critical act of the teacher in the presence of a sacred book, or a poem addressed to a muse, is to disable its explicit claims to authority. Transformation of the conceptual correlatives of the necessary conditions of institutional life into interpretive categories is a further stage of that struggle to control the meaning of the word which characterized the philological and text-critical establishment in its relation to its newly enfranchised student communities. The analogy between attitudes toward meaning based in institutional structure and theories of meaning apparently derived from the nature of literature itself calls attention to the fact that criticism cannot be just without taking the whole of its context into consideration. The class struggle cast in literary terms is the struggle for recognition *(der Kampf des Annerkenntnis);* it may not be mediable by a Marxian analysis (through the incorporation of the economic substructure into the interpretive issue), but whether it can be or not and whether the tradition is really about those classes into whose hands it is placed more or less without alternative is an issue for criticism to decide.

We are now approaching the end of a war, and therefore it is useful to note that response to war has been in modern times important in the growth of literary studies in their institutional form, and in the development of interpretive attitudes toward the canon. The very large literature of pedagogy and literary theory produced in the last few years identifies the present moment as an occasion of the sort which, after the Civil War in America and the First and Second World Wars, saw the development of a "new" criticism.[9] Presumably war precipitates a mimetic crisis requiring in its aftermath an effort to reconstitute images of the human person which are stable, reconciling (and therefore general), and at the same time useful (and therefore national, confirmatory of the survival of the group which may be subject to fundamental doubt by both victor and vanquished). The American Civil War produced, somehow, the American university, and with it for the first time departments of modern languages. Noah Porter, president of Yale, wrote an essay called "The New Criticism" in 1870:

> Formerly, criticism confined itself almost exclusively to the proportion of parts, the order of development, the effectiveness of the introduction, the argument and the peroration, and these with the illustration and explanation of the meaning of a work or a writer, constituted its entire aim. Now while it does not neglect the form, it thinks more of the matter, i.e., the weightiness and truth of the thoughts, the energy and nobleness of the sentiments, the splendor and power of the imagery, and the heroic manhood or the refined womanhood of the writer as expressed in his or her works . . . Instead of being judged by the mere accidents of form, and according to the capriciousness of a changing taste, it [literature] is both studied and tasted according to its perfect ideal.[10]

The ambiguous relation of the autodidact American author such as Melville, Whitman, Dickinson, or Hart Crane to the "perfect ideal" of literary and grammatical structure, or indeed to "heroic manhood" and "refined womanhood," calls attention to the difference between the civility which provided the first sanctions for English departments in America and what might loosely be called the literary truth. The new aestheticism noted by President Porter raises literature out of history by defining its imaginal and affective characteristics in ideal terms; it specifies that literary study will deal with and monitor private life according to eternal moral stereotypes, leaving the "future captain of industry," in

9. The singular character of *this* new criticism is, of course, its concern not only with literature as such but with its several orders of substructure both institutional and social.

10. Laurence R. Veysey, *The Emergence of the American University* (Chicago: University of Chicago Press, 1965), p. 182, n. 7. See also notes 9 and 11.

Andrew Carnegie's phrase, to learn "in the school of experience what is required for his future triumphs."

E. M. W. Tillyard was reluctant after the trenches to return to Cambridge as a classicist,[11] and on a larger scale, the general education movement in America after the Second World War shifted literary attention to the available moral content of literature so far as it bore upon a free society. At the present time it does not seem sufficient to advance once again toward a liberalization of attitude to the content of literature or toward the extension of the canon, though both of these are proceeding as they ought. Some further boundary of the literary presentation requires scrutiny. My point is that care must be taken not to create a new bondage for just those classes of persons to whom the university with its monopoly on language resource must mediate some aspect of freedom. It seems to be the case that when literature is taken into the university it becomes in important ways imponderable, either because it is made so by various versions of New Criticism, which by subsuming art under morally unusable categories gives and withholds great gifts simultaneously, or because it has lost its world, its situation in experience. In the first case, the theoretical and pedagogical custodianship of literature represents as a founding intent the will somewhere in society that the child not realize himself, a will to which the unworkable senses of "subjective," which the young throw up as a response to the irreconcilability of the inner and the social person in studies, responds. In the second case, institutionalization has eroded the relatedness or referentiality of literature, its boundaries both as value and act, and therefore its world; hence, the tenacity with which heteronomous compensation (grades, professional recognition) is retained, and I think quite rightly under the circumstances. It makes no difference to the liberal institution what the texts say, but how they are interpreted (who shall interpret them) seems clearly recognized on all sides as an episode in the class war. In President Porter's remarks we see idealist aestheticism replacing mental discipline as a way of controlling meaning by disabling it, much as a later New Criticism replaces text-making as a strategy for retaining control over meaning of words. Similarly, the ideal of

11. E. M. W. Tillyard, *The Muse Unchained: An Intimate Account of the Revolution in English Studies* (London: Bowes and Bowes, 1958).

universal creativity as a literary attitude may function not as an anarchic extreme of liberal pluralism but in effect as a new criticism, which by creating a weighted asymmetry between creation and reading sets students exclusively the impossible task of art, thus removing them from their just place in the struggle for a rational description of the world. It is one of the ironies of secularization that the ascription of redemptive qualities to art has tended to borrow from religion its usefulness as a means of social control and has led to that aura of false promises that gives so much of the anger in the current debate the bitter quality of disappointed love.

Returning to my illustration of the debate in poetry between open and closed structures, I wish to suggest that open structure may lack an analysis because it is not a poetic form at all but a gesture toward those social reciprocities which are the precondition of the intelligibility of form. There is ample suggestion in the "human universe" ambience of American postmodernism that the conditions of life and the nature of art as conflicting claims upon value have tended to destroy one another. In this matter the university, in its perhaps naïve custodianship of literature, has played a part. If in this process of fundamental retrenchment the critic is to intervene effectively, then I think that certain specific problems become his task.

Past and Present

Whether the present is unlike the past is a question the answer to which is generally both yes and no, an answer which leads to tolerable levels both of hope and despair. Whether this present is unlike the past that it knows, in ways different from the ways in which other presents have been unlike the pasts that they know, may be quite a different question. Professor Bate has written an elegant book about the way in which the fathers take up space, how strong men in the eighteenth century met that problem, and how we, too, are, as literary persons, both enjoined to admire and, by the terms of creativity and its covenants, prohibited from being like our predecessors.[12] In addition, Professor Bloom has recently proposed a theory of tradition as anxiety principle, as a con-

12. Walter Jackson Bate, *The Burden of the Past and the English Poet* (Cambridge, Mass.: Harvard University Press, 1970).

spiracy of the fathers against the lives of the children, an analysis
with which I am in some sympathy.[13] It is clear that the relationship between this present and its past is a question of some criti-
cality. To me it seems to demand not a new theory of tradition,
but a theory other than tradition. In part, as I have already suggested, the sense of the past as a principle of anxiety (the "covering cherub" of Bloom's analogy) is an imposed predicament
derived from the claims upon the meanings of words made by
those to whom the sponsorship of the culture of letters has been
assigned and who seem to exist to set the children at odds with the
fathers if only by the promotion of unceasing explanation. But
there may be additional reasons why the fact (which at other times
it has been reasonable to ignore) that all presents are nonidentical
with their pasts, and unaccountable in terms of them, should be
a more urgent fact in this present than in other presents. The problem of the past that, as Professor Bate indicates, becomes crucial
in the eighteenth century is, in my view, related to the process of
secularization and, in particular, to the disposition to transfer the
canonicity of religious descriptions of experience (a scripture is
an account of experience which by the privilege of canonicity is
true without alternative) to literature. The past is by its nature the
part of the world in which the struggle for precedence among
competing values and images is over; at the same time, it is not
merely a claim upon existential space, it is a statement about what
is true, acknowledgment of which as tradition is a necessary precondition of creativity, indeed of intelligible existence. The nature
of "literature" as a body of accounts which can be ordered taxo-
nomically calls attention in itself to a sufficient structural invari-
ance in the artistic forms of words. The question which must be
raised is not whether the great accounts have described too much
of experience to admit of creative novelty on our part, but whether
art as we receive it describes enough of what we must know in
order to be safe to deserve our credit. In other words, it is as
reasonable to attribute the burdensomeness of the past to its
mimetic insufficiency as to its mimetic universality. On this matter
I shall say something more later on.

Two conceptions of originality, of possible relationships to the
sources of life, are apparent in twentieth-century poetics. There is
Lawrence's "Poetry of the Present," "the unrestful, ungraspable

13. Harold Bloom, *Yeats* (New York: Oxford University Press, 1970).

poetry of the sheer present, poetry whose very permanency lies in its wind-like transit,"[14] which locates origins in the continuously disclosed, dimensionlessness of sensuous duration; and there is by contrast the spatially and temporally alien poetry of the fathers, however diversely ontologized by Eliot or Yeats, the well at the world's end. At the beginning of the century, the same distinction was defended by William James in his struggle for pluralism against "the sublimity of this noetic monism and of its vague vision of the underlying connection among all phenomena without exception": "Our sense of 'freedom' supposes that some things at least are decided here and now, that the passing moment may contain some novelty, be an original starting point of events, and not merely transmit a push from elsewhere. We imagine that in some respects at least the future may not be co-implicated with the past, but may be really addable to it, and indeed addable in one shape or another, so that the next turn in events can at any given moment genuinely be ambiguous, i.e. possibly this, but also possibly that."[15] All notions of tradition imply also a notion of descriptive canonicity extending from the past to the future and are monist in James's sense. The coimplication of art with the past may specify unfreedom as a condition of art just at those points, on those issues, where we most need to be free from preemptive accounts. Criticism which should, as we all agree, make free has from Pope through Arnold set the best above history.

> Still green with bays each ancient altar stands
> Above the reach of sacrilegious hands,
> Secure from flames, from Envy's fiercer rage,
> Destructive wars and all-involving Age.

Under such a model the business of the past as mentor is "To teach vain Wits a science little known, / T'admire superior sense, and doubt their own." This idea of the past as privileged to suppress the cognitive authority of individual consciousness in the phenomenal present, inducing doubt about the validity of the reader's own sense, disabling intuitiveness, and producing contempt by the individual for his fantasy, is pervasive in literary studies. The only justification for confidence in such an interven-

14. Lawrence, *"Poetry of the Present,"* p. 183.
15. William James, "The One and the Many," (1909) *The Moral Equivalent of War and Other Essays,* ed. John K. Roth (New York: Harper and Row, 1971), p. 164.

tion at the level of the best information which persons have about their world would be tested knowledge that the past is indeed like the present and that it substantiates all the vital human facts which must appeal to it as a structure without alternative for substantiation. Didactic common sense requires, therefore, that the business of criticism at present should be the testing of the structure of the canon against the structure of experience as if for the first time. It is at the limits of the terms of reference to experience that the cost of the noetic monism of tradition becomes apparent. There, as in the tormented human sea of Williams's "The Yachts," it may be possible to perceive the consequences of the naïve advocacy of greatness.

The perennial business of poetry has been the production of secular immortality, the lasting acknowledgment in which we know that we are known because there is an image of us in the consciousness of the other that is not a contingency of our death, that is to say, an image in art. The canons of art respond to a limited range of recognitions. The question as to whether this present is like the past in the same way that other presents were like their pasts is responded to in each person or class of persons by the intimate sense of being or not being visible to the consciousness of the other and hence to the self. The past may be burdensome or a principle of anxiety because in its presence we are invisible. If in the presence of the tradition we are in fact nowhere, then there is a conflict between our freedom and tradition itself as a way of conceiving the principles of the continuity of art and persons.

The Author

I am of the opinion that the teacher of literature ought to be a member of a universal class in the Hegelian sense, mediating between the goals of art and its possibilities.[16] That it should come to be otherwise is due in part to the dominance in academic criticism of genetic theory, that is, accounts of works which consist of state-

16. For a discussion of Hegel's "universal class" and its relation to bureaucracy, see Shlomo Avineri, *The Social and Political Thought of Karl Marx* (Cambridge: Cambridge University Press, 1968), pp. 41ff., especially p. 57.

ments about how they came to be. In particular, I think we must be interested in the relationship between academic bureaucratization and the peculiar status assigned as a matter of course to authors in relation to meanings. The most common way of getting meanings out of texts is the assignment of meaning-sponsorship to a continuously present authorial agent. I choose at random instances that come to hand from a new book on Homer: "The poet who perceived wonder in the simplest acts and feelings." "Thus at the very beginning of Greek literature Homer at one stride resolved." "Homer constantly reminds us." "It is so whenever Homer traces back the origin of his heroes."[17] This aoristic (insinuating, horizonless) use of the verb constructs a myth of the origins of the reader's understanding of the meaning of the work, in the form of an imaginary history of a meaning-intending agent. This myth assigns to the author the origin of that prior knowledge in the reader of the meaning of the whole, which in Diltheyan hermeneutics is the precondition of understanding at all. That such explanatory mythologies are not casual but central to the way in which works of literature are known, cared for, and possessed is amply shown by Professor Paul de Man in his recent discussion of Blanchot and Poulet.[18] That there is now a strong, eucharistic real presence in the explanatory aorist is indicated by the current vogue of biographical writing, and by the ever-increasing professional attention being given to literary explanation. The privilege of the professional reader has become the mind and acts of the author. Since the normal model for reading in the English tradition is the replacement of personal fantasy by the poet's verbal account,[19] the mind and act of the reader have also become, just

17. Paolo Vivante, *The Homeric Imagination: A Study of Homer's Poetic Perception of Reality* (Bloomington: Indiana University Press, 1970). Needless to say, I intend no invidious judgment on this very interesting work. The idol of discourse I allude to is the same Hirsch describes as "the speaking subject" (*Validity in Interpretation,* pp. 242, 244).

18. Paul de Man, *Blindness and Insight* (New York: Oxford University Press, 1971), pp. 64, 65, 96–98.

19. Elia in East India House established his very influential model for reading along the lines of a sort of internal colonization of mind, "I love to lose myself in other men's minds. When I am not walking, I am reading; I cannot sit and think. Books think for me." Severer versions of this attitude, for example reading as self-immolation, are discussed in de Man, *Blindness and Insight.*

to the extent that he is a good reader, part of that professional privilege. Since the paradigm of creativity that emerges from the explanatory habit on which I am commenting is the mythical creativity of an author as an individual, and since the author is an imaginary creature of the professoriate, instruction often becomes a competition as to whose creativity is legitimate. This is one reason why there is little interpretive pluralism in the classroom, or indeed anywhere in literary culture at present. Not questions of text but questions of meaning have become the battleground for dominance, and the student is driven, as I have said, to epistemologically desperate and morally false ideas of the total relativity of "the subjective" in order to protect himself from the authoritative interventions of his teachers at the most intimate levels of response and self-determination. The bureaucratization of intimacy based in the genetic hypothesis that comes to stand for interpretation tends to set the fathers against the children in the interest of tradition and its explainers.

The most subversive countergenealogy is the one which locates the origin of the work in the reader. Against it, philosophical criticism mounts the slogan, "The text means what the author intended it to mean," allowing an indefinite space outside the near redundance of text and meaning for significance.[20] In fact, unstable literary ontologies do lead to fuss about what will happen in the face of the assimilative reader, and literary ontologies become unstable when the basis of human reciprocity on which literary culture stands becomes deformed. Genetic theory involves some mistake about the source of art, but is surely right in its general concern with *source,* a word so obsessively abused in literary studies. Trilling in his essay "The Two Environments" alludes to Yeats's sentence, "The object of magic in all ages was and is to obtain control over the sources of life."[21] That is certainly also the object of literary culture. That there should arise a struggle for control of the sources of life among the living and also, as it were, between the living and the dead evidences the absence of a term in which all parties are united. It seems obvious to me that all the sponsoring groups in literary culture meet in a never completed

20. Hirsch, *Validity in Interpretation,* p. 25.
21. Lionel Trilling, *Essays on Literature and Learning* (New York: Viking Press, 1965), p. 221.

fullness of the communicability of selves, apprehension of which removes the afflictive tyrannies to which I have alluded; but there is in modern discourse no term of reference to such a state. The being of literature dwells in the collective where alone its ontologies become strong. In order to construct a mythology more truth-bearing than that of authorial presence, something must be said about the obstacles which have arisen in critical practice.

Access to the sources of life may be conceived to be obtained through style or story. Trilling speaks for style, the permanently characterizing, life-conserving trace of individuality:

> A true relation to the sources of life does not refer to rational criteria; it is expressed not in doctrine, not in system, ethics, and creeds, but in manner and style. We know whether or not a person is in touch with the sources of life not by what he says but by the way he says it, by the tone of his voice, the look in his eye, by his manner and style. So too with a society: we know if it is really in touch with the sources of life not by its mere practical arrangements but by the style of life that it fosters — in short by its culture, which we judge as a whole, rather as if it were a work of art.[22]

Walter Benjamin speaks for story, the collective *episteme* of narrative: "A ladder extending downward to the interior of the earth and disappearing into the clouds is an image for a collective experience to which even the deepest shock of individual experience, death, constitutes no impediment or barrier."[23] The division of literary analysis between style and story has become a boundary situation in critical perception because the ontology of the poem lies precisely at the point of meeting of these two kinds of theory where both are radically some third thing. They are, respectively, a horizontal and a vertical theory: the former from Longinus, incorporating the aoristic authorial presence, the social person ("the look in his eye"), freedom, "style"; the latter from Vico, incorporating the structural fiction, the generic person, necessity, "story."[24] Together, but not as a sum of the parts, they become

22. *Ibid.*

23. Walter Benjamin, *Illuminations* (New York: Harcourt Brace Jovanovich, 1968), p. 102. The translation is by Harry Zohn.

24. It is instructive in this regard to compare Longinus and Vico on the conception of "Homer."

the coordinates of a usable world, and therefore at their intersection a source of life. But the term *aesthetic,* which since Baumgarten we use for the collective form of private experience, is no longer a value-bearing category. It has become the place where the ghostly author and the custodians of art send the reader to lose his purposes, where being loses meaning by becoming beautiful. And the term *collective* has never been intelligible in literary discourse. It is evidence of the instability of literary ontology that *the work,* in which, in Jaspers's phrase, mankind rejoices in communicability, has no other name.

Literature, considered as something men do together, is a negotiation of the impossibility of speaking truthfully about the self as a whole self, not only the self in its conscious and unconscious interiority, but also in its scarcely apprehended continuities with nature. Consequently, it is not a self; nor does it represent a self in the singular sense, for it is a *donnée* of Western civilization that the self cannot accomplish its own recapitulation, remember its past lives, make its way unaided to its own source. Hence, men are pitched together in the common effort to tell one another about the self, like the heroes of Gilgamesh who read one another's dreams. Nor is the consequence of the collective effort to gain knowledge of the sources of life, which cannot be known intuitively or alone, an interpretation of life, but life itself, very life. The business of critical consciousness is the correct description of the means of life such that the complex reciprocal priority of work to reader and reader to work cancels neither term and such that there is no deformation of the symmetry by the interposition from the community of readers of an alien stake, as is so pervasively the case in the professional forms of literary culture.[25] Genetic hypotheses such as I have described separate the mind from genesis (the genesis comes to be *in* the other) and hence the self from its destiny and relations. All speech is, of course, an account of some small part of the whole situation of a speaker, a universal synecdoche. The most limited traditional vision of that synecdoche in art, and also its dominant form at the present time, is the lyric

25. The aoristic authorial presence defines the phenomenal issue of the priority of the work to the reader in an unmanageable way. It ignores the priority of the work to the author as well, making the fantasy-author, like the modern critic, an acosmic individual rather than a participator with the reader in the cosmos as a source of life and a large part of identity.

"I." In the small space of that figure men must move together, as best they can, toward the mastery of the sources of life. If competition for that space is irreducible, then the contrary of culture is not primitivism, barbarism or anarchy, but life itself. If, however, the proper description of art provides, as I think, a model for the common struggle of all men with the true enemies of life, then the high business of criticism is the elaboration of that description.

Cultural Membership

Traditional literary culture has as its spectral enemy Babel, the place where everybody speaks in his own language, and the collective enterprise which challenged heaven is ruined. English literature is itself a concession (part, as I shall suggest, of a movement which should be definitive of its nature as a study) to the legitimacy of pluralism in symbolic discourse. But there is a fundamental incompatibility between literary order and infinitely differentiating particularism that asserts as a right the autonomy and centrality of all accounts — merely because they are accounts of persons who *will* live, not by the delegation of the privilege of image to a central order, but in the likeness of their own god, their proper source. The very idea of study of literature in the mother tongue implies the anarchy of incestuous autonomy and imports no principle which excludes the claim to symbolic self-determination and indeed rule of any other matrix. Each student approached as a discrete source becomes an abyss which swallows up the interpretive enterprise of the responsible custodian of reality, and each particularism of class, *ethnos,* or sex defines claims against the background of a changeless, finite past, which, if acknowledged as sovereign, constitutes an inherent promise of everlasting mimetic scarcity. We are well aware that the love of art is a mistake about love if it is not subordinate to a love of persons and that the willingness on anyone's part to labor at art, that is to say, become a reader, makes the poem surely his. But the Babel of voices, interpretive claims, and concrete universes of recognition that then arises is a struggle of acknowledgment unanticipated by tradition. It is not clear that symbolic order can survive without a *genus mutum.*

We have remarked that shifts in the conception of literary
studies involving some relinquishment of the sovereignty of structure and tending toward the aesthetic, native, liberal, and interpretive are characteristic of postwar periods. There is an analysis of
such a period in the essay by Benjamin to which I have already
alluded.

> With the [First] World War a process began to become apparent
> which has not halted since then. Was it not noticeable at the end
> of the war that men returned from the battlefield grown silent —
> not richer, but poorer in communicable experience? What ten years
> later was poured out in the flood of war books was anything but
> experience that goes from mouth to mouth. And there is nothing
> remarkable about that. For never has experience been contradicted
> more thoroughly than strategic experience by tactical warfare, eco-
> nomic experience by inflation, bodily experience by mechanical
> warfare, moral experience by those in power. A generation that
> had gone to school on a horse drawn street car now stood under
> the open sky in a country-side in which nothing remained un-
> changed but the clouds, and beneath these clouds, in a field of
> force of destructive torrents and explosions, was the tiny fragile
> human body.[26]

It is within Benjamin's sense to say that the possession of an
image flows as a right from the right to life, and that "possession
of an image" might reasonably be described as a man's ability to
tell a story about himself, a story which begins in some way with
the sources of all life and ends in some way with the outcome of
all life.[27] In order to restore the resource of communicable experience and hence the reality of persons as storytellers, a new criticism arises. The problems with which it must deal involve certain
paradoxes. Since the canon of representation remains the same, it
is in interpretation that the will to renewal of the community is
expressed. But every interpretation is a crisis in the community,
a further challenge to the continuities of its understandings, a solicitation of Babel. In addition, since war, because of the trans-

---

26. Benjamin, *Illuminations,* p. 84.
27. A story by its transmissibility overwhelms the unknowability of
self to other, and by its objectivity the unknowability of the self to itself.

individual nature of its means and purposes, reduces in effect the value of the individual identity of all participants to zero, all prior contracts with respect to imaginal dominance and subordination require to be renegotiated, and there arises a factor of scarcity in the symbolic realm analogous to economic scarcity. New claims on cultural membership are put forward, and the profound hunger of all persons to be known raises questions not merely about the administration of the symbolic resource but about its fundamental adequacy. In practical teaching, questions arise as to the relation between the canon as it is understood by the teacher and the symbolic needs of the student, and these questions in turn raise other questions about the universality and particularity of literature itself. It seems clear to me that the interpretation of texts involves not so much the derivation of meanings as the mediation of representations as accounts of selves. The interpretation is true only if it is a tellable tale. Great anger on the part of the teaching community is occasioned by the insistence of the student that the images of which the teacher is a custodian are somebody else's tale, somebody else's immortality. But the idea of universality and the idea of literature are not identical, and this, too, constitutes a boundary situation in criticism involving the same terms which we have previously introduced as closure and aperture, style and story, genesis and existence.

In my view we can hypothesize a benign state of literary culture in which the entailments of its richest existence do not militate against the peace of the world, but we cannot enter that state, and for this reason: particularisms of all sorts assert that style is the source of life. Style is sovereign without being inclusive; as symbolic nationalism it is divisive, totalistic, asserting claims that intersect with the claims of others. Modernism established style as the distinguishing mark of literary authority. Universalism, by contrast, purports to be styleless, a pathway to the source of life unmediated by any individual person, global, serving identity at levels prior to the social, the literary theory of the national exile and the cosmic citizen. Like the notion of the collective, univers-true referent. In Frye's language, particularism defines art as dis-alism is a term of analysis and not of fact. In literature it has no placement, universalism as myth. If literary value resides wholly in the displacement, the perfected and unique language arrangement, then the profound, anthropogenetic values it mediates require, as their condition of being, retrenchment toward cultural nationalism, separatism, and the collision of classes, sexes, peoples in the struggle for dominance implied by the closed nature of personality expressed in traditional literary structures. Under such a regime literary education becomes a search for the points of convergence of the biogenetic origins of the individual and his symbolic culture. If the opposite is the case, then literary education must seek to loosen ties with the biological and indeed racial sources and conduct the student toward the universal resource where the struggle between choice and necessity is somehow lost in global individuality, where "the only abiding loyalty is one to mankind as a whole."[28] The latter is an abstract model of Renaissance education, the myth of origins of a ruling class whose relationship to the earth is presumptive. The former, earth-aspiring, essentially tragic countermodel defines the real situation of imaginative life.

Returning to the eighteenth century where we found the initial separation of poetry and criticism, we call to mind the Latin tag applied by Johnson to the achievement of Dryden, *"lateritiam invenit, marmoream reliquit."* This process of the transformation of the mother tongue from brick to marble requires some attention. The truly social man, in Renaissance educational theory, speaks a language other than his mother tongue, has in the process of socialization journeyed from *natura* to *natio,* from bondage in the feminine, earth and the realm of necessity, to acknowledgment of the father, the realm of freedom.[29] The resistance in this model of education to study of the mother tongue and also of natural science (another version of the realm of necessity) reflects the insistence that social man find his compelling loyalties elsewhere than in the earth. English studies, as an institution, was placed directly athwart the competing notions of man as self-affirming in the earth *(lateritia)* and man as self-affirming in the sky *(marmorea),* literature as fundamentally particularist or as fundamentally

28. Northrup Frye, *The Critical Path: An Essay on the Social Context of Literary Criticism* (Bloomington: Indiana University Press, 1971), p. 26. My general categories are comparable to Frye's "concern and "freedom." My conclusions differ from his.

29. Compare Ben Jonson's well-known poem of gratitude "To William Camden."

universalist, style and closure or myth and aperture, judgment or dream.

The global diffusion by technology and empire of English literature, the immense, heterogonous consequences of a literature with such eccentric geographical and political origins, obscures the fact that literary education in the mother tongue was to begin with a turning back upon earth origins — an entering into chthonian mythologies, an alignment of education with the potentially anarchic forces of genetic particularism.[30] The first consequence of the institutionalization of the mother tongue was, in effect, its masculinization (the mother tongue is by definition what you don't have to be taught), that is to say, the making of the language of the most intimate relationships an alien thing, part of the *natio,* or secondary social affiliation, rather than of the *natura,* the matrix. In America this effect was enhanced by the endemic colonial and Puritan sense that nothing meaningful is given from the earth.[31] Either English literature was a woman's language, anarchic, particularist, atavistic, and thus inimical to abstract order, or it was made over as a language of rule and subordination, ceasing to be the mother tongue as soon as it became teachable. Since English studies is one phase of modern nationalism, the appearance of classes of people who repudiate the symbolic appropriation or Augustan masculinization of the mother tongue, or who go behind the Renaissance model of the parvenu learner, or who declare that the collectivity served by what is called socialization is not their own, seems to me precisely anticipated by its nature as a movement and a fulfillment, rather than a betrayal of its implications. The clear preference at present for *natura* over *natio,* the ground over the figure, and the devaluation everywhere of federal symbols leading to a corresponding revaluation of older particularist accounts of the self poses the problem of the evolution of literary education. But English studies was, in fact, an initiative toward the freeing of human energies, both social classes and psychological states, and there is no reason fundamental to its

30. The rise of English studies in England and America runs parallel to national movements symbolic and political throughout the world, e.g., in Ireland, Italy, and Japan.

31. One notes the overriding emphasis on the teaching of writing at Harvard in the 1880's and 1890's. See Bliss Perry, *And Gladly Teach* (Boston: Houghton Mifflin, 1936).

theory or practice why it should not act as such unless it identifies itself with the peculiar, secondary political functions by which it was almost from the beginning preempted.

The problem for criticism is the issue of cultural membership and the more fundamental theoretical question of the intrinsic nature of the inveterate distinction between the particular and the universal. "Socialization" has acquired a negative valence because its rituals have ceased to be value-bearing, among them literary education. In order to become to itself an object of evolving rational concern through criticism, literary studies must abandon the inherently paradoxical notion that it transmits the mother tongue of anybody and join in the search for the mother tongue (its characterizing enterprise) now long lost. No one doubts that true socialization, collective human struggle, constant sustaining mutual recognition, immortality, is the enterprise of which literature is a part. Whether or not the paradoxes of particularism and universality, style and story, are inseparable from the literary fact is a question that lies not within art, but between art and the world of persons, which is its source and end. Only the most scrupulous attentiveness to the relation between person and story, and the most empathic attentiveness to the style of each teller can justify our day to day instruction, in the absence of the theoretical and social reordering of the discipline on which its beneficial evolution depends.

Concluding Observations

Greatness. The quarrel for prestige between the myth and the displacement in the ontology of the poem becomes objective only in the absence of the cultural person, the reader who reads to tell the tale; and the facilitation of such personhood is not advanced by misdefinitions. Art is not a solution to secularization for the reason that it is not an independent value. The notion that art is in itself capable of sustaining the value of persons is a romantic error, akin to the assignment of sovereignty to metaphor, a mistake of the part for the whole. The conflict between art and the attainment of cultural personhood becomes acute when the speaker in the poem, as in the romantic stereotype, becomes identified as the poet, so that the reader bent on participation is set the irrelevant task of "greatness" as a displacement and not an evolution of his own nature. The ontological destiny of the poem is the conservation of all names as part of the ontological destiny of civilization as a whole. In this destiny the English studies movement should be regarded as a phase in the mimetic establishment of the image life of all persons (not the reestablishment, for in this matter there is no desirable prior situation), the slow, troubled convergence of the canon of images toward the real universe of all selves who speak, and a phase in the withdrawal of consent from the feudal settlement that some should have stories and others live by "representation." Since the proper institution of literature is the culture as a whole, and since literature is reliant on the intactness of adjacent canons of religion, philosophy, and the gestures of ordinary life (all poetic languages being, as is obvious, versions of social languages), I think it reasonable to suppose that the appropriate, in my terms the "strong," critical negation at present may have nothing to do with literary fact at all, but with its boundaries and conditions. The reified idea of the great is indeed absurd if it is thought that greatness is a predicate of something exclusively characteristic of the poem or the poet as a principle of life. Poems are occasions of the greatness of persons. Conceived of as great objects, they become the tombs of possibility for generations and obstacles to the meditative self-recovery of individuals, obstacles which are ipso facto insuperable. The impoverishment of poems as meditative tools at present is apparent in the resort of the young to heterogeneous quasi-religious meditative disciplines. Greatness, when it seems to derive from the object alone, is a phantom from which it is consistent with dignity to flee.

Scarcity. The maxim on which my observations are based is that the end and nature of art is use and the validation of art the greatness of the person in its ·presence. Interpretation, therefore, is pragmatic, the preparation for being of the reader. The problem to which interpretation must speak now is the self-doubt as to existence of all persons. We live proleptically in the psychic aftermath of the Third World War, which has destroyed us all. This struggle for existence as image in the historical situation renders acutely problematic previously tolerable states of affairs, principal among them the background of image-scarcity against which the traditional labor for immortality takes place. The struggle is, in addition, exacerbated in so called postindustrial, secular societies by the withdrawal of opportunities to validate the self in labor at the means of life, and this acosmism is the same as that which arises in the absence of redemptive hope, sacred labor toward a god in whom world and man are united as in a common source. The interpretive struggle is for the medium of visibility; and the question must necessarily arise as to whether the medium itself is not predicated upon a hierarchy of the real and the unreal person as its very principle. The question is, to put it another way, whether there is any value to the image in the absence of imaginal scarcity and any study of literature which does not create such scarcity.

The state of the issue is obvious enough:[32] The canon of representation of traditional Western literature is a matrix in which all social persons and all experiences do not occur. The exclusionary principle is not casual but systematic. Not merely kings and not commoners, possessors and not slaves, but also the conquering imperium and not the conquered, the scribal culture and not the practic, the successor religion and not the predecessor, the strong and not the weak, the poet and not the dunce. The inveterate preference for the "sons of day" and for moderate states of consciousness has created a situation such that its reversal does not constitute a rectification (as the present state of the American novel demonstrates). Interpretation, the most important "weak" sense of critical, is the traditional solution;[33] but the unevolved state of the theory of reading which I have tried to illustrate suggests that participation, the life strategy of *methexis,* is involved at present in unfathomable complexities. This is also the remote cause of the difficulty of specifying the newly evolved open prosodies, prosody being the middle term between the individual and his transindividual resource. In the most hopeful view, the lodgment of the image in the social and theological station, where it becomes the self-validating instrument of a hierarchical culture in

32. I have discussed these matters in "Teaching Literature in a Discredited Civilization," *The Massachusetts Review* (Summer 1969).

33. I refer to the function of interpretation in religious cultures as a means of reversing the meaning of texts by subjectification of the referents (e.g., "The Bagavad Gita," a poem about aristocrats at war, transformed into a mental event becomes a poem about everybody's inner struggle).

which the visible is the only real, the imaginal the only visible, and art therefore not a criticism of life but a means of controlling its sources, may be a reparable state of affairs by the same evolution which has brought myself and you, the reader of my words, to the problem. But there still remains the extreme issue for criticism which I pointed to at the onset of my remarks when I observed that in postmodernism, the perfected form of the thing is the most problematic, the most dangerous by its closeness to the sources of life, as, for example, atomic physics, molecular biology, and the most original art. This reversal, from positive to negative, of the relationship between the imagination and the continuity of life is one of the chief perceptions of poetry since the war and has determined its withdrawal from modernist monumentality as from another reified value out of scale with human life and predatory upon it. The muse of Yeats is at last seen as the Teeth Mother whose new avatar is the exquisitely constructed fighter-bomber which executes the vengeance of the sky upon the earth.

In order for these matters to become a subject of criticism, the critic must divest himself of the inutile antinomies of culture and anarchy, civilization and primitivism, the educated and the mob, great art and its nameless contrary. This is not another case of the putting down of vermin.[34] Nor is it a matter of culture and its antistates or counterstates, instances of which demonstrate repeatedly that culture does not admit of alternatives and has no deeply significant variations of a merely oppositional sort. If the mono-myth is anything like what it is said to be,[35] namely the detachment of consciousness from its given concerns, the quest for the sources of life, and the return, then the business of criticism is with the administration of the sources in this way disclosed, and the critic is ipso facto a political man. But the mono-myth is not really of that order, for such a reading of it is patently an oneiric strategy for the self-compensation of the critic in view of the fundamental alienation imposed by literature itself or, in effect, by criticism as the only activity to which literature gives rise. A true critical task

34. My allusion is to an ambiguous application of a phrase of Pound's in Graham Hough's otherwise wholly admirable *The Dream and the Task* (London: Gerald Duckworth and Co., 1963) p. 41. I do not think it has been determined what constitutes the *trahison des clercs* just now.

35. For example, by Joseph Campbell.

is the reduction of just such reflexive monism, and the search for the implications of that pluralism which was the larger motive of the modern experiment of which English studies is a part. Only the search of the boundaries of the canon as a cooperative task can justify the continued promulgation of the tradition by those who secure their self-invention from it.

A Story about Relationship. The question, therefore, when gazing upon the canon, is why all this should not be otherwise, for art is like other things and not merely the unalterable likeness of other things. Only a misconception about the categories of past and present, such as I have pointed to earlier, removes art from the general evolutionary obligation of consciousness. All forms of art are interpretations of experience, like all states of consciousness. Because they specify the points of congruence between consciousness and meaning they are also as static structures predictions about experience. Neither tragedy nor comedy, for example, as interpretations of experience, foretells the negotiation of the human situation whole. In tragedy the gigantic human totality is extinguished or exchanged for an image as a consequence of contradictions which are an inherent, and if the term is ever appropriate, willed, aspect of the interpretation of experience implicit structurally in tragedy itself as a moment of consciousness. In comedy the gigantic totality is abandoned, relinquished in exchange for the measured and diminished consummation in human scale, the marriage. Tragedy displays act unenlightened and undiminished by knowledge — act before knowledge. Comedy shows act diminished but also enlightened by knowledge — knowledge before act. Literature is taught because it is a small part of the effort of some persons at self-invention toward a comic destiny.

But two things seem clear and underlie my remarks: First, literature without a profound and novel critical effort has become, as a study, an infelicitous abstraction from the process rather than a facilitation of it, in part because a burdensome sense of the past peculiar to literary culture has allowed consciousness to be caught by terms of discourse, such as tragedy and comedy, which deprive it of its proper evolutionary hopefulness. In the same way that the first critic supposed the tragic hero to be flawed, when in fact the universe itself denies the hero the consummation of his human will, so literary culture as an institution is disposed to display tragedy as the maxim which predicts the defectiveness of the human agent and the unalterability of those forces, including death, which will defeat him and which, as a structural proposition, literary culture sponsors. Second, comedy itself is no longer a viable model, for the elements in reality which must be suppressed to gain the consummation, like the serving women over whose dead bodies the remarriage of Penelope and Odysseus is celebrated, rise up in many forms and refuse to serve the triumph of the king.

If there is a mono-myth, then, it must be an as yet unknown but totally anticipated story about the relationship of all persons among themselves rejoicing in the truth of communicability which arises when meaning and being coincide. The business of teachers whose knowledge is literary is to work at the story in hopeful ways. The terms of the story will be as well illustrated in the right conduct of literary education as anywhere else, as well illustrated but no better.

The function of poetry (the conservation of the terms of personhood) is realized in the communities it forms. The simple, rather faithless associations in which we find ourselves telling one another about art is really all there is to it. Poetry constellates communities by pitching persons toward one another full of news. The competition, if there is to be any, is with respect to the fineness of the terms of reciprocation. So, we measure art against our highest intuitions of the concrete features of the nobility we desire for one another. What men seek for one another in literature is the safety which consists in telling a true story about the self, one which includes all the alliances of the self. And that must be a story which stretches from the origin of things to the end of things. Everyone must learn to speak the story for himself, and no one can do that except in the presence of others. When one can tell his story he becomes a person for persons. A man who can tell his own story facilitates the story of another and that ability is a meditative requirement for the teacher, his proper educational attainment. What people do for one another in literary communities is to describe the self. No amount of realistic zeal will assure the authority of the description. It is neither ratified nor disabled by passion or scholarship. What is required is the recollected self-awareness of the end of art — namely the person. In the matter of interpretation there are no rules; only the one function. The work of art has no other ontology than the relationship in which it is known. Poetry is in this sense the "human face divine," the beloved companion, the nothing in itself in whose presence we obtain ourselves. Anything else is something else. The strong sense I propose for criticism ought to unite such men as are concerned with art in the relentlessly conscious struggle with art as it is part of experience, guided by the final purpose which is the immortality of all being.

EDWARD W. SAID

On Originality

All things counter, original, spare, strange;

G. M. Hopkins

Anyone who has ever dealt seriously with literature has had to confront the problem of originality. There are a few principal ways in which originality as a quality or an idea seems essential to the experience of literature, but what I think counts as impressively is the sheer number of subsidiary insinuations of originality into our thinking about literature. For not only does one speak of a book as original, of a writer as possessing greater or lesser originality than another, but also of original uses of such and such a form, type, character, structure; moreover, specialized versions of originality are found put to use in all thinking about literary origins, novelty, radicalism, innovation, influence, tradition, conventions, and periods. There is no good reason to disagree now with Wellek and Warren: originality, they wrote laconically in 1949, is indeed "a fundamental problem of literary history."[1] But just how fundamental and how persistently elusive is the problem? Ought it to claim the analytic attention of the scholar, the teacher-writer and the student of literature?

1. René Wellek and Austin Warren, *Theory of Literature* (1949; rep. New York: Harcourt, Brace and World, 1968), p. 258.

I shall argue that originality as an element of literary experience is something worth examining, especially if one holds more than casually the belief that the study of literature has a crucial intellectual role to play in the contemporary university. Although I don't here discuss the originality of literature itself, some of what I say will point obliquely to that topic. But I should say immediately that in order for this interest to add up to more than a catalogue of examples (that is, Marlowe is original because . . . , or Dryden has originality because . . .), any interest in this privileged quality we associate with literature can really be sustained profitably only at a level of investigation not ordinarily associated with the practice of literary study, namely the theoretical. Now the going dogma is that literature is concreteness human, social, historical, and so forth, which is to say that literature affords us aesthetic instances of every variety of experience. Theory on the other hand is associated with abstractions and ideas, or with whatever amalgam of woolgathering that passes for philosophy when it is conceived of by the defensive literary student. This is not to say that theory has no influence among literary critics, for the extent to which Northrop Frye's criticism has power over students and teachers alike is a sign of their susceptibility (perhaps even vulnerability) to theoretical devices.

It is an instructive coincidence that what I mean by the theoretical level of investigation is connected historically in the West with perception of a notion of originality. A theme first taken up in Plato's dialogues, then again critically in Aristotle, is the relationship between the knowledge of Ideas (theory) and a man's life. Plato, Werner Jaeger says, "was the first to introduce the theoretical man as an ethical problem into philosophy and to justify and glorify his life."[2] Between Plato and the generation made up of Aristotle's students — Aristotle himself never abandoned his "Platonic legacy [of a belief in the moral value of the theoretic life] that had been so decisive for his attitude of research and his ideal of science"[3] — there occurred a fluctuation of belief

2. "On the Origin and Cycle of the Philosophic Ideal of Life," in *Aristotle: Fundamentals of the History of His Development,* trans., Richard Robinson (1934; rep. London: Oxford University Press, 1962), p. 429.
    3. *Ibid.,* p. 444.

that moved from the ideal of a contemplative life to arguments
for an active, practically involved life. And Jaeger points out that
stories about philosophers were used as evidence of the *originality,* the theoretically and contemplatively oriented *unusual*
behavior, of the philosophers among men. Thus,

> at first we find Socrates and Plato linking the moral world to the
> philosophical knowledge of being. Then in Dicaearchus' [a student
> of Aristotle] practical ideal, life and ethics are entirely withdrawn
> again from the rule of high philosophical speculation and restored
> to independence, and the daring wing of speculative thought is
> pinioned. With it fades the power of the ideal of theoretic life.
> When we meet it thereafter it is always the world of "pure science"
> and contrasted as such with the life of practice . . . Not until the
> destruction of scientific philosophy and metaphysics by skepticism
> could the theoretic life achieve renewal, now in the religious form
> of the contemplative life, which has been the monastic ideal since
> Plato's work of that name.[4]

From this debate comes the general division of work into active
on the one hand, and theoretical-contemplative on the other. In a
specialized form this division persists today in literary demotic as
the distinction between creative-original and critical-interpretive
writing. This generates another division, symmetrical to it, that
creative-original writing is primary, whereas any other kind is
secondary. Consistently enough, the study of literature in the
United States is conducted with these distinctions very much in
mind. A *writer*-author suggests the glamour of doing, of bohemia,
of *originality* close to the real matter of life (always we find the
closeness of reality and originality); a *critic*-scholar-author suggests drudgery, passivity, impotence, second-order material, and
faded monkishness. As the distinctions between original work and
secondary criticism have further multiplied in time, opinion has
not been kind to the critic, even if allowances have been made for
what the eighteenth-century English Augustans have called the
true critic. Today the student of literature is encouraged by the
curriculum and the ideology of study to bring himself out from
the haze of criticism and nearer the firm stones (Arnold's critical

4. *Ibid.,* p. 461.

imagery is still influential) of "creative writing": he tries for the concreteness and vivacity denied him, by definition, in study.

With this process so established, it perhaps seems an idle impertinence to introduce the Platonic and Aristotelian theoretic life as a life worth considering, if not actually living! Not if *theoria* is properly grasped. And not if the theoretical level of investigation can be shown to be capable now not only of dealing with such questions as originality, but also of being able to identify areas of study, problems of study, methods of study less shy of the whole range of experience available for modern writing. This latter capability of course constitutes relevance, but I intend a very disciplined sort that makes short work of modish and ill-defined subjects with a contemporary look. By theory and theoretical investigation applied to literature, I mean an active attention paid to concerns that are irreducible, that do not belong *to any but* verbal experience in general, and literature in particular. Only on this level can there be some hope for rigor and for the formulation of distinctive problems that are genuinely amenable to study. Most of the present courses and methods of literature are the product of a humanistic outlook no longer produced by the culture or even by the university. The study of authors and periods, occasionally of genres and themes, has always presupposed a knowledge of classical languages at least, and some sort of scholarly grounding in history, philology, and philosophy: this can no longer be assumed, for reasons too obvious to rehearse. Therefore both the student and the teacher have one alternative in the so-called appreciation of literature (for which such terms as *sensibility, impressiveness,* and *wit* serve as an intellectual scaffolding), and another in methodologies and techniques of study (for which machines erected from other systems first prepare the text then deliver it into interpretation). Theory, as I understand it, is more generous and capable of finer strictness than either of these alternatives.

Reading and writing are activities that theoretically and actually incorporate within them everything that one needs for the understanding and the production of a text. This is a truism only for someone who will not, for example, see that writing is the complex, orderly translation of innumerable forces into decipherable script; at bottom these forces converge around a *desire to write,* which is a choice made over the desire to speak, to gesture, to dance, and so on. So far as a theoretical view is concerned, then, a first question to be answered is why was writing intended in the case of a given text and not some other activity? Why that particular kind of writing and not another? Why, with relation to other similar writing, at that moment and not at another? Implied here is a sequence of rational choices made by the writer for which the evidence is a printed text. Strictly speaking, unconscious motivation is a boundary of sorts, but by no means — as Freud and more recently Jacques Lacan have demonstrated — a theater closed to the rational investigation of language. As for reading, there is a series of related questions: reading is always *for* a purpose that involves the writing in question. Why read this and not write? Reading in order to do what? Reading as development, or reading as appropriation?

Even in formulating these questions we leave behind much of the vagueness and privacy normally associated with uses of the word *originality.* Most of us do no more than experience originality as something that happens to a quality of our attention, which is enlivened or shocked by a literary work that pushes all others either into second place or out of sight. Since this sort of displacement is relatively common, originality might just as well be a name for an endless, perhaps occasionally violent, substitution of one experience for another. But rather than leave it at that, we can study writing itself as an activity in which identifiable forces play, as events taking place in a designated space, some being combined, others being displaced, still others being returned. Therefore the value of writing as an object of analysis is that it makes more precise, lively, and dramatic, the almost anonymous alternation of presence and absence we impressionistically and perceptually associate with originality. Presence and absence cease to be mere functions of our perception and become instead willed performances by the writer. Thus, presence, for example, has to do with such matters as representation, incarnation, imitation, indication, expression, whereas absence has to do with symbolism, connotation, unity, structure, and so forth. Writing can be seen then also as the setting in which the interplay of presence and absence *methodically* takes place. Rilke's description of the "fundamental element" of Rodin's art catches my meaning perfectly:

"This differently great surface variedly accentuated, accurately measured, out of which everything must rise."[5]

All this so far leaves one crucial issue somewhat unclear. What is the unit of theoretical interest; that is, what — how defined and demarcated a spatial or temporal interval — does one focus upon in a theoretical examination of writing or reading? If there is anything that centrally characterizes modern writing it is a dissatisfaction with and a problematization of traditional units of interest like the text, the author, the period, and even the idea. These are now seen at most to do provisional service as makeshift terms in an agreed upon shorthand covering textuality, but in reality they are but signs themselves in need of careful cryptanalysis. As Michel Foucault has asked, at what point does an author's text begin, at what does it end? Is a postcard or a laundry list written by Nietzsche a sequence within his integral text, or not? From the standpoint of writing, who is Swift, who is Shakespeare or Marx?[6] How can one apprehend a personality supposedly contained by graphemes on a page? In short, so expanded and diverse and specialized have the levels and dimensions of verbal apprehension become, and so sustained the exploitation of these levels by modern writing — witness the overwhelming use of parallels, echoes, fragments, parodies in Eliot, Joyce, Kafka, Mann, Borges, Beckett — that a newly adequate scheme for assembling them into intelligible units has to be sought.

Such comparatively recent schema as *style* (or idiolect) or *structure* have generated extraordinarily interesting disciplines (stylistics and structural analysis respectively).[7] These are affili-

5. *Rodin*, trans. Jessie Lamont and Hans Trausil (New York: Fine Editions Press, 1945), p. 11.

6. "Qu'est-ce qu'un auteur?" *Bulletin de la Societé francaise de Philosophie*, 63, no. 3 (July-September 1969), 79. It is appropriate to mention at this point that much in my text draws upon the work of a school of contemporary French critics and philosophers of whom Foucault is one; others are Jacques Derrida, Gilles Deleuze, Roland Barthes, and Philippe Sollers. For all of them, the notion of *écriture* is an important one; my word *writing* imperfectly translates the notion.

7. A celebrated example of structural analysis is to be found in Claude Lévi-Strauss, *Mythologies*, 4 vols. (Paris: Plon, 1964, 1966, 1968, 1972). The best recent work in stylistics, using "the history of words" as an analytic universal, is by Michael Riffaterre, *Essais de stylistique structurale* (Paris: Flammarion, 1971).

ated less with traditional disciplines like philology than with modern linguistics, which in turn is itself based upon the study of linguistic universals that enable linguistic performance. Systematic criticism such as Frye's, brilliantly resourceful though it is, also presumes a specific and innate literary faculty capable of generating a finely ordered "stubborn structure." My point here is that the kind of theoretical study I am suggesting will not, except in a very literal way, assume the universal and prior presence of imperatives pressing writers to write any more than it assumes the prior existence of units like the novel or the essay; rather what is assumed is a set of contingent circumstances or conditions from which came the decision, selected from among other courses of action, to write. The unit of study is determined by those circumstances that, for the writer in question, seem to have enabled, or generated, the *intention* to write.

The distinction I am making is well illustrated near the end of the *Phaedrus* (S.276), where Socrates marks off "an intelligent word . . . the living word of knowledge" from words "tumbled out anywhere . . . [with] no parent to protect them." The former are words deliberately sowed and cultivated; the latter are "written in water." Socrates's many-tiered argument is centered upon how it is that knowledge is formulated, disseminated, and acquired in words, a process he likens both to the slow, methodic cultivation of a garden and to the creation of a family by a solicitous father. Here again theory and originality coincide, for there can be no theoretical knowledge without a discernible origin: all true knowledge, whatever its form, exists within the domain of the knowable, which is also to say that the knowable is attained by "dialectical study," by seriousness, and above all, by caring for what is the mind's "legitimate offspring" (S.278). Socrates's merging of theoretical knowledge with man's most intimate production, his offspring, emphasizes what is too often forgotten, namely the proximity of a particular, concrete, human function and need to an abstract, theoretical, and general intention. Actually Socrates presses the relation more closely by saying that a theoretical capacity *fathers* practical works.

This really intimate connection between theoretical intention and existential performance seems to me quite literally one of the more fertile truths in Western thought. It is to be found in

Marx, obviously, but also in Hegel and Kant and Freud, as well as in any writing that brings together, as in the novel, continuity and originality. Socrates is not talking simply about the intention to yoke theory to practice, as the slogan has it, but he is also validating the direct relevance of an abstracted, hence vigilant, knowledge to a practical impulse. Or conversely and more interestingly, this truth presses responsibility for a theoretical extension *upon the practical intention.* That this has long gone neglected in literary studies is a function of what Georg Lukács and Roland Barthes, independently, have characterized as the reification, the mythologization of *things;* things seem not only present, given, natural, and unchanging, but they exclude the traces of their origin and that of any thought that might show them to have been the result of a *theory,* or a process designed exactly to show no theory or process at all.[8] Therefore, to study literature as given writing, canonized in texts, books, poems, works, dramas, and so forth, is to treat as natural and concrete that which derives from a desire — to write — that is ceaseless, varied, and highly unnatural and abstract, since "to write" is a function never exhausted by the completion of a piece of writing. Thus, only a theoretical interest in the abstract, a general interest in what is permanently knowable, though subject to numerous contingencies, can possibly deal with so apparently limitless an original (that is, irreducible) impulse. Indeed, one could argue persuasively, I think, that contemporary writing is best seen as an outstripping of practical occasions by theoretical desires; to write a novel or a story, thus, as in the case of fabulists like Borges, Pynchon, Barthelme, Garcia Marquez, is a desire to *tell* a story much more than it is one for telling a *story.*

A legitimate objection to this sort of argument is that I have confused knowledge of something like writing with the act of producing writing. After all, in the *Phaedrus,* in the *Ion,* in the *Republic* and the *Laws,* Plato separates the philosopher from the artist, the knower from the morally prone performer, the con-

---

8. Lukács, "Reification and the Consciousness of the Proletariat" in *History and Class Consciousness,* trans. Rodney Livingstone (Cambridge, Mass.; M.I.T. Press, 1971); Barthes, "Myth Today," in *Mythologies,* trans. Annette Lavers (New York: Hill and Wang, 1972).

templative from the actor. The reasoning is partially true. But in the main it overlooks how urgently Socrates in the *Phaedrus* brings together the lover and the lover of knowledge, the philosopher. He carefully withholds the epithet of *wise* from them,

> *Socrates.* . . . for that is a great name which belongs to God alone — lovers of wisdom or philosophers is their modest and befitting title.
> *Phaedrus.* Very suitable.
> *Socrates.* And he who cannot rise above his own compilations and compositions, which he has been long patching and piercing, adding some and taking away some, may be justly called poet or speechmaker or law-maker.   (S.278)

Less lyrically than Socrates, perhaps, we can translate "lovers of" to "desirers of" or "seekers after" writing. Hence the critic, as much as the novelist, is a writer who seeks writing in writing. On that theoretical and practical level, the search to produce writing unites (a) originality as an irreducible intention to perform a specific activity, with (b) originality as an irreplaceable action giving forth the writing. Whether one is the novelist producing his novel or the critic producing his work on that novel, in the terms I have been using both are equally original. To ask if one is more original than the other is to risk sociological conclusions of the same order as the talk about equality in *Animal Farm,* but even that kind of conclusion requires something more like Pierre Macherey's or Lucien Goldmann's strictness than Orwell's.[9]

Two examples of criticism based on some of these premises come to mind immediately, by Georg Lukacs and by the French classicist Jean-Pierre Vernant. Lukács, in *The Theory of the Novel,* undertakes an investigation of what original consciousness made the novel possible given a certain set of intellectual, psychological, and spiritual conditions. Lukács's discipline was in defining his task as the formulation for the first time of what the novelistic impulse originally was; he could do this only because, again for the first time, both the novel and Europe had reached

9. Macherey, *Pour une théorie de la production littéraire* (Paris: Maspero, 1966); Goldmann, *Le Dieu caché* (Paris: Gallimard, 1955).

stages of development that permitted explicit statements about
the novel in a non-novelistic form.[10] Vernant's papers on Greek
tragedy are based (like Nietzsche's analyses) on a presumption
that the tragedies were not substitutes for ideas, but were "things"
intended originally to perform an original function; thus, tragedy
takes place as an "invention . . . [that is] something radically new
in every respect." Tragedy occurs at a highly conditioned moment
when the Greek city "enacts itself on the stage . . . and most important, it enacts its own problematics." Vernant determines that
these problematics revolve around a difficult change in man's
communal conception of himself, a change that "could be neither
thought, lived, nor even expressed otherwise than through the
form of tragedy . . . All the problems of responsibility, of degrees
of intention, of the relationship between the human agent and his
acts, the gods and the world are posed by tragedy, and it is only
in the form of tragedy that they could be posed."[11]

Lukács's Hegelianism had not yet undergone its later Marxist
reworking, so that theory in the early phase of his thought still
inhabited a largely ideal realm. Not so in Vernant's theory
of tragedy's moment. For him language has a material status with
carefully regulated uses in the tragic form. Yet why do both
critics, one as much as the other, stress the extreme difficulty of
apprehending the forms they study? Because both novel and
tragedy are dated back to a pure origin, either spiritual or material, that cannot be immediately or fully grasped. Unlike Dilthey's
interpretive theory, these theories do not fall back upon a sympathetic intuition that overrides the sheer age of the documents
being studied. Both tragedy and the novel belong to a period lost
forever. Therefore the forms' originality, in the purest sense, is a
type of loss which the critic's writing attempts to convey.

Originality in one primal sense, then, has to be loss, else it
would be repetition; or we can say that insofar as it is apprehended

10. For an interesting essay developing this point, see Paul de Man,
Blindness and Insight (New York: Oxford University Press, 1971), pp.
51–59.
11. "Greek Tragedy: Problems of Interpretation," in Richard Macksey
and Eugenio Donato, eds., *The Languages of Criticism and the Sciences
of Man* (Baltimore: Johns Hopkins University Press, 1970), pp. 278, 279,
284, 285.

as such, originality is the difference between vacancy and repetition. Kierkegaard, for one, saw no contradiction (in religious experience) between repetition and originality, but generally we associate repetition either with debasement (for example, the first time tragedy, the second, farce) or with a challenging recurrence. Probably because he was a philologist, Nietzsche was obsessed with the study of genealogy in terms of different sorts of originality: thus, *Ursprung* (which corresponds with the notions I discussed above in connection with Lukács and Vernant) is an original pure, first, appearance; *Enstehung* signifies the historical emergence of a phenomenon, its *point de surgissement* (compare with the type of originality analyzed by Thomas Kuhn in *The Structure of Scientific Revolutions* and by Georges Canguihelm in his analyses of *singularity* in *Etudes d'histoire et de philosophie des sciences*,[12] and *Herkunft* designates the stock and the provenance from which originality arises.[13]

Yet Nietzsche, Marx, and Freud are writers in whose work there is a remarkable symmetry between attempts made to characterize originality (revolution, will to truth, the unconscious) and attempts made to regularize, pattern, and schematize the conditions of human experience. Thus, for every revolution there must be a set of recurring circumstances; as Foucault rightly says, the result is that true originality becomes an impossibility.[14] Human singularity, and hence any originality associated with human endeavor, is a function of the transpersonal laws that make up the patterns (psychological, economic, and intellectual) we call history, which is documented in thousands of written records. Therefore written history is a countermemory, a kind of parody of Platonic recollection that permits the discernment by contemplation of true, first *original* things. For Nietzsche, according to Foucault, the historical sense is parodic in its opposition to recol-

12. Thomas S. Kuhn, *The Structure of Scientific Revolutions,* 2nd ed. (Chicago: University of Chicago Press, 1970); Georges Canguihelm, *Etudes d'histoire et de philosophie des sciences* (Paris: Librairie Philosophique J. Vrin, 1968).

13. Foucault, "Nietzsche, la généalogie, l'histoire," in *Hommage à Jean Hyppolite* (Paris: Presses Universitaires de France, 1971), pp. 148, 154, 151.

14. Foucault, "Nietzsche, Marx, Freud," in *Nietzsche* (Paris: Editions de Minuit, 1967), pp. 184–185.

lection, it is dissociative with regard to continuity, it is destructive with regard to knowledge. Because originality becomes harder to discern, its characteristics are more and more finely defined. In the end originality has passed from being a Platonic ideal to becoming a variation on a pattern.

Language plays the great role in this change. Every utterance, no matter its singularity, has to be understood as part of something else; it is precisely against this order of regularity that Artaud rebelled. Nevertheless, the result of understanding is that the large pattern domesticates the single act, the order of language overtakes the idiosyncrasies even of script. So close is the liaison between intelligibility and language that Freud, for example, made verbal order the stage for his exploration of the unintelligible. To write therefore comes to mean *more* (Derrida's designation is supplementarity)[15] than to speak, for the appearance of writing alone gives assurances of regularity and meaning that the tumble and dispersion of speech denies. Writing, as Mallarmé was to discover, can even dispense with an author: *"L'oeuvre pure implique la disparition élocutive du poète, qui cède l'initiative aux mots, par le heurt de leur inégalités mobilisés; ils s'allument de reflets réciproques comme une virtuelle traînée de feux sur des pierres vives, remplaçant la respiration perceptible en l'ancien souffle lyrique ou la direction personnelle enthusiaste de la phrase."*[16] Originality is replaced with mobilized inequality. The Book, an unfinished and unfinishable repository of all writing, stands above all particular books.

We return now to a question asked earlier: what is the unit of writing in which we can study the play of repetition and originality? It can no longer be a work, or a text, or an author, since each of these, given an integral theoretic perspective, aspires to writing beyond such purely functional limits. But since one has neither the time nor the capacity to study all writing, it becomes

15. Jacques Derrida, *De la grammatologie* (Paris: Editions de Minuit, 1967), pp. 203–234.

16. "The pure work implies the disappearance of the poet-as-speaker, who cedes the initiative to words and to the shock of their mobilized inequality; they light each other up with mutual reflection, like a trail of live stones, replacing the perceptible respiration of the traditional lyric breath or the enthusiastic personal direction of the sentence." Stephane Mallarmé, *Oeuvres complètes* (Paris: Gallimard, 1945), p. 366.

necessary to analyze the intention, or where it can be decoded, the stated desire, from which a specifically demarcated set of writing originally derives. Here the example of modernist writing gives the theoretical critic of all other historical periods a difficult but cogent lesson, for one cannot teach or write about literature today without in some way being influenced by the contemporary literary situation. In no way does this situation have as coherent a defining characteristic as in its profound dissatisfaction with the units, the genres, the expectations of earlier times. Paradoxically, therefore, the *originality* of contemporary literature in its broad outlines resides in the refusal of originality, or primacy, to its forbears.

Thus, the best way to consider originality is to look not for first instances of a phenomenon, but rather to see duplication, parallelism, symmetry, parody, echoes of it — the way, for example, literature has made itself into a *topos* of writing. What the modern or contemporary imagination thinks of is less the confining of something to a book, and more the release of something from a book into writing. This release is accomplished in many different forms: Joyce releases the *Odyssey* into the verbal equivalent of twentieth-century Dublin, Eliot frees fragments from Virgil and Petronius into a whole set of jagged phrases, and so on. The writer thinks less of writing originally, and more of rewriting. The image for writing changes from *original inscription* to parallel script, from tumbled-out confidence to deliberate fathering-forth (in which Hopkins' alliteration signifies pattern, repetition, parallel), from melody to fugue. And since the writer no longer inaugurates a new locale, he tends to see his time as an interregnum. Philippe Sollers puts it this way: *"la vie de celui qui écrit est un 'interrègne,' et le travail apparement inutile ou le jeu qu'il poursuit sont en rapport avec le futur dont nous savons qu'il est le lieu de tout travail symbolique. La littérature appartient a l'avenir, et l'avenir, écrit Mallarmé, 'n'est jamais que l'éclat de ce qui eût du se produire antérieurement ou près de l'origine.' "*[17]

17. ". . . the life of him who writes is an 'interregnum,' and the apparently useless work he does or the game he plays is consonant with the future, which we know to be the site of symbolic work. Literature belongs to the future, and the future, wrote Mallarmé, is never more than the burst of that which must have been produced as anteriority, or as something close to the origin." *Logiques* (Paris: Seuil, 1968), p. 117.

Much of what I have been saying about the transformation of
the imaginative terms by which we can now understand originality
is indicated in the French critical phrase *le refus du commence-
ment*. Since our self-perception as writers has changed from being
"lonely begans" (Hopkins again) to being workers in the "already-
begun," the writer can be read as an individual whose impulse
historically has been always to *write through* one or another given
work, in order finally to achieve the independence, like Mallarmé,
of writing that knows no bounds. The Book is the myth, but
scarcely ever the reality, of writing. A parallelism, say between
Dublin and Attica, sustained over many pages and years leads the
writer not toward another book but rather toward writing-in-
progress. Still more fascinating is the case of Mann in *Doctor
Faustus*. The technique of that novel, as many critics have shown,
is the montage and the echo. Both Mann and his protagonist
master the art of doubling, inverting, imitating to infinity. Their
originality is to play this game until they achieve a state of *vacancy*
— the destruction of Western civilization and morals, the reversion of originality to silence by way of repetition. Adrian's pact
with the devil gives him the gift of artistic distinction over a period
of years, but since his earliest days, and since the novel's opening,
both Mann and Adrian have been fascinated with parallel and
parody, especially because even nature duplicates herself in the
most curious way: the inorganic mimics the organic, one form is
reproduced by another, and so on. Thus the fabric of the novel,
as well as its theme, is made of rewriting, one original *cantus
firmus* being imitated so many times as to lose its primacy.

Mann's treatment of all this in a novel has a very unusual ana-
logue in an essay by Leo Spitzer. Given first as a lecture at
Princeton in 1945 (and it is likely that Mann was present at the
time — at any rate, he was then working on *Faustus* and passed
through Princeton), "Linguistics and Literary History" is Spitzer's professional autobiography, his account of the development
of his philological theory and practice. He tells of a fascination he
has had, since coming to America, with the etymology of *conundrum* and *quandary*. Tracing the "extraordinary instability" of
their phonetic structure, Spitzer finds that an etymological search
reveals how "an agglomeration of mere sounds appears motivated." The two words derive from common French and Latin

roots, and their genealogy thus includes *calembour* (pun), *carrefour* (crossroads), *quadrifurcus* (Latin for crossroads), *calembourdaine* which in one development becomes *colundrum,* then *concundrum,* and in another parallel development becomes *conimbrum, conundrum, quonundrum, quandorum,* finally *quandary.* Hence he concludes that

> The instability and disunity of the *word-family* [conundrum-quandary] is symptomatic of its position in the new environment.
>
> But the instability apparent in our English words had already been characteristic of *calembredaine-calembour,* even in the home environment: this French word-family, as we have said, was a blend of at least two word-stems. Thus we must conclude that the instability is also connected with the semantic content: a word meaning "whim, pun" easily behaves whimsically — just as, in all languages throughout the world, the words for "butterfly" present a kaleidoscopic instability.[18] (Emphasis added.)

Now any reader of *Doctor Faustus* will immediately see how suggestive for the novel this entire line of reasoning is, especially the passage quoted above. For not only is the mature Adrian surrounded in Munich by a parody of his original *family* in Kaisersaschern, but his interests in doing as his father did, "speculating the elements," persist. Near the beginning of the book Zeitblom describes a butterfly "of transparent nudity," *Hetera esmeralda,* whose appearance and habits, like those of the leaf butterfly, are profoundly duplicitous:

> Hetera had on her wings only a dark spot of violet and rose; one could see nothing else of her, and when she flew she was like a petal blown by the wind. Then there was the leaf butterfly, whose wings on top are a triple chord of colour, while underneath with insane exactitude they resemble a leaf, not only in shape and veining but in the minute reproduction of small imperfections, imitation drops of water, little warts and fungus growths and more of the like. When the clever creature alights among the leaves and folds its wings, it disappears by adaptation so entirely that the hungriest enemy cannot make it out... For one cannot ascribe

18. *Linguistics and Literary History: Essays in Stylistics* (Princeton: Princeton University Press, 1948), p. 7.

the trick to its own observation and calculation. Yes, yes, Nature knows her leaf precisely: knows not only its perfection but also its small usual blunders and blemishes; mischievously or benevolently she repeats its outward appearance in another sphere, on the under side of this her butterfly, to baffle others of her creatures . . . This butterfly, then, protected itself by becoming invisible.[19]

These descriptions look ahead to Adrian's seduction by the prostitute, to a concealed motto in his music, to his pact with the devil, all ascribed generically to *Hetera esmeralda*. The butterfly's cunning is a function of Nature's, and the idea of an unstable butterfly clearly resonates through Spitzer's speculations on the nature of language. In the cases both of the philologist and of the novelist there is, moreover, no attribution of the process of duplication and repetition to anything more personal than "Nature." Thus, we might say that originality does not reside either in language or in the elements, since both make virtually impossible any attempt to determine the true from the copy. That is a conclusion on one level. On another level, as readers, we take note of Spitzer's personal intervention as a philologist, of Mann's as a novelist, of Adrian's as a Faust-figure, in the workings of an unstable medium so as to clarify in it the order of cunning symmetry. Hence the wielding of individual authority transforms the elements sufficiently to implicate the individual in a career of working them: Spitzer as philologist, Adrian as demonic musician.

Until now I have purposely left unasked the inviting question: did Spitzer influence Mann? For such a question inevitably raises the problem of originality; and indeed I seem to have been hinting that the critic has been, in a sense, more original than the original or the "creative" writer. But that is not the point. My argument is to stress the equal responsibility for originality in every vocation "working" language. From my theoretical point of view, Mann and Spitzer themselves recognize no originality per se, since nature and language are orders of duplication. Perceptually, on the other hand, originality is a quality discovered in whichever author of the two we discover first, as well as in impressions of novelty and force too subjective for sustained analysis. But because of the shift I discussed above from inscription to parallel script there is a

19. *Doctor Faustus*, trans. H. T. Lowe-Porter (New York: Knopf, 1948), pp. 14–15.

more crucial theoretic shift also in the conception of originality, which now becomes a sort of faculty for combinatorial play. A writer's responsibility is to control this play, which still leaves entirely up to him such matters as his point of departure, the center around which his writing is built, and so on. Nevertheless, these responsibilities of the writer are not implicit or abstract ideas heaped upon language by a critic, but are physically intrinsic to the writing itself. I mean essentially the actual senses of distance from or of closeness to a "subject" imparted to the writing, and the sense writing has of being materially co-extensive with what it is saying.

The latter sense needs emphasis. Traditionally the temporal convention in literary study has been retrospective. We look at writing as already completed. A critic therefore restores to a text its original meaning, one imagined to have been lost through time or technique. We are now even less likely to be interested in study that demonstrates a text's contemporary relevence except, as I said above, for modish reasons. But how much more challenging is a theoretic for study that takes writing as being produced for a future formed *in the writing:* this was Mallarmé's discovery. Thus, the ultimate, perhaps infinite goal of writing is a Book conceived of as a biblio-system, a kind of activated library, the effect of which is to stimulate further the production of forms of disciplined, gradually actualized freedom. If originality as a conception has had the power for too long of depressing time backwards into lost primacy at best, and regained utopias at worst, this is a good reason for reorienting our study systematically toward the future. As Foucault and Gilles Deleuze have said, so drastic a reversal of perspective has the effect of de-Platonizing thought.[20] For what could be more Platonic (in a debased way) than seeing literature as a copy, experience as an original, and history as a line moving from origin to the present? Once this type of linearity is revealed for the theology it really is, a secular reality for writing is enabled. Foucault's phrase for that reality is *l'ordre du discours* (the order of discourse), but we can recognize in it the proper, formidably complex originality of writing as it counters even nature.

20. Foucault, "Theatrum Philosphicum," *Critique,* 282 (November 1970), 75–95; Deleuze, *Logique de sens* (Paris: Editions de Minuit, 1969), pp. 292–306.

J . ROBERT BARTH, S.J.

A Newer Criticism in America:
The Religious Dimension

There are some of us who seem to blame Coleridge and Arnold for everything. And, who knows, perhaps we are right. In any case, I would like to begin by suggesting that there are two broad lines of development in the attitude toward literature in the nineteenth century and that both have left their mark on our own century. One has its roots, at least its more visible roots, in Arnold; the other in Coleridge.

Arnold, in his pursuit of "high seriousness," was preoccupied with the moral and societal dimensions of literature. He had little interest in formal structure or in the genesis of the literary work. His concern was with the implications of a work for the intellectual and spiritual growth of the individual and of society. Since his is a broad and humane view of literature, there is no wonder that it earned the respect of men of letters in his day — especially in an age which was so self-conscious about its own swiftly changing culture. Arnold gave the Victorian age a way of thinking about itself and its inadequacies.

I wish to thank the editors of the *Jesuit Educational Quarterly* for permission to use, in revised form, some paragraphs which originally appeared in that journal (October 1968).

Coleridge, too, had reflected deeply on some of the same problems of the culture of his own day. Like Arnold, he was, or tried to be, the conscience of society. His writings on church and state, on government, on the nature of science, on history and current affairs, on philosophy and religion, are all, at least in part, attempts to bring philosophical and moral principles to bear on the workings of modern society. The same is true of his literary criticism and his reflections on the nature of literature — and in this way he is close to Arnold. And it was precisely through the philosophical and moral aspects of his literature and criticism that he was most influential in the later nineteenth century. But at the same time Coleridge was much more the practicing artist than Arnold. He could not talk of literature without talking of formal structure and of the genesis of art — the shape and origin of the poem itself — as well as its implications for life and society. And, whatever the nature of his influence on the nineteenth century, it is his thoughts on the formal structure of literature that have had most influence on the twentieth century.

Criticism in our own century has had a complicated history, but it is possible to discern two fairly distinct lines of development: an Arnoldian tradition which emphasizes the moral and societal dimensions of literature, and a Coleridgean tradition which emphasizes formal structure. Each has been fruitful and important. The Arnoldian tradition has led to such very different critics as D. H. Lawrence; Irving Babbitt, Paul Elmer More and the new humanism; T. S. Eliot (at least one aspect of his criticism); and more recently, F. O. Matthiessen, F. R. Leavis, and R. W. B. Lewis. The Coleridgean tradition has produced critics like I. A. Richards and, in a fairly direct line from one side of Richards' work, the New Critics — critics like John Crowe Ransom, William Empson, R. P. Blackmur, Robert Penn Warren, and Cleanth Brooks.

Clearly, these obvious examples do not convey the complexity of twentieth-century criticism. One thinks of the expansive Christian humanism of Douglas Bush; the historical work of Vernon Parrington, Van Wyck Brooks, and Perry Miller; the broadly cultural analysis of Edmund Wilson; the archetypal criticism of Maud Bodkin and of Northrop Frye. But all these, despite their diversity of attitude and method, reflect what is important in the Arnoldian tradition. One central aspect of this tradition is expressed by Edmund Wilson when he writes that literary criticism ought to be "a history of man's ideas and imaginings in the setting of the conditions which have shaped them."[1] This is not to say that these critics are not concerned with formal structure, but only that this concern is put at the service of other considerations. One need only read Douglas Bush's *Mythology and the Renaissance Tradition,* for instance, to realize how study of formal structure can lead to reflections on history and society and the nature of man.

But for all this, it was the New Criticism which became popular in American classrooms during the 1940's and 1950's, and when reaction came in the 1960's it was against an essentially formalist criticism. It is this reaction, beginning in the late 1950's — particularly as it has taken place in the United States — that is my primary concern. Since this trend is essentially a reaction against the New Criticism, it might be referred to as a "newer criticism."

There is no doubt that the New Criticism, which held front stage in classes of literature for some twenty years, has contributed richly to the study of literature; it made critics approach the literary work, more than ever before, as an organic structure, after the Coleridgean model of the poem as organism, used so brilliantly in Coleridge's Shakespeare lectures. This criticism came to see literature as, in Nathan Scott's words, "a function of the interrelationships that knit the terms together into the total pattern that forms the unity of the work," illustrating in a fresh way what Cleanth Brooks called "the pressure of the context."[2] Some of the practitioners of the New Criticism — the followers, be it noted, rarely the originators — came in time to overemphasize the autonomy of the poetic fact, to forget that the poetic fact is not only a function of the interrelationships within the pressure of the poem, but also a function of "the relationships between the terms of the poem and some reality which is extrinsic to them."[3] Brooks's "context" came to be taken in a far more exclusive sense than he intended.

1. *Axel's Castle* (New York: Charles Scribner's, 1931), dedication page.
2. Nathan A. Scott, Jr., *Negative Capability: Studies in the New Literature and the Religious Situation* (New Haven: Yale University Press, 1969), p. 115.
3. Scott, *Negative Capability,* p. 115.

Within the past decade and a half, however, many critics, with-out rejecting or underrating the values of the New Criticism, have moved beyond the pressure of the immediate context. They have begun to come back to the belief that literature, whatever else it may be, is a way of knowing — and of knowing something out-side itself. This is a new emphasis, not a whole new movement; not a rejection of what was good in the past, but the re-poising of a balance. The New Criticism will remain with us, but will be en-riched by a fresh awareness of the relationship of the literary work to the world outside it.

Another way of expressing this phenomenon is that there has come to be a new realization of what was lost sight of for a time, that the philosophical and moral and religious values mediated through a work of literature become part of the literary work itself and are therefore a proper object of consideration for the critic. Not that literature is usurping the place of philosophy or theology. *Absit!* Literature is itself and nothing else; so are phi-losophy and theology. Each has its own tools and conventions, its own modes of inquiry. Nor is there any intention of separating the work of literature into form and content, as if the values expressed in it are apart from the text of the work itself — its structure, its metaphoric language, its poetic texture. Rather, the text itself — the words and sounds and formal structure — is of its very nature expressive of human values; this is, after all, part of the nature of words. And if the critic is to come to terms with this text in its fullness, he will necessarily take into account its implicit value judgments, its view of the world. Literature and literary criticism are rejoining the rest of the world, and, like the world itself, litera-ture is full of yeses and noes, of judgments and valuations, often about the most important things. And, though I have referred to it as a "newer criticism," there is really nothing very new in all this. We are simply returning to the tradition of the greatest critics of our language, like Coleridge, who wrote: "I never have been able to tame down my mind to think poetry a sport, or an occu-pation for idle hours."[4]

A striking manifestation of this new concern is the volume of

4. Samuel Taylor Coleridge, *Shakespearean Criticism,* ed. T. M. Raysor, Everyman's Library (London: Dent, 1960), II, 106.

English Institute essays of 1957, *Literature and Belief,* edited by M. H. Abrams. Here such critics as Douglas Bush, Cleanth Brooks, Walter Ong, and Nathan Scott, however much they differ in other respects, all agree on the profound relevance of religious values to literature and literary criticism. Indeed, Professor Abrams quotes approvingly Allen Tate's judgment that the essentially religious question of belief is today "the chief problem of poetic criticism."[5] Since that session of the English Institute, seminars, conferences, and symposia on religion and literature have been legion, with increasing participation by theologians as well as literary critics. Among numerous others, there have been the series of national conferences at Drew University in the 1960's, the three-day international conference on religion and literature sponsored by Boston College in 1970, and the annual meetings of the Conference on Christianity and Literature (as well as regional meetings each spring) for the past ten years.[6]

But even more important than such very public group manifestations of interest in the religious dimensions of literature, the work of individual critics coming to terms with literature has turned in this direction. Of course, their work is far from all of a piece. There are critics whose work tends toward study of thematic concerns: Nathan Scott, Jr., whose voluminous work has been influential on the work of many others;[7] Stanley Romaine Hop-

5. *Literature and Belief,* ed. M. H. Abrams (New York: Columbia University Press), p. vii.

6. I should also call attention to a number of collections of essays dealing with religion and literature: *Spiritual Problems in Contemporary Literature,* ed. Stanley Romaine Hopper (New York: Harper Torchbooks, 1957); *Symbolism in Religion and Literature,* ed. Rollo May (New York: Braziller, 1960); *The New Orpheus: Essays Toward a Christian Poetic,* ed. Nathan A. Scott, Jr. (New York: Sheed and Ward, 1964); *Mansions of the Spirit: Essays in Literature and Religion,* ed. George A. Panichas (New York: Hawthorn Books, 1967); *Literature and Religion,* ed. Giles B. Gunn (New York: Harper Forum Books, 1971). Another important discussion is J. Hillis Miller's essay "Literature and Religion" in *Relations of Literary Study: Essays on Interdisciplinary Contributions,* ed. James Thorpe (New York: Modern Language Association of America, 1967), pp. 111–126.

7. See *Modern Literature and the Religious Frontier* (New York: Harper, 1958); *The Broken Center: Studies in the Theological Horizon of Modern Literature* (New Haven: Yale University Press, 1966); *Craters of the Spirit: Studies in the Modern Novel* (New Haven: Yale University Press, 1968).

per;[8] M. H. Abrams, especially in his recent *Natural Super-naturalism*. There are others for whom close reading of the poetic text leads to broader philosophical, religious and human considerations and conclusions: Walter Jackson Bate, for example, in his definitive study of Keats; Cleanth Brooks in his study of Faulkner; J. Hillis Miller in his work on nineteenth-century poetry and fiction. Others focus on the theoretical problems of the nature and function of literary criticism: William Lynch, in *Christ and Apollo* and *Christ and Prometheus;* Sallie TeSelle, in *Literature and the Christian Life*. Still others, against the background of modern scriptural scholarship and interpretation, work toward an understanding of the hermeneutical matrix within which the reader "encounters" the author and his experience: Amos Wilder, writing of the place of modern scriptural hermeneutics in literary criticism;[9] Ray L. Hart, in his massive synthesis of modern views on "the dynamics of human speech and writing."[10]

For all the differences in methodology, one thing is common to these critics: they have left behind the false ideal of artistic autonomy that bewitched some of the later followers of the New Criticism. They define the poetic text not simply in terms of itself but in terms of its larger context as well, a context which stands outside the poem. As Amos Wilder writes of this departure from the New Criticism: " 'Meaning' is related not to the literary work as object, even when taken as a whole, but to that ultimate Real or Being itself which discloses itself in the work, in the language event of which the work is only the vehicle."[11] This is not to say that the poetic form is anything less than crucial, but simply that it is not all. As Richard Palmer has said: "The beginning point for literary interpretation must be the language event of experiencing the work itself — i.e., what the work 'says.' The saying power of a literary work, not its form, is the ground of our meaningful encounter with it, and is not something separate from the form but

8. See "The Problem of Moral Isolation in Contemporary Literature," in Hopper, *Spiritual Problems in Contemporary Literature,* pp. 153–170.

9. See *Early Christian Rhetoric: The Language of the Gospels* (Cambridge: Harvard University Press, 1971), pp. xi–xxx.

10. See *Unfinished Man and the Imagination* (New York: Herder and Herder, 1968).

11. *Early Christian Rhetoric,* p. xxvii.

rather speaks in and through the form . . . The saying done by a literary work is a disclosure of being."[12] It is this being which is disclosed — disclosed through the interrelationships and pressures of formal structure — that is coming under philosophical and moral and religious scrutiny.

The fact of the rapport between literature and religion is perhaps equally evident from the theologian's side. One thinks, for example, of the work of Harvey Cox of the Harvard Divinity School, of Tom Driver of Union Theological Seminary, of Preston Roberts of the University of Chicago Divinity School, or, for that matter, of Nathan Scott and Amos Wilder, whose work as literary critics has already been noted. The reasons here, however, are perhaps not so obvious. The reasons for the literary critic's interest are clear enough — the issue has been much discussed — but the reasons for the theologian's interest are not, I think, immediately evident.

Perhaps the question might be posed something like this: What are the principle points of tangency between the study of literature and the study of religion? Or, looking at it more directly from the theologian's point of view: To what theological problems can literature possibly contribute? Although I suspect there are many more, I am going to suggest three.

First of all, I take it that one of the problems to which modern theologians have been addressing themselves is the problem of the relevance of religious belief and doctrine to the individual believer. A great deal of recent theology is nothing if not personalist. The problem of belief, the problem of the relationship of the individual to the institutional church, the problems of authority, the problem (especially in the Catholic church) of personal responsibility vis-à-vis official teaching authority — all these focus in one way or another on the role of the individual person in the process of salvation.

This is one of the points of tangency between literature and religious studies. Literature commonly insists on the uniqueness of the individual person or fact or experience. One of its premises is the uniqueness of the concrete existent, and its product, the poetic fact — the epic, or lyric, or novel, or whatever — is essen-

12. Quoted by Amos Wilder, *Early Christian Rhetoric*, p. xxviii.

tially characterized by its uniqueness. Literature wants to know man with all his particularities of time and place and national culture, of temperament and personality and disposition, of age and shape and size — every object he sees, every experience he undergoes, every prejudice and every smile, every wart and every curve. Along with its evident concern to express human nature in its fullness, literature cares about individual finite realities in all their uniqueness. Literature cares for, to use Hopkins' term, the "inscape" of an object or person or experience.

> Each mortal thing does one thing and the same:
> Deals out that being indoors each one dwells;
> Selves — goes itself; *myself* it speaks and spells,
> Crying *What I do is me: for that I came.*

As William Lynch says in *Christ and Apollo,* this is what God himself has done in the Creation — expressed unique finite realities: "God's imagination has in His own creative act cut through all the lines of impossibility, penetrated into the last bit of mud at the hidden bottom of the sea, to illuminate the lines of possibility and reality."[13] And for the Christian, this is what Christ has done in becoming man: He took on "the dimensions and concreteness of an actual life." There is in Christ what Lynch calls an "absolute specificity." If one of the tasks of the theologian today is to make doctrine and theology relevant to the concrete world in which we live, he must know the temporal order in all its muddy actuality, so that he will not only know, but realize, that the world in which religious truth is to become *lived* religious truth is complex, exciting, comic, tragic, pathetic, beautiful, muddy, dynamic, and horrible — whether by turns or all together.

Apart from William Lynch, the best theoretician I have discovered on this whole matter of the relationship of religion and literature is the Protestant theologian Sallie McFague TeSelle. I would suggest, with Dr. TeSelle, that "theologians, particularly those involved in Christological theory, might benefit from a long hard look at the reality of man as depicted in the arts, for . . . it

13. William F. Lynch, S.J., *Christ and Apollo: The Dimensions of the Literary Imagination* (New York: Sheed and Ward, 1960), p. 27.

is literature and not Christology that enables us to see concretely what the reality of man's temporal life is all about."[14] If the theologian is to make religious belief significant for man's total human experience, then he must know the nature of that experience. Aesthetic experience is not religious experience, nor can it properly be a substitute for religious experience. This would be late in the day to revive Arnold's view of literature as a surrogate for religion. The point is that both are *human* experience. They come together in the mind, or more often perhaps in the imagination, of a concrete individual. If the theologian is to address the whole man in a meaningful way, he must know the nature of that man's human experience. As Dr. TeSelle writes, "through the aesthetic object we see the true structure of reality and see it profoundly for the first time . . . A novel or a poem does not usually offer a program of action or a philosophy of life, but it does present something for our contemplation."[15] If the theologian (or the student of theology) knows profoundly the nature of human experience, in all its complexity and all its definiteness, he can address himself more effectively to the problem of relating religious truth to man's total human experience.

The second area of rapport between religion and literature touches religion in terms of the current theological problem of language, which I take to be (in very general terms) the problem of finding language appropriate for modern man and relevant to him as a person — that is, language which somehow speaks to the whole man, not merely to the top of his head. Here again, literature can be of service to the theologian. Literature, like all art, is directed toward symbolic utterance. Its basic tool is metaphor, which, at its most intense, moves in the direction of symbol, whose fullest form is myth. To achieve such metaphorical and symbolic effect, literature works under the aegis not merely of the reason or will or senses, but of the imagination, which includes all of these and much more besides. "The poet," as Coleridge wrote, "described in *ideal* perfection, brings the whole soul of man into activity, with the subordination of its faculties to each other, according to their relative worth and dignity. He diffuses a tone and

14. *Literature and the Christian Life* (New Haven: Yale University Press, 1966), p. 43.
15. *Literature and the Christian Life*, pp. 105, 107.

spirit of unity, that blends, and (as it were) *fuses,* each into each, by that synthetic and magical power, to which we have exclusively appropriated the name of imagination."[16] The language made by such a faculty, expressing metaphor and symbol and myth, reveals not only mind but "the whole soul of man," and the energies it releases are from deep within man's spirit. Another factor influencing the relationship of religion and literature is the modern interest in the nature of symbolic language itself, raising the question of whether and to what extent such language corresponds to a reality. This in turn is closely bound up with the growth of myth criticism, which originally grew out of anthropological concerns but was later seen to be equally a function of language and of religion.

It would seem eminently useful then for the theologian and the student of religion to enter deeply into this artistic world and its language. They may well find there tools not only to convey, but even to investigate, a whole congeries of problems, values, emotional responses, and imaginative insights. As I. A. Richards wrote in his famous commentary on Coleridge's theory of the imagination: "The saner and greater mythologies are not fancies; they are the utterance of the whole soul of man and, as such, inexhaustible to meditation. They are no amusement or diversion to be sought as a relaxation and an escape from the hard realities of life. They are these hard realities in projection, their symbolic recognition, coordination and acceptance. Through such mythologies our will is collected, our powers unified, our growth collected."[17] What Richards says of "the saner and greater mythologies" is true of the greatest of the world's literature: of Homer and Virgil, of Dante and Milton, of Dostoevsky and Faulkner and T. S. Eliot. The best of literature engages the whole man, and it does so by the manipulation of language; surely the study of literature can be fruitful for the theologian in his search to find language which speaks to the whole man in the world of the twentieth century.

The third relationship which I see between religion and literature is to some extent implicit in the previous two, but it is im-

16. Samuel Taylor Coleridge, *Biographia Literaria,* ed. J. Shawcross (London: Oxford University Press, 1907), II, 12.

17. *Coleridge on Imagination* (Bloomington: Indiana University Press, 1960), p. 171.

portant enough to merit separate and explicit attention: it is the fact that both religion and literature are concerned with man's search for order in the world. Literature is, whatever else it may be, a search for the unity of order. As Shelley wrote in his *Defence of Poetry,* "there is a principle within the human being . . . which . . . produces not melody alone, but harmony." Even in the early ages of the world, "men dance and sing and imitate natural objects, observing in these actions, as in all others, a certain rhythm or order."[18] It may not be unity achieved, but to be literature or art it must be at least unity sought for. Poetry is, in Coleridgean terms, precisely the making of many into one.

Think, for example, of E. E. Cummings' familiar poem "anyone lived in a pretty how town." It is about a man and a woman, "anyone" and "noone," who fall in love and live their lives and die — and the pattern of their lives is paralleled by the ordered rhythm of the seasons, which reflects its order on their lives. Here is poetry precisely as a search for order, for pattern, for the rhythms of human experience. There is a pattern in men's lives, a rhythm, a cycle — birth, joy, sorrow, work, love, death — as there is in all the world —sun, moon, stars, rain — in the cycle of the seasons and the stars. The literature we read may be a poem, it may be a play, it may be a novel, but in each case, if it is literature, it will be a means not merely of encountering experience but of analyzing it, of ordering it, of seeing and expressing its patterns and rhythms, of learning to live with it and make it meaningful.

In the past, these functions of ordering and structuring experience were commonly taken to belong to the provinces of philosophy and theology, and, on the nonacademic level, of religion. It is their function, isn't it, to interpret reality for us, to structure experience, to offer a hierarchy of values? How does it come about then that people look less and less to philosophy and theology for the interpretation of reality, more and more to imaginative literature?

It has become a fact of life that most undergraduates today show little enthusiasm for the formal study of philosophy and

18. Percy Bysshe Shelley, "A Defence of Poetry," *The Selected Poetry and Prose of Shelley,* ed. Carlos Baker (New York: Modern Library, 1951), pp. 494–495.

theology as separate disciplines. Add to this the fact that the churches, by and large, have failed to communicate with younger people on anything approaching an intellectual level, and the result for many is a yawning vacuum in ethical and spiritual values. And yet ethical and spiritual problems remain, as they always will: there are moral decisions and spiritual commitments facing young people today which are of enormous import, not only for themselves but for the world in which they live. The ethical and spiritual vacuum will somehow be filled. It is for this reason, I believe, that more and more people look to works of the imagination — literature, art, the film — for hierarchies of value, for moral standards, for insights into the problems of the spirit which trouble them and will continue to trouble them. Literature and the arts today are a matter of serious quest and serious consequence.

Perhaps, in terms of what we have said already, there is something in the nature of literary art itself that makes this confrontation between literature and ultimate problems a natural and inevitable one. In a world which has become less ordered and unified — which has lost the vision of itself as an ordered hierarchy, a chain of being — perhaps order and structure can only be expressed adequately through art, which leaves the complexity of the world intact. Philosophy and theology necessarily abstract, order things in speculative terms, categorize. Art orders, but generally without abstracting, without categorizing; it leaves the reality, the experience, in all the richness of individual diversity.

And yet, is it really a new experience for men to look to literature for religious and philosophical insight? True, speculative philosophy and theology had long been given dominance in the academic world, as perhaps for too long religious dogma had been overemphasized at the expense of the human *experience* of religion. But if we return to the beginnings of a religion, we find that religion conveyed in imaginative art, which keeps alive the richness and complexity of the human experience which it expresses. Plato wrote dialogues, and his deepest experience is expressed in the form of a parable — the great parable of the cave: the cave wall, the shadows, the flickering firelight. And the sacred scripture itself, however inspired by God, is first of all a collection of literary works, which carry firmly impressed on them the marks of concrete human experience: books of wars and catalogues of tribes; narration of historical events; stories and parables; love songs and songs of the court; personal prayers and meditations; apocalyptic visions; images, metaphors, and symbols. Perhaps then our turning to literature as a source of values and order and enlightenment is only a return, part of a perennial return, to the essential source of all these things: the concrete, lived experience of men. Perhaps man always turns, at last, from the abstractions of speculation, however useful and necessary these may be, to the experience of his brothers in our common humanity, expressed and distilled in the language of poetry.

Having pointed out what I consider to be the principle relationships between religion and literature, I must now hasten to add a caveat or two. There are clearly pitfalls around which to walk warily: the one is a failure of aesthetic sensibility, the other of religious sensibility.

For the theologian approaching the work of literature, there is the danger of not sufficiently respecting the literary text, of merely touching the work lightly and then discussing the religious issue or problem suggested by it. To do so is a failure of aesthetic sensibility. The burden placed on the shoulders of the theologian who would also be a literary critic is no small one. His aim, for the moment, must become that of the critic, whose task is, in F. R. Leavis's phrase, to "enter into possession of" the literary text. Leavis writes in *The Common Pursuit:* "The business of the literary critic is to attain a peculiar completeness of response in developing his response into commentary; he must be on his guard against abstracting improperly from what is in front of him and against any premature or irrelevant generalizing — of it or from it. His first concern is to enter into possession of the given poem (let us say) in its concrete fullness."[19] Sallie TeSelle suggests that most theologians who attempt such criticism "come with a set of categories that are extrinsic to the piece of literature under consideration and impose these external categories upon it."[20] What the theologian must do, rather — probably with the help of the literary critic — is to "enter into possession" of the work, or perhaps better, to allow the work to take possession of him by enter-

19. *The Common Pursuit* (London: Chatto and Windus, 1958), p. 213.
20. *Literature and the Christian Life,* p. 44.

ing into it without the assertion of himself and his theological categories. Only when he has allowed the energies of the text itself, its imagery and texture and pressures of context, to work upon him and enter into him, will he be able to see the world from within the imagination of the artist — to see and value the world as the artist sees and values it. Only when he has done this may he legitimately begin to speak of the religious relevance of the artist and his work. Theologians might do well to recall what an old Boston lady said to Emerson, talking about the exalted religious sensibilities of an earlier age: "They had to hold on hard to the huckleberry bushes to hinder themselves from being translated."[21] Theologians who would read correctly the religious implications of literature must be careful to "hold on hard to the huckleberry bushes."

Another pitfall, closely linked with the first, is a failure of religious sensibility, by which a critic fails to understand the religious principles expressed or implied in a work of art. In a literary work which truly expresses religious values, there is a coming together of created reality and the transcendent God. Literature, as a work of the imagination, is essentially symbolic utterance. If what is expressed is, in some measure at least, religious vision, then what is symbolized is transcendent reality, incarnated in images of sense; the transcendent is expressed in and through creation. There is, to use Coleridge's term, a "consubstantiality" of created reality and transcendent reality.[22] Unless one has a strong sense of the several-leveled nature of the poetic act, and especially of the unity among the levels, there is the same danger we have seen, of not meeting the poetic act on its own terms, of translating it into concepts — or else of not perceiving the reality beyond the sense images.

There are surely critics who have failed to integrate religious experience and aesthetic experience, who have failed to recognize that both are legitimate forms of human knowing and that art can truly be an expression of transcendent reality. For them re-

21. Quoted by R. W. B. Lewis, "Hold on Hard to the Huckleberry Bushes," *Sewanee Review,* 67 (1959), 462.
22. On Coleridge's idea of "consubstantiality," see J. Robert Barth, S.J., "Symbol as Sacrament in Coleridge," *Studies in Romanticism,* 11 (1972), 320–331.

ligious experience is too utterly transcendent; creation and God do not really meet, either in the poetic act or elsewhere. God is far off from man and from the works, even the poetic works, of man. The result is a radical failure really to believe that religious experience can be expressed in literature. At best such experience can only be vaguely adumbrated, and then perhaps translated into conceptual language closer to man's more rational ways of knowing. The same failure occurs at times in the work of critics who come out of a strongly evangelical tradition. They are discerning about scriptural aspects of literature, whether imagistic or thematic, but fail to come to grips with the ontological reality of the poetic symbol. The symbol is not taken as symbol, but is translated into conceptual, nonsymbolic terms.

One occasionally finds this problem even in so good a critic as J. Hillis Miller, whose treatment of Gerard Manley Hopkins ultimately fails because it does not accept the possibility that Hopkins really did, as he so often asserts in his reflections on his own work, find the transcendent God in His creation.[23] Yvor Winters, too, fails disastrously with Hopkins for similar reasons.[24] Winters dismisses the greater part of Hopkins's poetry as "a chaos of details afloat in vague emotion," because he longs to conceptualize Hopkins's poetry, which obstinately refuses to be so constrained, which will not be boxed into clear and distinct ideas.[25] Hopkins's poetry is itself and nothing else, and it operates, without translation, on two levels at once: it expresses transcendent reality in and through the reality of the created world. God is, after all, present in His creation — and Christ did, after all, become man.

Perhaps in this context we may return to Coleridge and Arnold, who again — this time in a different way — diverge considerably. Arnold's view of literature, however implicitly, demands conceptualization. Poetry, for him, deals with great ideas: "the noble and profound application of ideas to life." Without them there is no "high seriousness." It is not enough for Chaucer to deal with creation; he must deal with creation conceptualized if he is

23. See *The Disappearance of God* (New York: Schocken Books, 1965), pp. 270–359, especially pp. 349–359.

24. See *The Function of Criticism* (Denver: Alan Swallow, 1957), pp. 101–156, especially pp. 103–104 and 139–146.

25. *The Function of Criticism,* p. 145.

to be ranked with the very great. And there is, too, in Arnold a
want of the symbolic sense; creation does not point to a world of
transcendent reality beyond itself. For Coleridge, there is no need
for the poet to conceptualize, to work at two removes from reality;
nature is symbolic, and to write of nature is already to write of
the transcendent. To know creation is to know God. The world
of creation is made up, after all, of

> The lovely shapes and sounds intelligible
> Of that eternal language, which thy God
> Utters, who from eternity doth teach
> Himself in all, and all things in himself.

We have indeed been moving in the direction of a newer criticism. But, as I have suggested, it is not really new at all. At its
best, modern criticism is returning to the Coleridgean tradition,
not the one-sided formalist view of Coleridge, but that of the complete Coleridge, at once sensitive to poetic form and open to the
deep human values — including religious values — which it incarnates. Once more the critic, like the poet, is bringing "the
whole soul of man into activity" through an act of the imagination.

Two

JOEL PORTE

The Problem of Emerson

"The more we know him, the less we know him." Stephen Whicher's wistfully encomiastic remark of two decades ago epitomizes the not entirely unhappy perplexity of a highly influential group of scholars and critics, beginning perhaps with F. O. Matthiessen, who, returning to Emerson's writings with enormous sympathy, intelligence, and sensitivity, attempted to discover a real human figure beneath the bland (or pompous, or smug) official portrait. Predictably, in view of the compensatory biases of modernist criticism, they found a "new" Emerson whose complexities belied that older optimistic all-American aphorist once dear to captains of industry, genteel professors of literature, and hopeful preachers in search of suitably uplifting remarks. Like the other great figures of the American Renaissance, Emerson was now found to be one of us — as richly evasive and enigmatic a figure, almost, as Hawthorne, or Melville, or Dickinson. Not only is Emerson incapable of being "summed up in a formula," Whicher insisted, "he is, finally, impenetrable, for all his forty-odd volumes."[1]

1. Stephen E. Whicher, "Emerson's Tragic Sense," in *Emerson: A Collection of Critical Essays,* ed. Milton Konvitz and Stephen Whicher (Englewood Cliffs, N.J.: Prentice-Hall, 1962), p. 39.

85

Though somewhat obscure, Whicher's statement is also highly instructive. I say obscure, because (as with Matthiessen and Perry Miller) Whicher's discouragement about his failure to fathom the secret of one of America's greatest authors implies not only an inability to get at the meaning of American culture at large, but also a personal failure that finally baffles speculation. What is instructive in the remark is its insistence on penetrating to the heart of Emerson *the man* (since, surely, one of the most astute Emersonians of the twentieth century was not admitting that he could make no sense of the master's works). Although I shall myself concentrate here on the problem of getting to the heart of Emerson's *writing,* I think there is something to be learned from Whicher's interest in Emerson's character, for it focuses attention on an important aspect of the Emerson problem.

For one thing, the meaning and value of Emerson's work have typically been overshadowed, and frequently undermined, by an emphasis on his example and personal force. Two of his most distinguished critics offer representative remarks in this regard. Henry James, Jr., speaking for those who had known Emerson, properly emphasized the manner in which he made his impression, "by word of mouth, face to face, with a rare, irresistible voice and a beautiful mild, modest authority."[2] This is an appealing portrait, suggesting an ethereal attractiveness that clearly made Emerson humanly persuasive. Santayana roughly seconds James's point, but his description of Emerson's authority sharpens the issue somewhat:

> Those who knew Emerson, or who stood so near to his time and to his circle that they caught some echo of his personal influence, did not judge him merely as a poet or philosopher, nor identify his efficacy with that of his writings. His friends and neighbors, the congregations he preached to in his younger days, the audiences that afterward listened to his lectures, all agreed in a veneration for his person which had nothing to do with their understanding or acceptance of his opinions. They flocked to him and listened to his word, not so much for the sake of its absolute meaning as for the

---

2. This and all subsequent quotations from Henry James are taken from "Emerson," in *The Art of Fiction and Other Essays* (New York: Oxford University Press, 1948), pp. 220–240.

atmosphere of candor, purity, and serenity that hung about it, as about a sort of sacred music. They felt themselves in the presence of a rare and beautiful spirit, who was in communion with a higher world.[3]

Santayana's clear impatience here with that atmosphere of high-minded religiosity that always vitiated the New England air for him is not intended, I think, to imply a disparagement of Emerson, to whom he was fundamentally sympathetic. Certain difficulties, nevertheless, are suggested in this description of Emerson's virtual canonization as one of the leading saints in the select American hagiology. ("He is a shining figure as on some Mount of Transfiguration," wrote George Woodberry in 1906.)[4] What would be the fate of Emerson's writings when that "fine adumbration," as James called him, should himself be translated to the higher world? Would his literary reputation endure the dissipation of his rare personal emphasis? Worse, could his writings weather the inevitable iconoclasm that tumbles every American idol from his pedestal? "I was never patient with the faults of the good," Emerson's own Aunt Mary Moody is quoted as saying.[5] And the mild saint seems to have written his own epitaph when he noted, in *Representative Men,* that "every hero becomes a bore at last."[6]

As we know, Emerson's fate, somewhat like Shakespeare's, was that he came to be treated as an almost purely allegorical personage whose real character and work got submerged in his

3. George Santayana, *Interpretations of Poetry and Religion* (New York: Scribner's, 1900), p. 217.

4. George Edward Woodberry, *Ralph Waldo Emerson,* repr. (New York: Haskell House, 1968), p. 1. In his *American Prose Masters* (1909) W. C. Brownell said that Emerson's presence was "suggestive of some new kind of saint — perhaps Unitarian." Twelve years earlier John Jay Chapman commented on the irony that this radical, who believed that "piety is a crime," should have been "calmly canonized and embalmed in amber by the very forces he braved. He is become a tradition and a sacred relic. You must speak of him under your breath, and you may not laugh near his shrine."

5. In Perry Miller, *The Transcendentalists: An Anthology* (Cambridge: Harvard University Press, 1950), p. 11.

6. Since the interested reader will have no difficulty locating quotations from Emerson's standard works (cited by name in the text), I have avoided the pedantry of elaborate documentation. References to Emerson's less accessible publications are duly noted.

function as a touchstone of critical opinion. More and more, the figure of Emerson merged with current perceptions of the meaning and drift of American high culture, and the emblem overwhelmed his substance. To the younger generation of the nineties, for example, notably John Jay Chapman and Santayana, certain aspects of Emerson represented the pale summation of that attenuated genteel tradition with which they had lost patience. As the polemical mood sharpened over the next quarter-century or so, Emerson became a kind of *corpus vile* useful mainly for the dissection of American culture. To the Puritan-baiting intellectuals of the twenties, he stood for little more than the final weak dilution in the New England teapot; but for the conservative New Humanists, who — like Fitzgerald's Nick Carraway — "wanted the world to be in uniform and at a sort of moral attention forever," Emerson was the pre-eminent voice of the American conscience and the patron saint, accordingly, of their rearguard action.[7] Even T. S. Eliot, though he sympathized with the general position of the school of Babbitt and More, wrote in 1919, while praising Hawthorne, that "the essays of Emerson are already an encumbrance";[8] and Eliot's key word suggests not so much a literary burden as a *monumental* physical weight — the Lares and Penates of Victorian culture which the brave new Aeneases of the twenties were determined to jettison:

> Matthew and Waldo, guardians of the faith,
> The army of unalterable law.

The American master seemed to keep watch over outmoded standards of conduct, not the new canons of poetry. As a result, "in those days [the twenties]," asserts Malcolm Cowley, "hardly anyone read Emerson."[9] Such a quirky exception as D. H. Law-

7. For a detailed history of this debate, see Richard Ruland, *The Rediscovery of American Literature* (Cambridge: Harvard University Press, 1967). Also useful in this connection is René Wellek's "Irving Babbitt, Paul More, and Transcendentalism," in *Transcendentalism and Its Legacy,* ed. Myron Simon and Thornton H. Parsons (Ann Arbor: University of Michigan Press, 1966), pp. 185–203.

8. Cited by F. O. Matthiessen in *The Achievement of T. S. Eliot* (New York: Oxford University Press, 1959), p. 24.

9. Malcolm Cowley, *Exile's Return* (New York: Viking Press, 1956), p. 227.

rence only proved the general rule, for this self-admitted "spiritual drug-fiend," despite his odd personal taste for Emerson, summarized the temper of the times when he argued, in 1923, that "all those gorgeous inrushes of exaltation and spiritual energy which made Emerson a great man now make us sick . . . When Professor [Stuart] Sherman urges us in Ralph Waldo's footsteps, he is really driving us nauseously astray." With a *"Sic transeunt Dei hominorum,"* Lawrence reluctantly ushered the tarnished deity from his niche.[10] The devils — Melville and Poe — were in, and the leading saint went marching out.

As I have noted, the "recovery" of Emerson that began largely in the forties and continues today is based on the sympathetic perception that beneath the seemingly ageless smiling public mask there lies a finite consciousness troubled with a tragic sense of contingency and loss — a little-known Emerson, as James said in 1887, with "his inner reserves and scepticisms, his secret ennuis and ironies." Indeed, most recently the saint has been turned not only inside out but upside down and shown to have a demonic bottom nature. In an improbable context of Siberian shamans become Thracian bards, Harold Bloom argues for a Bacchicly wild and primitivistic Emerson: "The spirit that speaks in and through him has the true Pythagorean and Orphic stink . . . The ministerial Emerson . . . is full brother to the Dionysiac adept who may have torn living flesh with his inspired teeth."[11]

The trouble with these strategies for redeeming Emerson is that they, too, like the Victorian apotheoses, are rooted in the character of the man (though in this case it is a presumably more appealing, because more complex, figure) and therefore depend for their force on our assenting to a particular reconstruction of Emerson's personality which may have little to do with the common reader's literary experience of Emerson. While praising Stephen Whicher's *Freedom and Fate: An Inner Life of Ralph Waldo Emerson,* Jonathan Bishop notes that "in the midst of one's appreciation for the achievement of this book, and the other works whose assumptions are comparable, one can still feel that

10. *A Dial Miscellany,* ed. William Wasserstrom (Syracuse, New York: Syracuse University Press, 1963), p. 151.

11. Harold Bloom, "Emerson: The Glory and the Sorrows of American Romanticism," *Virginia Quarterly Review,* 47 (Autumn 1971), 550.

the point of view adopted involves a certain neglect of the literary particulars."[12]

Though many literary particulars are brilliantly illuminated in Bishop's own book, which is undoubtedly the best modern reading of Emerson we have yet had, it unfortunately does not escape some of the typical difficulties of Emerson criticism. Predicated, like Whicher's work, on the notion that there is a "true, secret Emerson" who is the real and really interesting man we are after, *Emerson on the Soul* tells us that the reader's job is "to distinguish the excellent moments," which scarcely ever "exceed a page or two of sustained utterance" (though Bishop is uneasy with the old commonplace which argues that Emerson was little more than a sentence maker or at best a paragraph maker, he, too, sees little organic form in whole essays or books). This authentic Emerson — sometimes, indeed, by a kind of typographical mystification, identified as "Emerson" — predictably exhibits himself most freely in the private journals or letters. To arrive at these "interesting moments" in the public utterances, "one makes a drastic selection," avoiding "the dull tones, the preacherly commonplaces, the high-minded vapid identity" which obviously does not express the genuine Emerson we are seeking. The ability to recognize this profounder, more complex, more valuable tone may also serve as a kind of moral test of honesty in the reader, for "a coward soul is always free to interpret what Emerson says in a way that does not allow it to reach through to the places in him where matters are genuinely in a tangle." Rising to a pitch of almost religious fervor, Bishop claims finally that the authentic Emerson discoverable to our best selves can still serve as a hero and prophet for the American scholar. Thus, relying on a carefully controlled modern phenomenology of reading Emerson, Bishop reaches back fundamentally to join hands with the traditional notion that Emerson's highest value lies in the moral authority with which he utters permanent truths and thereby remains, as Arnold said, "the friend and aider of those who would live in the spirit."[13]

12. Jonathan Bishop, *Emerson on the Soul* (Cambridge: Harvard University Press, 1964), p. 6.

13. *Emerson on the Soul*, pp. 130, 15, 106, 184, 131, 151; Matthew Arnold, *Discourses in America* (London, 1889), p. 179.

II

It was usual for Perry Miller, when initiating his survey of American authors, to insist on the notion that "writing is written by writers." This innocent tautology was intended to convey the idea that the great figures being studied were not primarily to be considered as landmarks in the growth of American culture nor as so many statues in an imaginary pantheon whom it was our patriotic duty to revere, but rather as *writers* whose continuing claim on our attention resides in their exhaustless *literary* vitality. Writing is not necessarily written by famous authors, with beards and visitable houses; it is the fruit of patient labor by men and women fundamentally, and often fanatically, devoted to their craft. Books, as Thoreau says in *Walden,* "must be read as deliberately and reservedly as they were written." And such a reading is encouraged by thinking of authors primarily as writers, and only secondarily as famous hermits, spinsters, he-men, statesmen, spiritual leaders, madmen, madwomen, or the like.

Now, it is a curious fact that Emerson, who is often acknowledged to be the greatest, or at least most important, author of the American Renaissance and even of American literary history altogether, has manifestly not been accorded that careful scrutiny of his work *as writing* which Poe, Hawthorne, Melville, Thoreau, Dickinson, Whitman, and other more minor figures, have received in superabundance. The heart of the problem seems to lie, as I have already suggested, in the overwhelming, indeed intimidating, emphasis on Emerson's personal authority, his example, his wisdom, his high role as the spiritual father and Plato of our race. Even so sharp a critic as Henry James, with his exquisitely developed sense of writing as a craft, was blinded from seeing any pervasive formal excellence in Emerson's work by the "firmness" and "purity," the "singular power," of Emerson's moral force — his "particular faculty, which has not been surpassed, for speaking to the soul in a voice of direction and authority." Though James assumed Emerson's "importance and continuance" and insisted "that he serves and will not wear out, and that indeed we cannot afford to drop him," he did so only as a special tribute to this great man, allowing him to be "a striking exception to the general rule that writings live in the last resort by their form; that they owe a large part of their fortune to the art with which they

have been composed." Despite occasional "felicities, inspira-
tions, unforgettable phrases," James felt it was "hardly too much,
or too little, to say of Emerson's writings in general that they were
not composed at all." He never truly achieved "a fashion and a
manner" and finally "differs from most men of letters of the same
degree of credit in failing to strike us as having achieved a style."
James concluded his survey of Emerson's career by positing a
large and significant *if:* "if Emerson goes his way, as he clearly
appears to be doing, on the strength of his message alone, the
case will be rare, the exception striking, and the honour great."

It should be a matter of some interest, and no little amusement,
for us to note that Henry's scientific brother was moved to make
precisely the claim for Emerson, at the centenary celebration,
which the distinguished novelist and critic had withheld. "The
form of the garment was so vital with Emerson that it is impossible to separate it from the matter. They form a chemical combination — thoughts which would be trivial expressed otherwise,
are important through the nouns and verbs to which he married
them. The style is the man, it has been said; the man Emerson's
mission culminated in his style, and if we must define him in one
word, we have to call him Artist. He was an artist whose medium
was verbal and who wrought in spiritual material."[14] Perhaps it
was the unsatisfied artist in William James himself, as Santayana
describes him,[15] who was enabled to make these observations
about Emerson which, though almost universally ignored, have
scarcely been bettered: his "thoughts . . . would be trivial expressed otherwise"; his "mission culminated in his style." William
James's valuable hints have not been picked up, and Henry's
prescient *if* has progressively exerted its force. Emerson, as any

14. William James, "Address at the Emerson Centenary in Concord,"
in *Emerson: A Collection of Critical Essays,* p. 19. W. C. Brownell's comment manages to echo both James's at once. Though "no writer ever
possessed a more distinguished verbal instinct, or indulged it with more
delight" than Emerson, his style is that "of a writer who is artistic, but
not an artist." Emerson had "no sense of composition; his compositions
are not composed. They do not constitute objective creations. They have
no construction, no organic quality — no evolution . . . art in the con-
structive sense found no echo in Emerson's nature." See *American Prose
Masters,* ed. Howard Mumford Jones (Cambridge: Harvard University
Press, 1963), pp. 125–127.

15. In *Character and Opinion in the United States* (1920).

candid teacher of American literature can report, has manifestly *not* made his way "on the strength of his message." He has become the least appreciated, least enjoyed, least understood — indeed, least read — of America's unarguably major writers. Even most intelligent and willing students, dropped in the usual way into the great *mare tenebrum* of Emerson's weightier works, gratefully return to shore, dragging behind them only out of a sense of duty a whale of a précis of Emerson's "message," which, they will usually admit, contains little meaning and less pleasure for them. Nor have students of Emerson's writing received much practical help from well-intentioned critics who, while praising Emerson as a prophet of romanticism, or symbolism, or existentialism, or pragmatism, or organicism, sadly concede that the master's reach exceeded his grasp so far as exemplifying the particular *-ism* in successful works of literary art is concerned. Seen from this perspective as a flawed genius whose theory and practice were always disjunct, Emerson may exasperate by seeming to promise more than he can perform. As Charles Feidelson says, "what he gives with one hand he takes away with the other."[16]

I have myself, to echo the conclusion of *Nature,* come to look at the world of Emerson with new eyes and been greatly gratified and exhilarated to discover a kind of verification of my views

16. Charles Feidelson, Jr., *Symbolism and American Literature* (Chicago: University of Chicago Press, 1953), p. 150. An example of how much Emerson needs protection from his "friendly" critics is afforded by this quotation from Norman Foerster's "Emerson on the Organic Principle in Art": "To Emerson . . . it was a fundamental conception capable of answering all our questions about the nature and practice of art. It is true that in his own writing, his own practice of art, Emerson was notoriously deficient in the organic law in its formal aspect; his essays and poems are badly organized, the parts having no definite relation to each other and the wholes wanting that unity which we find in the organisms of nature. Rarely does he give us even a beginning, middle, and end, which is the very least that we expect of an organism, which, indeed, we expect of a mechanism. Yet if he could not observe the law of organic form, he could interpret it; in this matter his practice and theory are not equivalent — happily, he could see more than he could do" (*Emerson: A Collection of Critical Essays,* pp. 109–110). The Emerson who was too impotent artistically to produce even a respectable machine is thus "praised" for envisioning what a truly living art might be! Though one might be tempted to say something harsh about such jejune remarks as these, Professor Foerster's blandly thoughtless "happily" simply baffles judgment.

in the — surprisingly — delighted reactions of students. The Emerson we now see, I am convinced, has always existed; indeed it is the same Emerson whom William James was moved to praise as an artist. This Emerson's interest and appeal reside in the imaginative materials and structures of his writing — in his tropes and *topoi,* his metaphors and verbal wit, in the remarkable consistencies of his conceiving mind and executing hand. What I am prepared to state categorically is that the familiar rubrics of Emersonian thought, the stock in trade of most Emerson criticism, though undeniably there, are a positive hindrance to the enjoyment of Emerson's writing. Though some Emersonians will undoubtedly continue until the end of time to chew over such concepts as Compensation, the Over-Soul, Correspondence, Self-Reliance, Spiritual Laws, *et id genus omne,* the trouble with such things is that they are not very interesting. They make Emerson seem awfully remote, abstract, and — yes — academic. My experience has been that when these topics are mentioned the mind closes, one's attention wanders . . . Similarly, the now standard debate over Emerson's presumed inability, or refusal, to confront evil (usually capitalized) has had the unfortunate effect first of making him seem shallow compared, say, to a Hawthorne or a Melville; and, second and more importantly, it has frequently shifted discussions of Emerson to a high plane of theological or metaphysical argument where one's ordinary sense of reality, and the powers of practical criticism, falter in pursuit. Evil with a capital has a way of teasing the imagination into silence.

My thesis then is simple: Emerson, as he himself frequently insisted, is fundamentally a poet whose meaning lies in his manipulations of language and figure. The best guide to change, or growth, or consistency in Emerson's thought, is his poetic imagination and not his philosophic arguments or discursive logic. The alert reader can discover, and take much pleasure in discovering, remarkable verbal strategies, metaphoric patterns, repetitions and developments of sound, sense, and image throughout Emerson's writing. One finds an impressively unified consciousness everywhere in control of its fertile imaginings.[17]

17. There are some valuable observations on "Emerson as literature" in James M. Cox, "Emerson and Hawthorne: Truth and Doubt," *Virginia Quarterly Review,* 45 (Winter 1969), 88–107. Professor Cox writes of "metaphor as action" in Emerson's work.

As an initial illustration of what I am claiming for Emerson's work, I would momentarily leave aside the juiciest plums — *Nature,* the "Divinity School Address," the great essays — and turn briefly to a book for which, probably, only the most modest assertions of imaginative unity can be made, hoping, nevertheless, that its example will prove instructive. Like most nineteenth-century travel books, *English Traits* cannot be expected to succeed entirely in transcending the somewhat episodic nature of its author's peregrinations and his own normal desire, with his varied audience in mind, to include something of interest to everyone. Typically, since such an omnium-gatherum will amiably avoid pushing toward overwhelming conclusions and let its appeal reside precisely in its miscellaneous character, any search for organic form seems defeated at the outset. Still, we are dealing with the inescapable consistencies of Emerson's shaping imagination.

In the preface to a recent edition of *English Traits,* Howard Mumford Jones confronts Emerson's difficulty in making a unified book of his heterogeneous materials and complains specifically that Emerson spoiled the natural form of his work by beginning with a chapter on his first, earlier visit to England and concluding, not logically with "Results," but anticlimactically with his "Speech at Manchester."[18] I believe, however, that the sympathetic reader of *English Traits* can supply some possible justifications for Emerson's procedure. The opening chapter is an expression of disappointment with England, and this is the keynote of the book. Here, the disappointment, though it has a personal basis, is emblematic of the young American's unfulfilled expectations of the Old World and prophetic of his developing hope for America. He

18. *English Traits,* ed. Howard Mumford Jones (Cambridge: Harvard University Press, 1966), p. xv. Though Philip Nicoloff, in his exhaustive study of *English Traits,* also sees little justification for the opening and concluding chapters (indeed, he claims that the whole book is "not so shapely a production as has often been suggested, either in its entirety or in its parts"), he does find an intellectual pattern in *English Traits* based on Emerson's belief in the necessity of racial and historical evolution — growth and decline. Emerson's theories thus led him to see England as an exhausted species passing on its genetic heritage to the country of the future, i.e., America. My argument here is that the metaphoric structure of *English Traits* precisely reinforces this doctrine. See Philip Nicoloff, *Emerson on Race and History* (New York: Columbia University Press, 1961). Cf. also Ralph Rusk, *The Life of Ralph Waldo Emerson* (New York: Columbia University Press, 1957), pp. 393ff.

goes abroad eager to meet certain great men — Landor, Coleridge, Carlyle, Wordsworth — and finds them sadly isolated,
mutually repellent, and embittered, "prisoners . . . of their own
thought" who cannot "bend to a new companion and think with
him." They thus fail as poets in Emerson's own high sense (as
"liberating gods," that is, who help man "to escape the custody
of that body in which he is pent up, and of that jail-yard of individual relations in which he is enclosed"). Their vaunted originality somehow evaporates for the young seeker: Coleridge's talk
falls "into certain commonplaces"; Wordsworth expiates his "departure from the common in one direction" by his "conformity in
every other." Significantly, both Carlyle and Wordsworth talk
much of America, turning Emerson's thoughts back whence he
came and pointing us forward to Emerson's peroration in Manchester, where he will, as delicately as possible, summarize his
negative reaction to this "aged England," this "mournful country," with its pathetically atomistic island mentality, its conformity to custom, its played out spirit, and suggest that if England
does not find new vigor to restore her decrepit old age (as the
weight of his whole book tends to prove it cannot), "the elasticity
and hope of mankind must henceforth remain on the Alleghany
ranges, or nowhere."

The huge, virtually endless American continent is the mysterious force against which Emerson measures the fixed, finite, island
prison, the "Gibraltar of propriety," which is England. Here we
have the central imaginative structure of *English Traits*. Though
initially England seems "a paradise of comfort and plenty," "a
garden," we quickly learn that this miracle of rare device, like
Spenser's Bower of Bliss, is a false paradise where "art conquers
nature" and, "under an ash-colored sky," confounds night and
day. Coal smoke and soot unnaturally make all times and seasons
of one hue, "give white sheep the color of black sheep, discolor
the human saliva, contaminate the air, poison many plants and
corrode the monuments and buildings." This is the epitome of the
fallen modern world of industry, where "a terrible machine has
possessed itself of the ground, the air, the men and women, and
hardly even thought is free." Everything, we are told, "is false
and forged," "man is made as a Birmingham button," and "steam
is almost an Englishman." The whole island has been transformed

into the thoroughfare of trade where all things can be described, in Emerson's eyes, as either "artificial" or "factitious": the breeds of cattle, the fish-filled ponds and streams, the climate, illumination, heating, the English social system, the law, property, crimes, education, manners, customs — indeed, "the whole fabric." All is "Birminghamized, and we have a nation whose existence is a work of art — a cold, barren, almost arctic isle being made the most fruitful, luxurious and imperial land in the whole earth."

In this setting, we are not surprised to learn that the two most mysterious and imponderable of life's gifts, religion and art, are particularly vulnerable to the general fate. Since these two subjects touch the quick of Emerson's concern, it is especially fascinating to note in this regard how the fundamental paradigm of America (as revealed in and through its transcendental minister, Emerson) against which all is being tested palpitates within Emerson's language and metaphors. True religion is utterly missing from England, for it is an alien and frightful thing to the English: "it is passing, glancing, gesticular; it is a traveler, a newness, a surprise, a secret, which perplexes them and puts them out." We should keep this consciously orphic sentence in our ear as we glance at the next chapter, "Literature," on the way to Emerson's culminating vision of America. Speaking of English genius, Emerson notes: "It is retrospective. How can it discern and hail the new forms that are looming up on the horizon, new and gigantic thoughts which cannot dress themselves out of any old wardrobe of the past?" Now, the alert student of Emerson will recognize here an unmistakable echo of the opening paragraph of *Nature* ("Our age is retrospective . . . why should we grope among the dry bones of the past, or put the living generation into masquerade out of its faded wardrobe . . . There are new lands, new men, new thoughts"). What this echo should tell us is that the very same living, prospective, titanic American nature which, Emerson insisted in 1836, would inspire a new poetry and philosophy and religion of "revelation," as opposed to the backward-looking, dead, limited British tradition — that "great apparition," as he terms it in *Nature,* is fully present to Emerson's imagination twenty years later in *English Traits* as he attempts to explain what the English spirit dares not face and isolates itself from.

Walking the polished halls of English literary society, Emerson seems to find himself "on a marble floor, where nothing will grow," and he concludes that the English "fear the hostility of ideas, of poetry, of religion — ghosts which they cannot lay . . . they are tormented with fear that herein lurks a force that will sweep their system away. The artists say, 'Nature puts them out.'" Recalling the opening paragraph of *Nature* and hearing still that orphic sentence from the preceding chapter on religion, we may now feel confirmed in our intuition about Emerson's real point: that great force which threatens the English and "puts them out" is equivalent to the religio-poetic mystery of American nature.

Emerson's metaphoric confrontation between England and America, which represents the true symbolic thrust of *English Traits,* culminates most forcefully and appropriately in the fourth chapter from the end, entitled "Stonehenge." Traveling with Carlyle, who argues that the English have much to teach the Americans, Emerson concedes the point but does not budge from his instinctive belief: "I surely know that as soon as I return to Massachusetts I shall lapse at once into the feeling, which the geography of America inevitably inspires, that we play the game with immense advantage; that there and not here is the seat and centre of the British race; and that no skill or activity can long compete with the prodigious natural advantages of that country, in the hands of the same race; and that England, an old and exhausted island, must one day be contented, like other parents, to be strong only in her children." Emerson's conviction that the English mind is simply rendered impotent by, and turns away self-defensively from, the enormously perplexing forces that embosom and nourish us seems strengthened by his visit to Stonehenge itself. "The chief mystery is, that any mystery should have been allowed to settle on so remarkable a monument, in a country on which all the muses have kept their eyes now for eighteen hundred years." Ignoring this strange and unsettling secret at the heart of its own island, the English mind leaves Stonehenge "to the rabbits, whilst it opens pyramids and uncovers Nineveh." Emerson completes this series of speculations and, in a very real sense, the point of his whole book in a fine paragraph toward the end of "Stonehenge" that at once expresses his own sense of America's ineffable power and his firm belief that the Englishman is unable to comprehend it:

On the way to Winchester, whither our host accompanied us in the afternoon, my friends asked many questions respecting American landscapes, forests, houses, — my house, for example. It is not easy to answer these queries well. There, I thought, in America, lies nature sleeping, overgrowing, almost conscious, too much by half for man in the picture, and so giving a certain *tristesse*, like the rank vegetation of swamps and forests seen at night, steeped in dews and rains, which it loves; and on it man seems not able to make much impression. There, in that great sloven continent, in high Alleghany pastures, in the sea-wide sky-skirted prairie, still sleeps and murmurs and hides the great mother, long since driven away from the trim hedge-rows and over-cultivated garden of England. And, in England, I am quite too sensible of this. Every one is on his good behavior and must be dressed for dinner at six. So I put off my friends with very inadequate details, as best I could.

In the face of such a passage as this, the critic of Emerson may be commended most for appreciative silence.[19] I want only, with these lines in mind, to underline my previous point about this book and Emerson generally: namely, that the excellent moments in his writing are not, as has so often been said, incidental gems in a disjointed mosaic, but typically the shining nodal points in a carefully woven imaginative web.

19. Still, the impulse to comment on this strange paragraph is hard to resist, though it may threaten to carry one far afield. Emerson's desire to express what he seems to feel is the primitive source of America's natural power leads him into a quasi-Frazerian fantasy in which he creates a myth-figure, "the great mother," who has the sort of terrifying appeal of that Yeatsian "rough beast" which "slouches toward Bethlehem to be born." Emerson's rank goddess seems to live in a solitude which is at once sad from the human point of view (*tristesse*) and yet necessary, for what man — even a mammoth American hero — could marry such a creature, a thing of night and water which "sleeps and murmurs and hides" like some holy outcast? The operative word here is *sloven,* not simply because it contrasts America's sprawling disorder with England's enclosed neatness, but more crucially because it suggests a kind of fecund dirtiness and lewdness ("lewd" is in fact an old meaning of the word) which constitutes the secret force of the American earth. Thus, Emerson seems to see the two countries in sexual terms, England being an "aged" and "exhausted" woman worn out "with the infirmities of a thousand years," whereas the American mother maintains a frightening but fertile attractiveness. With her will mate Emerson's superhuman national Poet, whose thought, "ejaculated as Logos or Word," arises like the mother's body from the dark and dank substratum of human life ("Doubt not, O poet, but persist. Say 'It is in me, and shall out.' Stand there, balked

III

Although some Emerson scholars in our own time have noticed
that certain motifs or metaphors are central to Emerson's literary
project, their perceptions have by and large been ignored in practical Emerson criticism. Three important examples, all from
Emerson scholarship now more than two decades old, will illustrate my point. In *Emerson's Angle of Vision,* Sherman Paul
taught us that "for Emerson the primary agency of insight was
seeing"; the eye "was his prominent faculty." Another valuable
perception was offered by Vivian C. Hopkins in *Spires of Form,*
where she asserted that "Emerson's own term of 'the spiral' ad-
mirably hits the combination of circular movement with upward
progress which is the heart of his aesthetic. Optimism controls
Emerson's idea of the circle becoming a spiral, ever rising as
it revolves upon itself." Finally, Stephen Whicher, writing on
"Emerson's Tragic Sense," noted that "something resembling the
Fall of Man, which he had so ringingly denied, reappears in his

---

and dumb, stuttering and stammering, hissed and hooted, stand and
strive, until at last rage draw out of thee that *dream*-power which every
night shows thee is thine own; a power transcending all limit and privacy,
and by virtue of which a man is the conductor of the whole river of
electricity"). One moves directly from all of this to "Song of Myself":

> I am he that walks with the tender and growing night;
> I call to the earth and sea half-held by the night.
> Press close barebosomed night!
> Press close magnetic nourishing night . . .
> Smile O voluptuous coolbreathed earth!
> Earth of the slumbering and liquid trees! . . .
> Smile, for your lover comes!

I am also reminded of another American genius who combined spiritual fastidiousness with a taste for the "arrant stinks" of the new world.
Wallace Stevens' aesthetician of *mal,* like the Emerson of the paragraph
we have been examining,

> sought the most grossly maternal, the creature
> Who most fecundly assuaged him, the softest
> Woman with a vague moustache and not the mauve
> *Maman.* His anima liked its animal
> And liked it unsubjugated, so that home
> Was a return to birth, a being born
> Again in the savagest severity . . .

The Collected Poems of Wallace Stevens (New York: Knopf, 1957),
p. 321.

pages."[20] I want to suggest, very briefly, how useful an awareness of three such motifs as these, often in combination with one another, can be, not only for the illumination of individual essays and books, but also for an understanding of change or development overall in Emerson's work.

Although every reader of *Nature* since 1836 has taken special notice of the famous eyeball passage, either to praise or to ridicule its extravagance, surprisingly few students or even teachers of Emerson, in my experience, are aware that in this metaphor resides the compositional center of gravity of the essay.[21] Despite Emerson's insistence in this crucial paragraph that his purpose is to "see all," to become nothing more nor less than *vision,* readers of *Nature* seem generally not to notice that in the magnificent opening sentence of the piece — "Our age is retrospective" — the key word means precisely what it says and is rhetorically balanced by the title of the last section — "Prospects." It is a question of seeing in a new way, a new direction. Emerson is inviting us to behold "God and nature face to face," with our own eyes, not darkly and obscurely through the lenses of history. *Nature* concerns the fall of man into perceptual division from his physical environment. Salvation is nothing less than perceptual reunification — true *sight* externally and *insight* internally. The Poet, the *seer,* as Emerson was to suggest in the essay of that name, is a type of the savior "who re-attaches things to nature and the Whole" through his vision:

20. Sherman Paul, *Emerson's Angle of Vision* (Cambridge: Harvard University Press, 1952), pp. 72–73; Vivian C. Hopkins, *Spires of Form: A Study of Emerson's Aesthetic Theory* (Cambridge: Harvard University Press, 1951), p. 3; Stephen Whicher, "Emerson's Tragic Sense," in *Emerson: A Collection of Critical Essays,* p. 42.

21. Notable exceptions are: Kenneth Burke, "I, Eye, Ay — Emerson's Early Essay 'Nature': Thoughts on the Machinery of Transcendence," in *Transcendentalism and Its Legacy,* pp. 3–24; Tony Tanner, *The Reign of Wonder* (New York: Harper and Row, 1967), chapter 2, "Emerson: The Unconquered Eye and the Enchanted Circle"; Richard Poirier, *A World Elsewhere* (New York: Oxford University Press, 1966), chapter 2, "Is There an I for an Eye?: The Visionary Possession of America." See also Warner Berthoff, *Fictions and Events* (New York: Dutton, 1971), " 'Building Discourse': The Genesis of Emerson's *Nature,*" especially pp. 209–213. This trenchant essay, much less restricted in scope than its title suggests, is the best general introduction to Emerson that I know.

As the eyes of Lyncaeus were said to see through the earth, so the poet turns the world to glass, and shows us all things in their right series and procession. For through that better perception he stands one step nearer to things, and sees the flowing or metamorphosis . . . This insight, which expresses itself by what is called Imagination, is a very high sort of seeing, which does not come by study, but by the intellect being where and what it sees; by sharing the path or circuit of things through forms, and so making them translucid to others.

The echoes of *Nature* in this passage from "The Poet" tell us that we can all become our own poet-savior by becoming pellucid lenses, transparent eyeballs, and perfecting our vision. "The eye is the best of artists"; "the attentive eye" sees beauty everywhere; wise men pierce the "rotten diction" of a fallen world "and fasten words again to visible things," achieving a viable "picturesque language"; "a right action seems to fill the eye"; "insight refines" us: though "the animal eye" sees the actual world "with wonderful accuracy," it is "the eye of Reason" that stimulates us "to more earnest vision." Mounting to his splendid peroration in "Prospects," Emerson reminds us that "the ruin or the blank, that we see when we look at nature, is in our own eye. The axis of vision is not coincident with the axis of things, and so they appear not transparent but opake." A cleansing of our vision is all that is required for "the redemption of the soul." In such a case, Emerson says at the start of his last paragraph, we shall "come to look at the world with new eyes." Since "what we are, that only can we see," we must make ourselves whole again. Emerson culminates his quasi-religious vision with a ringing sentence that catches up the Christian undertone of the essay and assimilates it to the naturalistic premise of America's nascent literary hopes: "The kingdom of man over nature, which cometh not with observation, — a dominion such as now is beyond his dream of God, — he shall enter without more wonder than the blind man feels who is gradually restored to perfect sight." Emerson's last word, of course, underlines once again the point of the whole essay. And the important allusion here to Luke 17:20-21 (unfortunately not noted in the new Harvard edition of *Nature*) tells us that the visionary perfection we seek has stolen upon us unawares and lies waiting within.[22]

This heady faith, expressed in the controlling metaphor of *Nature,* which believes that clarified sight can literally reform our world, for the most part governs the first series of Emerson's *Essays* and is embodied in the opening sentence of "Circles": "The eye is the first circle; the horizon which it forms is the second." Emerson's meaning, enforced here by a favorite pun and emphasized throughout "Circles" (when a man utters a truth, "his eye burns up the veil which shrouded all things"; when the poet breaks the chain of habitual thought, "I open my eye on my own possibilities"), is that the self, represented here by the creative eye, is primary and generative: it *forms* the horizon — goal, world view — that it sees. This is the "piercing eye" of Uriel which, in the poem of that name, is described as "a look that solved the sphere." But, as we know, by the time Emerson came to write "Uriel" in the mid-1840's his "lapse" had already taken place and his own reference to the "ardent eye" (as Thoreau was to term it) is consciously ironic.[23] Indeed, and this is my central point, as we move into his second series of *Essays* and beyond, we may verify the fundamental shift in Emerson's optative mood brought about by his "sad self-knowledge" through simply observing the transformations that his visual metaphor undergoes. In the crucial "Experience," for example, Emerson accedes to the notion of the Fall of Man, redefining it as "the discovery we have made

22. Emerson uses the same sentence from Luke in "Experience." Cf. M. H. Abrams, *Natural Supernaturalism: Tradition and Revolution in Romantic Literature* (New York: Norton, 1971), p. 47; see also pp. 411ff. For an understanding of the Romantic context of *Nature,* one could hardly do better than to study Professor Abrams' brilliant exposition of the central Romantic motifs (the transvaluation of religious "vision"; the reinterpretation of the fall of man; the significance of the Romantic spiral). Since I cannot quote as much of this absorbing book as I should like, I shall content myself with simply recommending it to all students of Emerson. Professor Abrams's key text, by the way — Wordsworth's "Prospectus" for *The Recluse* — might have served Emerson as doctrine for *Nature.*

23. Compare my own "Transcendental Antics," in *Harvard English Studies* 3, ed. Harry Levin (Cambridge: Harvard University Press, 1972), pp. 180–182.

that we exist" — the discovery, that is, that the individual consciousness is limited and contingent. "Ever afterwards we suspect
our instruments. We have learned that we do not see directly, but
mediately, and that we have no means of correcting these colored
and distorting lenses which we are." Emerson now has only
a "perhaps" to offer concerning the "creative power" of our
"subject-lenses," and he serves up his own optimistic perception
from "Circles" in a new, markedly qualified, form: "People forget
that it is the eye which makes the horizon." What we have created
is no more than an optical illusion. Emerson further confirms his
diminished sense of personal power later in the book, in the first
paragraph of "Nominalist and Realist," when his trope reappears: "We have such exorbitant eyes that on seeing the
smallest arc we complete the curve, and when the curtain is lifted
from the diagram which it seemed to veil, we are vexed to find
that no more was drawn than just that fragment of an arc which
we first beheld. We are greatly too liberal in our construction of
each other's faculty and promise." It is worth noticing, by the
way, how the quintessentially figurative nature of Emerson's
imagination has unerringly guided him to the witty choice of
"exorbitant" in this passage.

But an even more impressive example, in this regard, of the
progressive metamorphosis of Emerson's metaphor as his perceptions changed may be found in "Fate." By 1852, when the essay
was completed, Emerson had so qualified his views that Nature,
which sixteen years before was the book of life and possibility,
became now "the book of Fate." In 1836 Emerson asserted in
"Prospects" that "nature is not fixed but fluid. Spirit alters,
moulds, makes it . . . Every spirit builds itself a house, and beyond
its house a world, and beyond its world a heaven." Now he was
forced tragically to concede that "every spirit makes its house; but
afterwards the house confines the spirit." Faced with this crushing
sense of limitation, Emerson returned to his favorite metaphor in
a new, notably ironic, mood:

> The force with which we resist these torrents of tendency looks
> so ridiculously inadequate that it amounts to little more than a
> criticism or protest made by a minority of one, under compulsion
> of millions. I seemed in the height of a tempest to see men over-

board struggling in the waves, and driven about here and there. They glanced intelligently at each other, but 'twas little they could do for one another; 'twas much if each could keep afloat alone. Well, they had a right to their eye-beams, and all the rest was Fate.

Here sight, as Jonathan Bishop has remarked well, "the sense especially associated with the intellectual freedom of the Soul, has dwindled until it can provide only a bare proof of impotence."[24] The rhetorical procedure in "Fate," to be sure, is insistently dialectic, but this old Emersonian game of yin and yang is rather mechanically worked out, and a balance is not struck for the reader, I think, because we sense clearly where the weight of Emerson's own imagination leans. When, a few pages later, he argues for the power of individual will by saying, of the hero, that "the glance of his eye has the force of sunbeams," we can hardly fail to recall the convincing paragraph I have quoted. Intelligent glances may serve as a kind of spiritual consolation to drowning men, but eyebeams and sunbeams alike seem insubstantial as levers against the overwhelming force of Fate.

An analogous indication of discouragement in Emerson's optimistic philosophy may be seen in the fortunes of another central metaphor — that of the ascending spiral or upward-pointing staircase (or ladder). In this case, I believe we can actually pinpoint the shift in Emerson's attitude as occurring somewhere between the composition of "The Poet" and "Experience" (which is to say somewhere between late 1842 and early 1844). I think it is even possible to assert in this regard that although "The Poet" stands first in the second series of *Essays,* the ebulliently hopeful mood and metaphoric coordinates of that piece place it with the first book of *Essays,* whereas "Experience," which is printed directly following "The Poet," actually marks a new departure in both tone and imagery.

Emerson's first collection of *Essays* is largely controlled by figures of ascension. In "Self-Reliance" we read that "the soul *becomes*," that power "resides in the moment of transition from a past to a new state, in the shooting of the gulf, in the darting to an aim." The inchoate metaphor develops in "Compensation," where

24. *Emerson on the Soul,* p. 210.

Emerson affirms that "the soul refuses limits," for "man's life is
a progress, and not a station." The law of nature "is growth," and
"the voice of the Almighty saith, 'Up and onward for evermore!' "
The method of man is "a progressive arrangement," we are told in
"Spiritual Laws"; and this means, as regards the affections (in
"Love"), that we must pass from lower attractions to higher ones:
"the lover ascends to the highest beauty, to love and knowledge
of Divinity, by steps on this ladder of created souls." Since, in
"Friendship," we "descend to meet," we must make room for one
another's merits — "let them mount and expand" — parting, if
need be, so that we may "meet again on a higher platform." This
is the "spiritual astronomy" of love, as it is the law of the soul's
progress in "The Over-Soul" ("the soul's advances are not made
by gradations, such as can be represented by motion in a straight
line, but rather by ascension of state"). Emerson's figure develops
further, in the first series of *Essays,* with "Circles," which is essentially devoted to working out a set of variations on the notion of
man as "a self-evolving circle," a rising spiral, who scales the
"mysterious ladder" of upwardly mobile life. In a very real sense,
however, the figure culminates in "The Poet," for he is the Christ-
like hero whose *logos* breaks our chains and allows us to "mount
above these clouds and opaque airs" in which we normally dwell.
Poets are "liberating gods" who preach *"ascension,* or the passage
of the soul into higher forms . . . into free space." Released by this
extraordinary savior, we live the heavenly life of the redeemed
imagination: "dream delivers us to dream, and while the drunken-
ness lasts we will sell our bed, our philosophy, our religion, in
our opulence."

This divine bubble is punctured sharply in "Experience" as
Emerson, in typical fashion, picks up his own language and places
it in a startling new context: "Dream delivers us to dream, and
there is no end to illusion." The imagination is now seen as a kind
of devil of deceit who provokes the fall of man into a "middle
region" of uncertainty and confusion:

> Where do we find ourselves? In a series of which we do not
> know the extremes, and believe that it has none. We wake and find
> ourselves on a stair; there are stairs below us, which we seem to
> have ascended; there are stairs above us, many a one, which go
> upward and out of sight. But the Genius which according to the

old belief stands at the door by which we enter, and gives us the lethe to drink, that we may tell no tales, mixed the cup too strongly, and we cannot shake off the lethargy now at noonday. Sleep lingers all our lifetime about our eyes, as night hovers all day in the boughs of the fir-tree. All things swim and glitter. Our life is not so much threatened as our perception. Ghostlike we glide through nature.

Vision is darkened here. Indeed, Emerson's mood is sinister, almost Poesque, as he, too, in a sort of "lonesome October," wanders "in the misty mid region of Weir" which we find in "Ulalume." Or, to use the terms of Wallace Stevens, Emerson is trapped in something like a "banal sojourn," a time of indifference, when man's depressed spirit dumbly mutters: "One has a malady, here, a malady. One feels a malady."[25] That malady can perhaps best be described as loss of affect, a contemporary version of acedia; a dejected state in which Emerson cannot even feel that this terrible threat to perception is a threat to life because his very sense of self is "ghostlike." This is the form evil takes in Emerson's lapsarian mood. The optimistic spiral has collapsed upon itself and Emerson, having set his "heart on honesty in this chapter," finds himself forced down his ladder into "the foul rag-and-bone shop of the heart." Though it would be more than mildly misleading to suggest that the Emerson of "Experience," and after, truly joins hands with Yeats in giving voice to a peculiarly modern sense of discouragement and dislocation, it is nevertheless fair to say that the Emerson who began to conceive of existence in such grayly tragic terms as these took a large step toward insuring that his writing could have a continuing life for twentieth-century readers.

IV

Most Emersonians would probably agree that to redeem Emerson by resorting to what Newton Arvin calls a "cant of pessimism" is to do him a disservice.[26] This is not to say that the expression we find, in such an essay as "Experience," of a kind of existential *nausea,* a feeling that reality eludes us and that we are all, as

25. *The Collected Poems of Wallace Stevens,* p. 62. Cf. "The Man Whose Pharynx Was Bad," p. 96.
26. Newton Arvin, "The House of Pain," in *Emerson: A Collection of Critical Essays,* p. 59.

Sartre says,*"superfluous,* that is to say, amorphous, vague, and sad"[27] — that the expression of such things in Emerson is not particularly valuable. This side of Emerson deepens our interest in him, making us feel that his sense of the way life can be sometimes corresponds more nearly to our own. But, if we resist the temptation to overemphasize Emerson's journals and letters and pay attention mainly to those published works by which the world has known him for more than a century, the fact remains that the "House of Pain" was not Emerson's dominant structure and should not constitute his major claim on us.

My own intent has been to show that the problems which have perennially dogged Emerson's reputation and hindered a true appreciation of his work can largely be obviated if we focus our attention on his writing *as writing.* His work, I am saying, does have this kind of interest to a high degree; and a fundamentally literary approach to Emerson can yield surprising dividends of reading pleasure and a new understanding of what he was about. As a final short demonstration of my argument, I propose to examine a familiar — in some ways, too familiar — specimen brick from the Emerson edifice, the "Divinity School Address." Like most monuments of Emerson's prose, this piece has been so solidly in place for so long that we tend to overlook what is really in it. Though it is normally spoken of in terms of Emerson's evolving career, or the Unitarian-Transcendentalist controversy, or its doctrine (or the absence thereof), its real interest, it seems to me, lies in its exhibition of Emerson's skill as a literary strategist and of his mastery of organic form.

On the first of April preceding that momentous July evening when Emerson delivered his bombshell, he told a group of divinity students informally that "the preacher should be a poet."[28] That is precisely and totally the "doctrine" of his address, which is both

27. Jean-Paul Sartre, *Nausea,* trans. Lloyd Alexander (New York: New Directions, 1964), p. 177.

28. See *The Journals and Miscellaneous Notebooks of Ralph Waldo Emerson,* ed. William H. Gilman et al. (Cambridge: Harvard University Press, 1960–), V, 471 (this edition is abbreviated hereafter as *JMN*). A valuable treatment of the evolution of Emerson's notion of the preacher-poet, especially in relation to the Unitarian background, is Lawrence I. Buell, "Unitarian Aesthetics and Emerson's Poet-Priest," *American Quarterly,* 20 (Spring 1968), 3–20. See also Frederick May Eliot, "Emerson and the Preacher," *Journal of Liberal Religion,* 1 (Summer 1939), 5–18.

an exposition and an enactment of that belief. The key concept, and word, in the address is *beauty,* for Emerson was determined to prove that "the institution of preaching — the speech of man to men" (which is also, we should note, the institution of literature) is utterly nugatory if moral truth is separated from the delight of living. The "new Teacher" whom Emerson called for in the last sentence of his speech was charged with showing "that the Ought, that Duty, is one thing with Science, with Beauty, and with Joy." Accordingly, those two final words, beauty and joy, govern Emerson's startlingly heretical portrait in the address of the archetypal preacher, Christ, who is offered to us as a kind of first-century aesthete, replete with "locks of beauty," who was "ravished" by the "supreme Beauty" of the soul's mystery and went out in a "jubilee of sublime emotion" to tell us all "that God incarnates himself in man, and evermore goes forth anew to take possession of his world." The man who is most enamored of the "beauty of the soul" and the world in which it is incarnated is called to serve as "its priest or poet," and Emerson urges such men to feel their call "in throbs of desire and hope."

It is precisely the absence of any evidence of such emotions that characterizes the unnamed formalist preacher whom Emerson describes in a striking *exemplum* about halfway through the address:

I once heard a preacher who sorely tempted me to say, I would go to church no more. Men go, thought I, where they are wont to go, else had no soul entered the temple in the afternoon. A snowstorm was falling around us. The snowstorm was real; the preacher merely spectral; and the eye felt the sad contrast in looking at him, and then out of the window behind him, into the beautiful meteor of the snow. He had lived in vain. He had no one word intimating that he had laughed or wept, was married or in love, had been commended, or cheated, or chagrined. If he had ever lived and acted, we were none the wiser for it. The capital secret of his profession, namely, to convert life into truth, he had not learned. Not one fact in all his experience, had he yet imported into his doctrine. This man had ploughed, and planted, and talked, and bought, and sold; he had read books; he had eaten and drunken; his head aches; his heart throbs; he smiles and suffers; yet was there not a surmise, a hint, in all the discourse, that he had ever lived at all. Not a line did he draw out of real history. The true preacher can always be known by this, that he deals out to the people his life, — life passed through the fire of thought.[29]

Emerson, the preacher, moves in thought down into the congregation and reminds himself of a typical parishioner's experience: boredom.[30] If habit had not brought him to the church, he would scarcely have gone, for there is nothing to attract him, no promise of reality, no pleasure. The true preacher, the true poet, bases his verbal art on personal experience in the actual world that surrounds us all, thus transmuting "life into truth." Otherwise, words are mere counters that leave us untouched. Emerson's real genius here, however, lies in the business of the snowstorm. Playing the role of listener, he allows his wandering attention to move outside the window and find its sole available pleasure in the "beautiful meteor of the snow."[31] Perhaps only a New England consciousness could invent such a phrase; but then Emerson is writing of what he knows and loves (as in his poem "The Snow-Storm"). The fine irony of the passage is that the preacher should seem *spectral* compared even to the frigid and ghostly reality of snow. What Emerson has done himself is to insist on some sort of interpenetration between that which goes on inside the church and the beautiful world outside. His example suggests that the skillful preacher will attempt to do the same.

29. The hapless preacher referred to here was actually Barzillai Frost, and Emerson's experience is recorded in *JMN*, V, 463. Conrad Wright's "Emerson, Barzillai Frost, and the Divinity School Address," *Harvard Theological Review*, 49 (January 1956), 19–43, contains an absorbing discussion of the event. Noticing that Frost was only one year younger than Emerson, Professor Wright conjectures that Emerson viewed Frost as the lifeless preacher he himself might have become had he not left the Unitarian ministry in 1832. The vehemence of Emerson's reaction to Frost in his journal certainly does suggest a complex personal dimension to what, in the address, is presented simply as a generic problem in contemporary preaching.

30. Compare Robert Spiller's introduction to the address in *The Collected Works of Ralph Waldo Emerson*, vol. 1, *Nature, Addresses, and Lectures*, ed. Robert E. Spiller and Alfred R. Ferguson (Cambridge: Harvard University Press, 1971), p. 71.

31. It is worth noting that the journal passage which Emerson worked up here for the address, though it parallels the finished paragraph rather closely, does not mention "the beautiful meteor of the snow." That represents the touch of the poet, shaping remarks into literature.

Now, in our backward movement through the address, let us confront the magnificent strategies of the opening passage. On what was apparently a splendid Sunday evening in July 1838, Emerson mounted the pulpit in Divinity Hall to speak, nominally, to the senior class in divinity; but they were a small group, and the room was packed with faculty members and friends. Emerson's intent, as I have noted, was to *demonstrate* that "the preacher should be a poet," that religious truth and human pleasure must coexist, and that the two worlds of chapel and physical universe are mutually enriching. Accordingly, in a prose that is consciously purple, Emerson began his address by inviting this sternly theological audience to allow its attention to wander, as his own had wandered on that boring Sunday in winter, beyond the chapel window to the ripe world of nature outside:

> In this refulgent summer it has been a luxury to draw the breath of life. The grass grows, the buds burst, the meadow is spotted with fire and gold in the tint of flowers. The air is full of birds, and sweet with the breath of the pine, the balm-of-Gilead, and the new hay. Night brings no gloom to the heart with its welcome shade. Through the transparent darkness the stars pour their almost spiritual rays. Man under them seems a young child, and his huge globe a toy. The cool night bathes the world as with a river, and prepares his eyes again for the crimson dawn. The mystery of nature was never displayed more happily. The corn and the wine have been freely dealt to all creatures, and the never-broken silence with which the old bounty goes forward, has not yielded yet one word of explanation. One is constrained to respect the perfection of this world, in which our senses converse.

An example of how inattentive even some of the most devoted Emersonians have been to the master's art is provided by Stephen Whicher's comment: "the address itself was calculated to give no offense, on grounds of vocabulary at least, to a Unitarian audience."[32] It is precisely in its vocabulary that the barefaced effrontery of Emerson's gambit resides. There is probably not another

32. *Freedom and Fate: An Inner Life of Ralph Waldo Emerson* (Philadelphia: University of Pennsylvania Press, 1953), p. 74. In "The Rhetoric of Apostasy," *Texas Studies in Literature and Language,* 8 (Winter 1967), 547–560, Mary Worden Edrich argues persuasively that Emerson's language throughout the address was carefully calculated to shock.

place in all his writings where Emerson is so consciously arch. The only astute comment I have found on this passage belongs to Jonathan Bishop: "the immediate rhetorical motive, evidently enough, is shock: an address to a small group of graduating divinity students is not supposed to begin by an appeal to the sensual man."[33] Emerson's stance, as Bishop says, is that of a "voluptuary," and the word is well chosen. Following the "unusually aureate" (Bishop's term) *refulgent* — which suggests a kind of shining forth, or epiphany, in the summer's beauty — Emerson explodes his real charge in the sentence: *luxury*. We must remind ourselves that Emerson's audience, trained in theology, was not likely to overlook the implications of that red flag, for *luxuria,* one of the seven deadly sins, means lust. Although that technical meaning, of course, is not Emerson's, a calculated air of aesthetic indulgence permeates this opening remark.[34]

In the sentences that follow, Emerson has measured out his language with extreme care to one end: the creation in words of

33. *Emerson on the Soul,* p. 88.
34. It is interesting to survey definitions of *luxury* in American dictionaries which Emerson might have consulted. Webster's first edition (1806) gives simply "excess in eating, dress, or pleasure." By 1830 this entry has been expanded, and the first meaning is "a free or extravagant indulgence in the pleasures of the table; voluptuousness in the gratification of appetite; the free indulgence in costly dress and equipage." The Latin sense of *luxuria,* "lust; lewd desire," is offered as definition number 4 and marked obsolete. However, the 1832 American edition of Johnson's dictionary gives as its first meaning "voluptuousness; addictedness to pleasure," and cites Milton ("lust; lewdness"). As late as 1846 Worcester's dictionary gives "voluptuousness" as the first meaning. Emerson's own use of the word in the 1820's and 1830's tends to lean, not surprisingly, in Milton's direction. Thus, in 1821–22, "wealth induces luxury, and luxury disease" (*JMN,* I, 300); in 1831, "I am extremely scrupulous as to indulging my appetite. No <splendour> luxury, no company, no solicitation can tempt me to <luxury> excess ... because ... I count my body a temple of God, & will not displease him by gratifying my carnal lust?" (*JMN,* III, 225). In a letter to Carlyle in 1834 Emerson says, "to write luxuriously is not the same thing as to live so, but a new & worse offence. It implies an intellectual defect also, the not perceiving that the present corrupt condition of human nature (which condition this harlot muse helps to perpetuate) is a temporary or superficial state. The good word lasts forever: the impure word can only buoy itself in the gross gas that now envelopes us, & will sink altogether to the ground as that works itself clear in the everlasting effort of God." See *The Correspondence of Emerson and Carlyle,* ed. Joseph Slater (New York: Columbia University Press, 1964), p. 108.

an unfallen world of the senses where formal, traditional religion is unnecessary because nature provides its own sacraments. It is hard to see how Emerson's frank appropriation of religious terms and concepts could have failed to offend much of his audience. The rays of the stars are *"almost* spiritual"* (Is not heaven then *really* above our heads? Conversely, can a natural phenomenon *almost* approach spiritual truth?). Man, returned to the innocence of childhood, is bathed by the cool night as in baptismal waters, whereby his eyes are *prepared* for the dawn (a familiar type of the coming of Christ).[35] The technical term *mystery* is applied to nature; but unlike theological mysteries, this one is openly and happily "displayed." In the next sentence, Emerson announces that the central sacrament, the Eucharist (over which, of course, he had created a controversy when he left the Second Church of Boston six years earlier), is "freely dealt to all creatures" by nature — without condition or exclusion. Then, to a congregation still committed to the belief that the creation is fully expounded in the Bible, Emerson states that no "word of explanation" has been provided — and implies that none is needed. Finally, this Christian audience, all children of the Puritans, are told that they are "constrained to respect," not (as we should expect) the dogmas and duties of their faith, but rather the *perfection* of *this* world, a totally natural world, the one "in which our senses converse." Can we really doubt that to most of Emerson's listeners all of this seemed the sheerest effrontery (although to many others since it has seemed merely a flowery portal, the blandly poetic induction to a serious theological dissertation)? But it is clear that Emerson's aim was not fundamentally to offer an insult but to enact a meaning which would develop organically in the course of his address and to which he would "come full circle" at the end: namely, as we have noted, that Ought and Beauty, Duty and Joy, Science and Ecstasy, Divinity and the World, must merge in the new hypostatic unity of a living religion of the soul.

There is "a sort of drollery," Henry James remarks, in the spectacle of a society in which the author of the Divinity School address could be considered "profane." What they failed to see,

35. See, for example, Jonathan Edwards' *Images or Shadows of Divine Things,* ed. Perry Miller (New Haven: Yale University Press, 1948), entry nos. 40, 50, 54, 80, 85, 110, and 111.

James continues, is "that he only gave his plea for the spiritual life the advantage of a brilliant expression." Emerson, of course, has long since ceased to be thought profane (except perhaps in the curious pronouncements of such an eccentric critic as Yvor Winters). The problem is exactly the reverse: it is Emerson's pieties that have damned him. What I have tried to argue here is simply that we can, in search of a living Emerson, make much better use of the advantage of which James speaks. Emerson *is* a great writer. He has only to be read.

DANIEL AARON

Ambrose Bierce and the American Civil War

Abatiss, n. Embarrassing circumstances placed outside a fort in order to augment the coy reluctance of the enemy.

Army, n. A class of non-producers who defend the nation by devouring everything likely to tempt an enemy to invade.

Bayonet, n. An instrument for pricking the bubble of a nation's conceit.

Bomb, or Bomb-Shell, n. A besieger's argument in favor of capitulation, skillfully adapted to the understanding of women and children.

Foe, n. A person instigated by his wicked nature to deny one's merits or exhibit superior merits of his own.

Freedman, n. A person whose manacles have sunk so deeply into the flesh that they are no longer visible.

> Ambrose Bierce,
> *The Enlarged Devil's Dictionary*

Most northern writers who lived through the years of the American Civil War hated slavery, despised southern traitors, and welcomed the integrated nation destined to emerge after the federal victory, but their self-appointed roles as bards and prophets removed them too effectually from theaters of conflict. For reasons of age (many were in their thirties), temperament, health, family responsibilities, they disqualified themselves from military service and supported the Great Cause as soldiers of the pen.

The effusions of these warriors in mufti like Richard Henry Stoddard, Thomas Bailey Aldrich, George Henry Boker, and Edmund Clarence Stedman are forgotten with good reason. Although talented and in many ways sympathetic men, their elegies, eulogies, satires, and ballads on the theme of war were largely rhymed propaganda ground out for the home front. A few of them made some effort to see the real war. Bayard Taylor, traveler, lecturer, and poet, visited some military camps before accepting a diplomatic post in Russia. Stedman wrote a vividly "literary" account of the Bull Run disaster for the *New York World* and reported the Union defeat at Ball's Bluff — his last glimpse of real battle.[1] Neither they nor the vehemently patriotic civilian writers broke through the smoke of ideology to behold the war's immensity and horror.

For literary men who took small interest in politics, the War was an annoying interruption,[2] and it was task enough to water the gardens of the muses during the four-year drought. "These war times are hard on authors," Bayard Taylor complained: "the sword of Mars chops in two the strings of Apollo's lyre."[3] It was also hard not to be caught up in the issues of the war or to ignore its presumed consequences. Whatever their political and aesthetic differences, the literary publicists belonged to the elect of "acute

1. E. C. Stedman, *The Battle of Bull Run* (New York, 1861).
2. R. H. Stoddard remarked almost petulantly that an anthology "of amatory verse from the best English and American poets" which he and Bayard Taylor were preparing might have succeeded but for the "impending shadow of our great Civil War." *Recollections Personal and Literary,* ed. Ripley Hitchcock (New York, 1903), p. 274. Some years later Stedman recalled how Stoddard, Taylor, and others "found their music broken in upon by the tumult of national war." *Poets of America* (Boston and New York, 1885), p. 379.
3. M. Hansen-Taylor and Horace Scudder, eds., *Life and Letters of Bayard Taylor* (Boston, 1895), I, 381.

large-active minds" who saw in the war a chance to establish "a centralization of thoughts, feelings, and views on national subjects." They were the conscious and unconscious adjuncts of these scientists, scholars, clergymen, political theorists, journalists, and politicans bent upon converting "a loose aggregate of sovereign or semi-sovereign states" into "a single central object of love and devotion."[4]

The dream of a nation directed by an ideal aristocracy gave them an elevated view of the war and encouraged them not only to write poetic exhortations but also to campaign on the home front against Copperheads, to write and disseminate "correct" opinion to the nation's press, to address meetings and assemblies.[5] Toward the southern enemy they presented a stern collective face. None would have disagreed with Charles Eliot Norton's description of enemy leaders as "men in whom passions have usurped the place of reason, and whose understanding has been perverted, and well nigh, in moral matters, extinguished by long training in the seclusion of barbarism, and long use in the arts of self-deception."[6] All looked upon slavery as the ugly stigma of that barbarism, and while differing in their notions of the Negro and his capacities, they were ready to prolong the war if necessary to assure slavery's extinction. All, after first misgivings about the "ignorant, ungainly, silly, Western Hoosier,"[7] Abraham Lincoln, eventually backed him and in the end exalted him. He figured in their poems and orations as a benign distillation of the common man, but it is hard to imagine them any more at ease with Uncle Abe than with the common soldiers they sincerely but distantly applauded.

When Walt Whitman made his famous prediction that the real Civil War would never get into "the books," he was thinking, per-

4. Wolcott Gibbs to F. L. Olmsted, November 6, 1861 (Olmsted Papers, Library of Congress). In the same spirit, Stedman wrote to his mother in 1861: "So soon as this fight is over, we propose to shoot ahead of Great Britain in arms, navies, art, literature, health, and all other elements and appendages of national greatness," *Life and Letters,* I, 245.

5. Charles G. Leland, *Sunshine in Thought* (1862), facs. ed. (Gainsville, Fla.: B. Y. Spencer, 1959).

6. Norton to Olmsted, September 16, 1866 (Olmsted Papers, Library of Congress).

7. Leland, *Memoirs* (London, 1893), II, 22.

haps, of these genteel writers whose "perpetual, pistareen, paste-pot work" omitted the terrors of the field and camp. A few writers, however (probably unknown to him) had a first-hand acquaintance with mass killing and organized atrocity and did put the "real War" into their books — the war that choked several millions with blood. One of them was Ambrose Bierce.

II

Ambrose Bierce not only choked on the blood of the Civil War. He practically drowned in it. For the remainder of his life it bubbled in his imagination and stained his prose.

Toward Grant, the "Butcher," in some of whose campaigns he had taken a microscopic part and whom he had seen shedding "the blood of the grape and grain abundantly" with his staff during the battle of Missionary Ridge,[8] Bierce maintained a reserved respect. He knew from experience, as Grant's toadies did not, that the General blundered on occasion. Nonetheless, in 1886 he memorialized the "admirable soldier" as a hard and cruel agent for a hard and cruel God.[9] Presumptuous civilians might try to invest the Civil War with divine intentions, to see "what the prophets say they saw." Too "simply wise" to dispute chance or fate, Grant submitted without any inward struggle to duty:

> The cannon syllabled his name;
>   His shadow shifted o'er the land,
>   Portentous, as at his demand
> Successive bastions sprang to flame!
>
> He flared the continent with fire,
>   The rivers ran in lines of light!
>   Thy will be done on earth — if right
> Or wrong he cared not to inquire.
>
> His was the heavy hand, and his
>   The service of the despot blade;
>   His the soft answer that allayed
> War's giant animosities.[10]

8. Paul Fatout, *Ambrose Bierce: The Devil's Lexicographer* (Norman, Okla.: Oklahoma University Press, 1951), pp. 48–49.
9. Carey McWilliams, *Ambrose Bierce: A Biography* (New York: Archon Books, 1967), p. 55.

The eighteen-year-old Ambrose Bierce from northern Indiana, the second in his county to enlist after Lincoln's call to arms, was not the author Ambrose Bierce who wrote these lines. "When I ask myself what has become of Ambrose Bierce the youth, who fought at Chickamauga," he told a friend, "I am bound to answer that he is dead. Some little of him survives in my memory, but many of him are absolutely dead and gone.[11] The "deceased" Bierce was a country boy with a patchy education. Possibly some of the bookishness of his father, an ineffectual farmer, rubbed off on the son. A two-year apprenticeship as a printer's devil and several terms in a Kentucky military school may also have disciplined his mind. But when he was mustered into the Ninth Regiment of the Indiana Volunteers, nobody expected very much from him. His friends and neighbors knew him only as a solitary, undemonstrative boy who preferred books to games and who showed few signs of ambition or ability.

"At one time in my green and salad days," he later recalled, "I was sufficiently zealous for Freedom to be engaged in a four years' battle for its promotion. There were other issues, but they did not count much for me."[12] That was Bierce's way of saying he had once had illusions. The Bierce clan was antislavery, and none more so than Lucius Verus Bierce, Ambrose's favorite uncle and the only member of the family of any public distinction. It was this same General Bierce of Akron who furnished his friend John Brown with supplies and weapons for Brown's Kansas business.[13] On the evening of Brown's execution, Lucius Bierce addressed a mass meeting in which he equated the martyr's alleged fanaticism, folly, madness, and wickedness with virtue, divine wisdom, obedience to God, and piety. John Brown, he predicted, would "rise up before the world with his calm, marble features, more terrible in

---

10. *The Collected Works of Ambrose Bierce,* 12 vols. (New York and Washington, D. C.: Neale Publishing Company, 1909–1912), IV, 132.
11. Walter Neale, *Life of Ambrose Bierce* (New York: W. Neale, 1929), p. 158.
12. Fatout, *Ambrose Bierce,* p. 36.
13. "These were the identical weapons used in the Pottawatomie affair." McWilliams, *Ambrose Bierce,* p. 28. See also G. W. Knepper, *Travels in the Southland: The Journal of Lucius Versus Bierce, 1822–1823* (Columbus Ohio: Ohio State University Press, 1966), pp. 24–26.

death, and defeat, than in life and victory."[14] Whether or not his
nephew read the oration, he applauded its sentiments. Eventually
an older and disenchanted Bierce conjured up some retributive
ghosts of his own.

III

Bierce's biographers agree the war was the central experience of
his life to which he constantly returned, a time of bale and bliss,
and an ordeal that brought some coherence to the hitherto random
pattern of his youth. Of all the literary combatants of the Civil
War, none saw more action or steeped himself so completely in
the essence of battle.[15] For no other writer did it remain such an
obsessive presence. "To this day," he wrote in 1887, "I cannot
look over a landscape without noting the advantages of a
ground for attack or defense . . . I never hear a rifle-shot without
a thrill in my veins. I never catch the peculiar odor of gunpowder
without having visions of the dead and dying."[16] The sight of
Richmond in 1912 dejected him as it had Henry James when the
author of *The American Scene* visited the city several years before. "True, the history is some fifty years old, but it is always
with me when I am there, making solemn eyes at me."[17] There is
no reason to question his quiet assertion that prefaces a recollection of Chickamauga, the graveyard of his idealistic youth: "I had
served at the front from the beginning of the trouble, and had seen
enough of war to give me a fair understanding of it."[18]

Outside a few letters and diary notes, very little remains of
Bierce's on-the-spot recording of the war years. His account of
them is largely restrospective, often glazed with nostalgia and set
down after he had trained himself to write. Yet thanks to an almost

14. McWilliams, *Ambrose Bierce,* p. 29.
15. Namely, at Shiloh, Murfreesboro, Stone River, Chattanooga, Kene-
saw Mountain (where he was seriously wounded), Missionary Ridge,
Franklin and in lesser engagements. Enlisting as a private, he rose to first
lieutenant and upon his mustering out in January 1865 was brevetted
major for distinguished service. He was often cited for bravery in the
dispatches; experienced the excitement of capture, brief incarceration,
and escape; and as a Treasury agent in postwar Alabama he once again
participated in a kind of sporadic war.
16. Fatout, *Ambrose Bierce,* p. 159.
17. McWilliams, *Ambrose Bierce,* p. 311.
18. *Collected Works,* I, 270.

uncanny visual sense cultivated by his wartime duties as topo-
graphical engineer, he managed to fix in his mind the terrain he
had traversed and to map his stories and sketches so that the
reader can visualize every copse or ravine or stream he mentions.
He also absorbed the business of war, the details of the soldier's
trade conspicuously missing from the war chronicles of those who
picked up their information second-hand. This "solidity of speci-
fication," as Henry James might say, gave his war fiction the "illusion of reality."

The word *illusion* is used advisedly here, because Bierce's tales
of war are not in the least realistic; they are, as he doubtless intended them to be, incredible events occurring in credible surroundings. Triggered like traps, they abound in coincidences and
are as contemptuous of the probable as any of Poe's most bizarre
experiments. Bierce's soldiers move in a trance through a pre-
figured universe. Father and son, brother and brother, husband
and wife, child and servant, separated by chance or conviction,
murderously collide in accidental encounters. The playthings of
some power, they follow a course "decreed from the beginning of
time."[19] Ill-matched against the outside forces assailing them, they
are also victimized by atavistic ones. Bierce's uncomplicated men-
at-arms, suddenly commandeered by compulsive fear or wounded
by shame, destroy themselves.

Yet each of Bierce's preposterous tales is framed in fact and
touched with what Poe called "the potent magic of verisimili-
tude." Transitions from reality to sur-reality seem believable not
only because the Civil War was filled with romantic and implausi-
ble episodes, but also because of the writer's intense scrutiny of
war itself. The issues of the war no longer concerned him by the
time he came to write his soldier stories. They had practically disappeared in the wake of history. But the physical and psychological consequences of constant exposure to suffering and death, the
way men behaved in the stress of battle — these matters power-
fully worked his imagination, for the war was only meaningful to
Bierce as a personal experience. If war in general became his
parable of pitifully accoutered man attacked by heavily armored
natural forces, the Civil War dramatized his private obsessions.

19. *Ibid.*, II, 76.

IV

Like John W. De Forest, Bierce smuggled personal experiences into his fiction (the tales are usually laid in localities he had fought over), but he left no personal records so complete as De Forest's *A Volunteer's Adventures. Bits of Autobiography,* composed some time after the events described, touches only a few of the high points in Bierce's career as a soldier. All the same, it complements the war fiction and hints of his fiery initiation.

From the moment he enlisted, Bierce conducted himself like the trusty and competent soldiers who figure in his stories. The sketches are not self-celebrations, however, and tell little of his personal exploits; they are the emotion-tinted memories of an untranquil man. He looks back to "the autumn of that 'most immemorial year,' the 1861st of our Lord, and of our Heroic Age" when his regiment from the Indiana lowlands encamped in the Great Mountain country of West Virginia. During the first months of his " 'prentice days of warfare," he and his friends in the "Delectable Mountains" assumed the responsibility of personally subduing the rebel fiends. They felt omnipotent and free, in charge of their respective destinies. The proximity of the enemy added just the necessary "spice of danger." Only a few incongruities marred the idyll: a soldier named Abbott killed by "a nearly spent cannon shot" on which his name was stamped (an incident scarcely less improbable than one of Bierce's horrendous fictional coincidences) and the discovery of "some things — lying by the way side" whose "yellow-clay faces" would soon be made anonymous by rooting swine.[20]

Subsequent campaigns in the West seasoned the green recruit, and unremitting encounters with death raised first doubts in his mind about the propriety of dying "for a cause which may be right and may be wrong."[21] Bierce was attached to the Army of the Ohio under General Buell and took part in the dash from Nashville to assist Grant's mauled divisions at Pittsburg Landing. Shiloh, his first major battle, began with a sequence of exhilarating bugle calls, reached a climax in a tempest of hissing lead and "spouting fires" and ended in "desolation" and "awful

20. *Ibid.,* I, 225–233.
21. Fatout, *Ambrose Bierce,* p. 52.

silence." War was no longer new to him, but his surcharged recollection of confusion, of troops demented by shell-shock, of the night march when he and his men, soaked to the skin, stumbled in darkness over the bodies of the dead and near dead, testify to the sustained intensity of the impact:

> Knapsacks, canteens, haversacks distended with soaken [sic] and swollen biscuits, gaping to disgorge, blankets beaten into the soil by the rain, rifles with bent barrels or splintered stocks, waist-belts, hats and the omnipresent sardine-box — all the wretched debris of the battle still littered the spongy earth as far as one could see, in every direction. Dead horses were everywhere; a few disabled caissons, or limbers, reclining on one elbow, as it were; ammunition wagons standing disconsolate behind four or six sprawling mules. Men? There were men enough; all dead, apparently, except one, who lay near where I had halted my platoon to await the slower movement of the line — a Federal sergeant, variously hurt, who had been a fine giant in his time. He lay face upward, taking in his breath in convulsive, rattling snorts, and blowing it out in sputters of froth which crawled creamily down his cheeks, piling itself alongside his neck and ears. A bullet had clipped a groove in his skull, above the temple; from this the brain protruded in bosses, dropping off in flakes and streams. I had not previously known one could get on, even in this unsatisfactory fashion, with so little brain. One of my men, whom I knew for a womanish fellow, asked if he should put his bayonett through him. Inexpressibly shocked by the cold-blooded proposal, I told him I thought not; it was unusual, and too many were looking.[22]

When Bierce wrote "What I Saw at Shiloh," he was already practicing to disguise the violence of his revulsion from organized killing by irony, understatement, and bravado. He succeeded no better than Hemingway. Like Sergeant Byring in "A Tough Tussle," the repugnance he felt toward the mangled dead was at once physical and spiritual, and his bitter joking about spilled guts and brains, his facetiousness in the presence of corrupted flesh, was his response "to his unusually acute sensibilities — his keen sense of the beautiful, which these hideous things outraged." Neither Bierce nor his sergeant found any dignity in death. "[It] was a

22. *Collected Works,* I, 236, 256, 267, 269, 254–255.

thing to be hated. It was not picturesque, it had no tender and solemn side — a dismal thing, hideous in all its manifestations and suggestions."[23] The half-buried corpses at Shiloh angered him: "Their clothing was half burnt away — their hair and beard entirely; the rain had come too late to save their nails. Some were swollen to double girth; others shriveled to manikins. According to degree of exposure, their faces were bloated and black or yellow and shrunken. The contraction of muscles which had given them claws for hands had cursed each countenance with a hideous grin." And at the conclusion of this disgusting tableau, he burst out: "Faugh! I cannot catalogue the charms of these gallant gentlemen who had got what they enlisted for."[24]

The sight of men tumbling over like tenpins as the lead thudded against flesh, the piling up of bodies in "a very pretty line of dead," the postures of soldiers flattened out beneath "showers of shrapnel darting divergent from the unassailable sky," parodied the fracas between men and nature. Their fate and his was to wait "meekly to be blown out of life by level gusts of grape — to clench our teeth and shrink helpless before big shot pushing noisily through the consenting air." Neither Blue nor Gray was made to stand up to this kind of chastisement. In Bierce's Civil War, lead always scores "its old-time victory over steel," and the heroic invariably breaks "its great heart against the commonplace."[25]

At Chickamauga, the setting of one of his most macabre and powerful tales, he observed a fragment of the fierce, seesaw battle as a staff officer in General W. B. Hazen's command.[26] And at Pickett's Mill, too minor a disaster to find a place in Sherman's

23. *Ibid.*, III, 108–109.
24. *Ibid.*, I, 262.
25. *Ibid.*, I, 258, 259, 265.
26. "In such circumstances the life of a staff officer of a brigade is distinctly 'not a happy one,' mainly because of its precarious tenure and the unnerving alternations of emotion to which he is exposed. From a position of that comparative security from which a civilian would ascribe his escape to a 'miracle,' he may be dispatched with an order to some commander of a prone regiment in the front line — a person for the moment inconspicuous and not always easy to find without a deal of search among men somewhat preoccupied, and in a din in which question and answer alike must be imparted in the sign language. It is customary in such cases to duck the head and scuttle away on a keen run, an object of lively interest to some thousands of admiring marksmen. In returning — well, it is not customary to return." "Killed at Resaca," *Collected Works*, II, 96.

memoirs but important enough to be "related by the enemy," he stored up additional facts about the art of war. Here ignorant armies clashed by day. The Indiana veterans, unaware of what was going on in front of or behind them, fought alongside regiments of strangers. Their commander — "aggressive, arrogant, tyrannical, honorable, truthful, courageous" — had not flinched at the criminal order that would sacrifice his feeble brigade. His valorous troops, though virtually cut to pieces, pushed to the "dead-line," the stretch of "clear space — neutral ground, devoid of dead" beyond which men vulnerable to bullets could not pass. Veterans of this caliber and experience had by now learned almost instinctively to divine the hopeless and to retire in good order.[27]

Bierce survived a number of other engagements, only some of which he wrote about. "There are many battles in a war," he remarked, "and many incidents in battle: one does not recollect everything." The war itself, however, had pressed so deeply into his consciousness that he did not need to recollect it. Again and again he came back to it, sometimes to the accompaniment of rhetorical music. "Is it not strange," he asked, "that the phantoms of a blood-stained period have so airy a grace and look with so tender eyes? — that I recall with difficulty the danger and death and horrors of the time, and without effort all that was gracious and picturesque?" One suspects that it was not all that difficult for him to recall the terrors so meticulously and relentlessly recorded in his prose. What he desperately yearned for were his adventurous youth and his lost illusions. ("Ah, Youth, there is no such wizard as thou! Give me but one touch of thine artist hand upon the dull canvas of the Present; gild for but one moment the drear and somber scenes of today, and I will willingly surrender an other life than the one that I should have thrown away at Shiloh.") But he could not reproduce the ecstasy as authentically as the pain.[28]

V

The war left Ambrose Bierce stranded in a civilian world. He ungraciously adjusted to it, but between his retirement from the army and his disappearance into Mexico in 1913, he remained a prickly alien. The unformed (and he would have said "mis-

27. *Ibid.*, I, 290, 284, 291.
28. *Ibid.*, I, 324, 269.

informed") youth emerged after four years of fighting as one of those "hardened and impenitent man-killers to whom death in its awfulest forms is a fact familiar to their every-day observation; who sleep on hills trembling with the thunder of great guns, dine in the midst of streaming missiles, and play cards among the dead faces of their dearest friends."[29] In short, he was a veteran, and no civilian who had not undergone this terrific initiation could claim membership in Bierce's mystic company.

The civilian — untested, insulated from the quintessential experience of violence and death — inhabited a different country and spoke in a different tongue. He was likely to be a patriot, an idealist, an amateur; he believed in God and Providence, hated the enemy, and had not an inkling of the soldier's austere trade.

"An Affair of the Outposts" personifies the civilian in the governor who for strictly political reasons comes from the "peaceful lands beyond the sea of strife" to visit Grant's bedraggled army after the battle of Pittsburg Landing. The governor misreads the hieroglyphics of war. To his unpracticed eye, the apparent disorder of the camp suggests "carelessness, confusion, indifference" whereas "a soldier would have observed expectancy and readiness."[30] Trapped in a melee, he is just unterrified enough to appreciate "the composure and precision" of the troops, but he is more shocked than enlightened by the sordidness of battle: "Even in his distress and peril the helpless civilian could not forbear to contrast it with the gorgeous parades and reviews held in honor of himself — with the brilliant uniforms, the music, the banners, and marching. It was an ugly and sickening business: to all

29. "A Son of the Gods," *Collected Works*, II, 63.
30. Elsewhere Bierce observes: "An army in line-of-battle awaiting attack, or prepared to deliver it, presents strange contrasts. At the front are precision, formality, fixity, and silence. Toward the rear these characteristics are less and less conspicuous, and finally, in point of space, are lost altogether in confusion, motion, and noise. The homogeneous becomes heterogeneous. Definition is lacking; repose is replaced by an apparently purposeless activity; harmony vanishes in hubbub, form in disorder. Commotion everywhere and ceaseless unrest. The men who do not fight are never ready." *Ibid.*, II, 198. Here, perhaps, is an allegory of war and peace. After Appomattox, veteran and nonveteran alike wanted to instill some of this military discipline and precision into civilian life. Edward Bellamy's "Industrial Army" in *Looking Backward* is an example of such thinking.

that was artistic in his nature, revolting, brutal, in bad taste." The great man is rescued from capture by the heroic sacrifices of the Tenth Company but passes off his near misadventure with a witticism whose irony he is too obtuse to recognize: "At present — if you will permit an allusion to the horrors of peace — I am 'in the hands of my friends.' "[31]

In a society where such men held high place, war seemed superior to the indecencies of peace. The veterans, bestialized by battle and forced into the imbecile business of killing, evoked in Bierce a tenderness notably absent in his dealings with the rest of the world. It made no difference to him whether they broke under the ordeal or survived it; they contended against the uncontendable. The strong in his stories are always broken in any case. The men he most admired were stern paternal figures, like General Hazen, who made a religion out of duty, lived what they preached, and shared the fate of all who lived "a life of strife and animosities."[32] Such men were out of place in postwar America where civilian precepts and values suffocated the soldierly ones.

Bierce's idealism, although not completely extinguished at the end of the war, was already guttering. His work as a government treasury agent in Alabama in 1865 and a glimpse of corruption in New Orleans snuffed it out. Once he had believed in "a set of infinitely precious 'principles' — infallible criteria — moral solvents, mordant to all base materials." The carpetbaggers who enriched themselves and the ex-soldiers who looted "the people their comrades had offered their lives to bring back into the Union," helped to rout such fancies from his mind.[33] "O Father of Battles," he begged in later years, "pray give us release / From the horrors of peace, the horrors of peace!"[34]

Corrupt civilians aroused his contempt, bloody-minded civilians his rage. Bierce never sympathized with the southern cause, but like Whitman he honored Confederate veterans as unfeignedly as he did his northern comrades in arms, for they belonged to his bloodied fraternity. "What glorious fellows they were . . . These my late antagonists of the dark days when, God forgive us, we

31. *Ibid.*, 158, 164.
32. Fatout, *Ambrose Bierce,* p. 149.
33. McWilliams, *Ambrose Bierce,* pp. 67–68.
34. *Collected Works,* IV, 118.

were trying to cut one another's throat." So Bierce wrote long after when battle seemed to him a "criminal insanity.[35] He regretted his role of death-dealer and looked upon his former enemies as superior to the breed who survived them:

> They were honest and courageous foemen, having little in common with the political madmen who persuaded them to their doom and the literary bearers of false witness in the aftertime. They did not live through the period of honorable strife into the period of vilification — did not pass from the iron age to the brazen — from the era of the sword to that of the tongue and pen. Among them is no member of the Southern Historical Society. Their valor was not the duty of the non-combatants; they have no voice in the thunder of civilians and the shouting. Not by them are impaired the dignity and infinite pathos of the Lost Cause. Give them, these blameless gentlemen, their rightful part in all the pomp that fills the circuit of the summer hills.[36]

Bierce's tribute concluded his plea to provide markers for the shallow and forgotten graves of the Confederate dead. "Is there a man, North or South," he asked, "who would begrudge the expense of giving to these fallen brothers the tribute of green graves?" Apparently there were, just as there were the "Vindictives" of the Bloody-Shirt unwilling to return captured Rebel flags. He gently chided GAR veterans for fearing that concessions to old foes smacked of treason. He and his fellow soldiers had not fought to capture banners but to teach the South better manners. Let kings keep trophies, he said. "The freeman's trophy is the foeman's love, / Despite war's ravage."

> Give back the foolish flags whose bearers fell,
>   Too valiant to forsake them.
> Is it presumptuous, this counsel? Well,
>   I helped to take them.[37]

He was less genial to the superpatriots and self-righteous moralists, inflexible judges of right and wrong. Rejected ideas, he

35. *Ibid.,* I, 341.
36. *Ibid.,* XI, 398.
37. *Ibid.,* IV, 331–337.

warned them, constantly double back to "mock the new"; they
run "recurrent in an endless track." And angered by one who
opposed the decorating of Confederate graves, Bierce wrote:

> The wretch, whate'er his life and lot,
>> Who does not love the harmless dead
>> With all his heart, and all his head —
> May God forgive him, *I* shall not.[38]

VI

The war educated Bierce, enlightened or undeceived him in
the same sense that Melville's shattered veterans were enlightened
by exploding shells and undeceived by bullets. It also left him
a casualty, permanently warped and seared like one of Hawthorne's damned seekers who is crushed rather than tempered
by revelation. A universe where such atrocities could happen
remained hostile to him as did the God who allegedly managed
human affairs. Once he had swallowed the "fascinating fallacy
that all men are born equal," had believed that words meant what
the dictionary said they did.[39] He had heard the cry for help
when he was "young and full of faith" and in keeping with others
of that "sentimental generation" had willingly taken more than
his fair share of hard knocks. But "The Hesitating Veteran"
asked himself in the light of the aftermath whether it had been
worth it:

> That all is over now — the reign
>> Of love and trade still all dissensions,
> And the clear heavens arch again
>> Above a land of peace and pensions.
> The black chap — at the last we gave
>> Him everything that he had cried for,
> Though many white chaps in the grave
>> 'Twould puzzle to say what they died for.
>
> I hope he's better off — I trust
>> That his society and his master's
> Are worth the price we paid, and must

38. *Ibid.*, V, 64.
39. *Ibid.*, III, 361.

> Continue paying, in disasters;
> But sometimes doubts press thronging round
> ('Tis mostly when my hurts are aching)
> If war for Union was a sound
> and profitable undertaking.
>
> No mortal man can Truth restore
> Or say where she is to be sought for.
> I know what uniform I wore —
> O, that I knew which side I fought for![40]

Bierce the veteran did know what side he fought for even though Bierce the devil's lexicographer might treat the pastime of war with Biercean irreverence. If he knew little about the controversies leading up to the war when he enlisted, according to his friend and confidant Walter Neale, he decided "after he had reached years of discretion . . . that he had fought on the right side."[41] But the war turned him into a "hired assassin" and a bleak determinist. In his last visits to the battlefields — once in 1903 and again in 1913 — retracing "old routes and lines of march" and standing "in my old camps," he tried but only partially succeeded in recapturing the elation of what he called "my Realm of Adventure."[42] The ache of despair overmatched the pleasures of nostalgia.

By this time, Bierce's misanthropy was not "a reasoned philosophy of despair but a conditioned reflex."[43] His response to

---

40. *Ibid.*, IV, 116–118.

41. *Life of Ambrose Bierce,* p. 102. According to Neale, Bierce enlisted to free the slaves: "There was besides, the moral urge, the chivalric impulse, and the excuse to justify bloodshed. Of course, the dominating urge was lust for war, the opportunity for adventure, the call to the blood of youth" (193–194). Had Bierce known the Negro as well in 1861 as he did in 1906, "he might have been tempted to fight for the South — this jocosely" (190). And again: "He grew to dislike negroes intensely as a race, despite his fascination, although he did not extend his antipathies to individuals. But how he 'loathed their black hides, their filthy persons, and their odiferous [sic] aroma!' " (189). Neale, a Virginian, was deeply prejudiced against Negroes himself. His allegations about Bierce's distaste for blacks, Hindus, American Indians, Chinese, and Japanese must be taken with this in mind.

42. McWilliams, *Ambrose Bierce,* pp. 319–320.

43. S. C. Woodruff, *The Short Stories of Ambrose Bierce: A Study in Polarity* (Pittsburgh: University of Pittsburgh Press, 1964). p. 115.

the war had always been intensely personal, never philosophical, and he generalized his pessimism into universal law. The war remained for Bierce hardly more than a lurid stage set for a private drama. It left the grander spectacle untouched and unfelt, but few writers registered the shock of war's terrors with a comparable fidelity.

William Dean Howells: Realism and Feminism

When Hamlin Garland looked back on the 1880's he remembered literary Boston "divided into two parts, — those who liked Howells and those who fought him, and the most fierecely debated question at the clubs was whether his heroines were true to life."[1] Howells had had a ready answer for his critics; he had never created an ideal woman because he was waiting for the Almighty to begin.[2] And in the meantime he was not going to pander to a reading public which was four-fifths female and thoroughly depraved in its tastes.

Women, Howells suspected, were born with "insatiate nerves," and when kept from experiencing life for themselves, craved cheap thrills and mock heroics in the books they read.[3] He refused to go as far as those realists who spoke of "Iron Madonnas" and lamented the day the "Young Girl" had sealed the lips of

1. Hamlin Garland, *A Son of the Middle Border* (New York: Grosset and Dunlap, 1927), p. 383.
2. Edwin Cady, *The Road to Realism: The Early Years of William Dean Howells* (Syracuse: Syracuse University Press, 1956), p. 232.
3. William Dean Howells, *My Mark Twain* (New York: Harper and Brothers, 1910), p. 176.

133

fiction.[4] What could not be said to ladies should not be said at all, as far as Howells was concerned, although he was unwilling to put complete trust in the ability of American females to exercise a wise censorship over the nation's literature. After all, he pointed out, it had been the lady authors who tipped the balance in favor of greater license when, in 1889, the *New York Herald* asked prominent writers how they felt about discussing "certain facts of life" in fiction.[5]

Howells recognized that women were discriminated against in American society, and in the early nineties, came out in favor of suffrage and broader job opportunities. He was confident that once women were required to accept real responsibilities, they would abandon their novel-inspired dreams in favor of a hardy realism. And their sacrifices would be well worth it. Only by overcoming a peurile idealism could American girls of all ages hope to become full-fledged adults.

However, despite Howells's conviction that it was time for his countrywomen to grow up, he never responded to the feminist complaint that it was hard to grow up without models. He would have us believe that the ladies who rejected his conflicted heroines (and those of James and De Forrest) were the vicarious consumers of Veblen's vision, when in fact his most outspoken female critics were dedicated to reshaping American society by enlarging woman's sphere. Unlike Howells, who believed that the stimulation women got from romantic and sentimental literature was purely masturbatory, Elizabeth Cady Stanton, Frances Willard, and Gertrude Atherton were convinced that they could never have understood woman's true potential or conceived of alternate life styles for their sex without the help of Corinne and Jane Eyre. What would the coming generations of American women be like if they were raised on the pap of William Dean Howells's antiheroines? Mrs. Stanton, Miss Willard, and Mrs. Atherton shuddered to think.

At eighty, Elizabeth Cady Stanton was as addicted to novels as she had been as a girl when she mastered the art of ironing her

4. Hjalmar Hjorth Boyesen, *Literary and Social Silhouettes* (New York, 1894), p. 49. See also William Dean Howells, *Criticism and Fiction, and Other Essays,* Clara Marburg Kirk and Rudolph Kirk, eds. (New York: New York University Press, 1959), p. 73.

5. Howells, *Criticism and Fiction,* p. 69.

underwear by sitting on it in order to devote more time to the works of Madame de Staël.[6] A lifelong fan of the Brontës, George Eliot, and George Sand, Mrs. Stanton was given a complete set of Howells by her children to occupy her on a transatlantic voyage in 1883. The crossing was unusually rough, but Mrs. Stanton found the Howells hardest to stomach. "It seems to me there is a lamentable want of common sense in all his women," she wrote in her diary. "They may be true to nature but as it is nature under false conditions, I should rather have some pen portray the ideal woman, and paint a type worthy of our imitation."[7]

Mrs. Stanton later relented somewhat in her opinion of Howells; by 1895 she felt that she had to acknowledge his support of woman suffrage. Moreover, the utopian *Traveller from Altruria* had pleased her better than his earlier efforts. But she never changed her mind about how crucial it had been to her own development to have been exposed to the heroics of *Corinne*.[8]

Frances Willard, an active suffragist like Elizabeth Stanton, although better remembered as the founding president of the Woman's Christian Temperance Union, felt her eighteenth birthday had been the turning point of her life: "Mother insists that at last I *must* have my hair 'done up woman fashion,' " she wrote in her diary: "She says she can hardly forgive herself for letting me 'run wild' so long. We've had a great time over it all, and here I sit like another Samson 'shorn of my strength.' That figure won't do, though, for the greatest trouble with me is that I shall never be shorn again. My 'back hair' is twisted up like a corkscrew; I carry eighteen hairpins; my head aches miserably; my feet are entangled in the skirt of my hateful new gown . . . Altogether, I recognize the fact that my 'occupation's gone.' "[9]

Desperate to find some way of turning adulthood to her advantage, toward evening on her birthday Frances Willard sat "quietly in her mother's rocking-chair, and began to read Scott's 'Ivanhoe.' " When Mr. Willard came home he reminded her that his daughters were forbidden to read novels, and she quietly re-

6. Elizabeth Cady Stanton, *Eighty Years and More* (New York, 1898), p. 47.

7. Theodore Stanton and Harriet Stanton Blatch, *Elizabeth Cady Stanton: As Revealed in Her Letters, Diary and Reminiscences,* 2 vols. (New York: Harper and Brothers, 1922), II, 213.

8. Stanton, *Elizabeth Cady Stanton,* II, 310.

9. Frances Willard, *Glimpses of Fifty Years* (Chicago, 1889), p. 69.

plied, "You forget what day it is." Later she recalled that he had been "dumbfounded."[10] But this was just the first skirmish in a longer struggle over what she should read — and implicitly over what kind of woman she should be.

Shortly after her eighteenth birthday, she spent a month in the home of a neighboring family and there discovered the novels of Charlotte Brontë. She had already devoured *Jane Eyre* and *Shirley* in "feverish haste," and was just in the middle of *Villette,* "when a long shadow fell across the threshold where I was sitting, unconscious of everything about me, and my father's tall form bent over me; he took the book from my hand, and as he saw the flush on my cheeks his brow was clouded. 'Never let my daughter see that book again, if you please, madam,' he said to the lady of the house, who, not knowing his rules, had hardly noted my proceedings; the book was taken from me and to this day I have never finished reading 'Villette.' "[11]

Mr. Willard was a conservative man who had moved his family from Oberlin to Wisconsin only when his health made a change imperative; he did not want any pioneers in sex roles in his family. And while in retrospect Frances Willard saw that it was just as well that she had not been raised on romantic fiction, she nonetheless deplored the "blindness and fatuity" of "our current writer of the W. D. Howells and Henry James school." Unable to envision the new American woman, the realists' writings seemed no less "conventional" to her than "the style of art known as Byzantine." Howells and James were a "dreary pair," whose books it might be hoped would "put a period to the literary sentence of their age."[12]

When she wrote these withering sentences in the 1880's, Frances Willard was not calling for stories of intrigue and lust, but for a kind of feminist realism, something akin to socialist realism, in which the ideal American woman would be portrayed and the lessons of her new and larger life inculcated in future generations. She wanted to read about the new Jane Eyres who,

10. Willard, *Glimpses,* p. 72.
11. *Ibid.,* pp. 87–88.
12. Frances Willard, *How to Win: A Book for Girls* (1888), excerpted by Aileen Kraditor, ed., *Up From the Pedestal* (Chicago: Quadrangle Books, 1968), pp. 316–317.

after graduating from Cornell, would carry their genius for making THE WHOLE WORLD HOMELIKE into medicine, business, and the affairs of state. Significantly, she, like Mrs. Stanton, modified her opinion of Howells when he began to write in a utopian vein, addressing him as "Dear Brother: (For since Altruria you are that.)"[13] Although she had become a socialist of sorts by the 1890's her new fellow feeling seemed to have less to do with politics than with her hope that Howells had been permanently converted to the ideal in fiction.

Mrs. Stanton might be taken to represent the mid-nineteenth-century radical wing of the organized woman's movement which survived in America until 1900 largely because of the longevity of its leaders. She and her closest associates were not interested in making the world homelike, but in lobbying for those social and political changes which they believed were necessary if women were to have room to explore their individual potential. They were self-righteous, elitist, and incurably romantic in their conviction that the most important thing in life was to express your own deepest feelings, to be heroic, even Byronic, if your inner voices spoke, as theirs did, in the accents of Corinne.

In contrast, Frances Willard represents the more conservative wing of the nineteenth-century woman's movement: those feminists who argued their right to the vote on the basis of good behavior, not great souls. Mrs. Stanton relished outrageous womanhood — the irregular careers of George Sand and George Eliot meant as much to her as their novels — while Miss Willard's favorites were the quiet women who did not smoke, drink, or swear and who could be relied upon to make the world safe for family life.

Between the years when Elizabeth Stanton had discovered Madame de Staël and the late 1850's when she began to work full time for woman's rights, she had spent a decade and a half at home with a houseful of children. Later she felt that without her immurement in Seneca Falls she would never have known how impossible it was for women to develop their potential within the confines of the nuclear family. Frances Willard did not marry,

13. Frances Willard to William Dean Howells, November 22, 1895 (Howells Collection, by permission of the Harvard College Library).

and her progress from college student to president of the female college of Northwestern to W.C.T.U. president was relatively rapid and smooth. But with nothing to stop her, she still had difficulty imagining a career pattern appropriate for a powerful woman.

"I have been called ambitious," she wrote in the final pages of her autobiography, "and so I am, if to have had from childhood the sense of being born to a fate is an element of ambition. For I never knew what it was not to aspire, and not to believe myself capable of heroism."[14] Frances Willard could remember lying on the prairie grass as a girl, asking God what was to become of her, for "a woman, and most of all a woman shy and sensitive, could not determine on a 'career' except as a writer of books." At one point she pleaded with her father to let her go and teach the freedmen, "but he was more careful of his daughters than any other father I ever knew, and shook his head saying, 'Stay at home — that is your natural and proper place until you have a home of your own; I am able to take care of you.' "[15]

At the age of twelve she *had* been allowed to read *Robinson Crusoe* and *Swiss Family Robinson,* as well as several lesser known adventure books with such titles as *Wild Western Scenes* and *The Green Mountain Boys.* These tales, she later recalled, "produced on my imagination the same effect that they would upon a boy's. Above all things in earth or sky I wanted to be, and meant to be, a mighty hunter."[16] In 1858 she enrolled in Northwestern Female College, and as a classmate later remembered, "Frank" was seen as the ally of the college administration, counteracting

The tendency to silly escapades and moonlight walks with the "University boys" . . . In fact she came to be something of a 'beau' herself — a certain dashing recklessness about her having as much fascination for the average school-girl as if she had been a senior in the University, instead of the carefully dressed, neatly gloved young lady who took the highest credit marks in recitation, but was known in the privacy of one or two of the girls' rooms to assume

14. Willard, *Glimpses,* p. 687.
15. *Ibid.,* p. 688.
16. *Ibid.,* p. 50.

the "airs" of a bandit, flourish an imaginary sword, and converse in a daring, dashing way supposed to be known only among pirates with their fellows.[17]

Who can wonder that Frank, who had been carefully shielded from all novels with "love interest" (that is, significant women), should first have found an outlet for her ambitions in mock-heroic male impersonation? And who can doubt that she was enchanted in the second year of her college career when she began to read *The Memoirs of Margaret Fuller Ossoli?* "I think her views are so essentially correct," she recorded in her journal in the spring of 1859; "they appeal so directly to my consciousness of right and fitness. Oh, to have known such a person! Oh, to possess such a mind! We of the lower stratum are improved, refined, by such communication."[18] Margaret Fuller, the "American Corinne," and the heroines of Charlotte Brontë had been invaluable to her when she tried to envision a womanly role commensurate with her girlhood ambitions.

Unlike Elizabeth Stanton and Frances Willard, Gertrude Atherton was repelled by organized feminism. Her idea of a heroine was not a self-sacrificing zealot who went to jail in the name of female solidarity, but a powerful and sensual creature, the offspring of her own "passionate interest in novels," a combination Ouida and Jane Eyre.[19] Mrs. Atherton's career as a romantic novel reader and writer was not interrupted by child-bearing or a sexual identity crisis, but by her own aristocratic sense of herself which led her to believe that she was destined to marry into one of the first families of California. Soon bored and angry with the role of wife, she took revenge on her husband and his relatives by writing a lurid novel about a family which closely resembled theirs. The Athertons never mentioned *The Randolphs* in her presence — nor did they invite her to San Francisco for the social season. " 'Everybody' was furious with me — an unknown chit — for 'taking them in,' " she gloated in her memoirs. They were "convinced there was something radically

17. *Ibid.*, p. 100.
18. *Ibid.*, p. 103.
19. Gertrude Atherton, *Adventures of a Novelist* (New York: Liveright, 1932), pp. 468–469, p. 29.

wrong with a young wife and mother who wrote at all, much less
a wicked, improper, scandalous, and altogether abominable story
like *The Randolphs of Redwoods*."[20]

Yet this first novel was tame in comparison to the second, in
which she wrote of "Cavour, King Vittorio Emanuele, d'Aźeglio,
Mazzini, Garibaldi, Napoleon III, Morny, de Maupa, and all that
crew; Thackeray, Charlotte Brontë — everyone else of that time I
could crowd in, besides innumerable imagined characters. The
heroine was all I should have liked to be myself: the most fascinating and beautiful of women, widowed at an early age that she
might go abroad and play a great role in European politics. A
melánge of Madame de Staël, Madame Récamier, and Lady Bles-
sington."[21] Mrs. Atherton, unlike Frances Willard, distinguished
sharply between James and Howells. A total convert to James by
the time she had finished her historical romance, she felt that it
was a pity Howells "had ever lived, for he was a blight on
American letters."

> He founded the school of the commonplace, and to any young
> writer who hated the commonplace as I did, the Howell's tradition
> was an almost insurmountable obstacle on his upward path. Those
> who followed in his footsteps were reasonably sure of success, not
> only because the critics, largely of his own ilk, decreed that realism
> (littleism would have been a better word) was the fashion, but
> because the majority of fiction readers were necessarily common-
> place and enjoyed reading about their own kind. James, even in his
> first manner, was too aristocratic, too lofty and detached, to com-
> mand as large a following as Howells.[22]

In 1905 she published *The Bell in the Fog and Other Stories*,
dedicating them "To the Master Henry James," the thinly dis-
guised hero of her title story. Having become a cult object himself, arousing raptures in the initiated, Orth-James makes a
fetish of the portraits of two children, long dead, which hang in
his newly purchased "ancestral home." Eventually he stops
"mooning like a barren woman" over the jolly little chap and his

20. Atherton, *Adventures,* p. 100.
21. *Ibid.,* p. 101.
22. *Ibid.,* pp. 101–102.

sister Blanche (whose pouting mouth is "like a little scarlet ser-
pent") long enough to write a bestseller based on his researches
into the children's short histories.[23] Yet something keeps him
from killing off the girl. Only after meeting Blanche redivivus on
the estate next door does he discover that the child in the portrait
had lived long enough to marry and commit adultery with a
neighboring yeoman. Think of "having all that pent up within her
two centuries ago!" Orth-Atherton reflects. "And at the mercy of
a stupid family, no doubt, and a still stupider husband."[24]

In her memoirs, Gertrude Atherton recalled having an argument with a friend over which one of them James would prefer
and losing on the basis of a line in *Roderick Hudson* "in which
the heroine was almost gloatingly described as having 'a mass of
dusky hair over a low forehead.' "[25] But who was that passionate
Blanche in "The Bell in the Fog" if not the author herself, cun-
ningly transformed into a six-year-old blonde to tempt the pru-
rience of Henry James? Perhaps because she had been reading
Ouida instead of Margaret Fuller in her formative years, perhaps
because of her own beauty, Mrs. Atherton was conscious of the
way a woman might use sex to her advantage. And while Henry
James might be vulnerable to her charms (at least if she approached him in the guise of perpetual girlhood), Howells the
family man could never be seduced.

In a rambling article entitled "Why Is American Literature
Bourgeois" (1904), Gertrude Atherton spoke with contempt of
writers who lacked the "magnificent audacity" of those who had
built the Central Pacific Railway. What hunters were to Frances
Willard, the railroad barons were to her. Realism was an Eastern
cartel which had monopolized the literary market until the Spanish-American War stirred up "an apparently insatiable demand
. . . for history and romance, fighting men and picturesque women,
incident, adventure, a total repudiation of the little and the
obvious."[26]

23. Gertrude Atherton, *The Bell in the Fog and Other Stories* (New
York: Harper and Brothers, 1905), pp. 7–9.
24. Atherton, *Bell,* p. 33.
25. Atherton, *Adventures,* pp. 110–111.
26. Gertrude Atherton, "Why Is American Literature Bourgeois,"
North American Review (May 1904), p. 775.

Even before Gertrude Atherton had seized upon the railroad men as the stuff of dreams, Mrs. Stanton had embraced Theodore Roosevelt, becoming an enthusiastic advocate of American imperialism. She had sensed at the time what Gertrude Atherton would later describe as literary history: the Spanish-American War had been just what the country needed to keep it from a drastic devaluation of heroism.[27] In *The Bostonians* James announced that moral heroics had gone out of style after the Civil War, but Mrs. Atherton, writing from the vantage point of California, could afford to ignore the disheartening parallels he sketched between the history of antebellum causes and the decay of New England commerce. Similarly, Howells in *A Woman's Reason* used the dwindling China trade to represent the declining American taste for zeal and commitment.

After her father's import business collapses and he dies, Helen, the title character in *A Woman's Reason,* is saved from a career as a milliner by the reappearance of her shipwrecked lover. In *The Bostonians* James allowed Verena to be bundled off by the chauvinist Ransom into what seems certain to be an unhappy marriage, but Howells was more tender of his American girl. Helen is not left to struggle through — and perhaps find herself — but instead is mated to the perfect antiromantic hero who, despite his adventures, refuses to admit that he has done anything special.

Stories like this were hardly the stuff of which feminists were made. In fact, even Howells's staunchest female supporters conceded that he had an unfortunate tendency to project truths along negative lines. "Mr. Howells does not so much aim at making us love virtue," Anna Laurens Dawes apologized, "as to make us hate vice." By appealing to his readers' heads rather than their hearts, she explained in *The Andover Review,* he failed to make his novels substitutes for more traditional conversion experiences.[28] Elizabeth Stanton, Frances Willard, and Gertrude Atherton were the heirs, in certain respects, of Jonathan Edwards and Charles Grandison Finney. Like the revivalists, they believed that a change of heart, a passionate commitment to some reality be-

27. Atherton, *Adventures,* pp. 780–781.
28. Anna Laurens Dawes, "The Moral Purpose in Howells' Novels," *Andover Review* (January 1889), p. 35.

yond everyday experience, was the only source of personal salvation and the only hope for womankind. Unless women were converted to a new mode of being, their lives were not worth living. And the keys to the kingdom, as far as they could tell, were to be found in secular literature.

Howells, in contrast, was the heir of Horace Bushnell and Catharine Beecher, who had decried the idea of dramatic conversion even before the Civil War, substituting instead a thoroughly domesticated version of the religious life in which children were gradually, almost imperceptibly, brought to Christ in their own homes. Both Bushnell and Beecher were profoundly suspicious of women's rights — Catharine Beecher was particularly disturbed by the rhetoric of the woman's movement which represented, to her way of thinking, the kind of emotional arousal that was the opposite of sweet reason and self-sacrificing virtue.[29]

Elizabeth Stanton had ultimately rejected her father's Calvinism (after Judge Cady had made it clear how he defined woman's place, it was hard for her to believe that his God would number her among the elect), yet she never lost her taste for oratory, a taste developed as a girl while reading of the *improvvisatrice* Corinne and listening to the stirring performances of Finney and the abolitionists. Frances Willard's own childhood memories of Finney were somewhat confused with her adult impressions of Dwight L. Moody, but she was perfectly clear in her own mind that life without passionate commitment was unbearable.

Insofar as evangelical religion stressed individual emotional experience, it unquestionably improved the position of women in the Protestant church. In fact, evangelical religion, Quakerism (with its emphasis on the inner voice), and romantic and sentimental literature, shared a set of common assumptions about the way humans could know truth, assumptions which were enormously powerful in the hands of American feminists in the mid-nineteenth century. They gave these women a self-righteousness, and better still, a healthy self-esteem that enabled them to declare on the basis of their own holy intuitions that conventional wisdom about sex roles was not to be trusted.

29. Catharine Beecher, "An Address to the Christian Women of America," *Woman Suffrage and Woman's Profession* (Hartford, 1871), p. 200.

But by the time Howells became a suffragist there were second- and third-generation feminists in the field who were willing to do without the old romanticism and the evangelical rhetoric of souls and to rely on political savvy alone to get the vote. Unfortunately, in their concentration on tactics, these new realists in the woman's movement lost sight of first principles, and to the degree that they managed to convince Americans of both sexes that the vote was the be-all and end-all of woman's cause, they deserve much of the blame for the collapse of the organized woman's movement after the Nineteenth Amendment was passed.

Certainly Howells himself cannot be held responsible for undermining feminism in America, despite the darkest suspicions of some of the old guard in the suffrage ranks. But it does seem reasonable to ask whether his egalitarianism was in fact tainted by a desire to get even with the opposite sex. Edwin Cady has interpreted Howells's "realism" about women as a laudable attempt to set them "free to become simple, equal participants in modern culture."[30]

> [Aided by] his extraordinary partnership with keen witted Elinor Howells, he was fascinated by the feminine psyche and the (from a male point of view) illogical but often sagacious processes of feminine thought. He believed women to be morally and esthetically superior to men and very much wanted them in every aspect of life, to be stimulated to give the very best of their gifts to a sorrowfully needy world. Bad education and foolish romances encouraged women to be childish, he thought, and he aimed to use his access to the feminine novel-reading audience to correct that. A feminist in the best of all senses, he wished to help women become freer psychologically and intellectually, more honest, more mature, more realistic, healthier.[31]

There is a strong element of truth in all this; certainly it is a description of intention that Howells himself would have recognized. And yet there is another side to the picture, the man who took pleasure in designing the rites of initiation for women, in providing the means by which they would be forced to give up their

30. Cady, *Road to Realism,* p. 232.
31. *Ibid.,* p. 233.

most cherished fantasies and to face the horrors of American life.
Part of Howells dreamed of the Altrurian future when both men
and women would make the home the center of their existences;
another part wanted women to learn here and now that you cannot go home again. The oral imagery which he used to describe
those women who devoured novels like opium eaters is one clue
to his rage over the fact that women were homehow exempted
from having to assert themselves. They were allowed to remain
innocent, to be girlish, even infantile, while men frequently had
to compromise their very lives in order to make a living.[32]

   Dr. Breen's Practice is in many respects the most revealing of
Howells' efforts to place women in his fiction, and it is even more
intriguing in the context of two other novels about lady physicians
written in the 1880's, Elizabeth Stuart Phelps's *Doctor Zay* and
Sarah Orne Jewett's *A Country Doctor*. In her first feminist novel,
The Story of Avis, Elizabeth Phelps told of a beautiful artist who
married against all her better instincts only to find that her instincts
had been right. She is the nesting sparrow whose "cramped
muscles ache for flight." It is her daughter Wait who, like Sir
Galahad, will possess the coveted Sangreal; Avis (Sir Launcelot)
will be fulfilled through her.[33]

   Elizabeth Stuart Phelps may have been thinking of her own
mother when she devised this ending, for Mrs. Phelps had died
before fulfilling her literary promise, and her daughter had
assumed her name as well as her career. *Doctor Zay,* however,
seems to have more to do with wish fulfillment than autobiography. The doctor marries, but only after careful negotiations with
a fiancé who realizes that he has been getting a distinctly feminist
message from his mother all his life, and the reader is left with
a vision of Dr. Zay and her mother-in-law walking off into
the sunset.

   32. "One of the advantages of the negative part assigned to women in
life is that they are seldom forced to commit themselves. They can, if
they choose, remain perfectly passive while a great many things take
place in regard to them; they need not account for what they do not do."
William Dean Howells, *The Lady of the Aroostook* (Cambridge, Mass.,
1882), p. 52. See also William Dean Howells, *The Kentons* (New York:
Harper and Brothers, 1902), p. 19.
   33. Elizabeth Stuart Phelps, *The Story of Avis* (Boston, 1877), pp.
42, 457.

Sarah Orne Jewett read Elizabeth Stuart Phelps's novels, although she did not share her taste for those prolonged scenes in which Avis and Dr. Zay debate their futures. Jewett thought of the heroine of *A Country Doctor* as an eagle; her imagination was dominated by the idea of singleness, of one true calling for each individual. In contrast, Elizabeth Phelps was fascinated by forced options. It is in the crisis of choice that her characters come alive, and her own late marriage, at forty-four to a twenty-six year old minister, seems to have been the result of a long-unsatisfied desire to be forced to choose. The less single-minded a woman was, the more torn, the more important she seemed to Phelps's revivalistic imagination.

Perhaps it was her lust for complications that appealed to William Dean Howells when he published her stories in *The Atlantic* and the various collections he edited. Certainly Launcelot-Galahad allegories were not what he was looking for in literature. And he had mixed feelings when she wrote in the fall of 1881 to tell him of her plans for *Doctor Zay*. Howells replied that he had nearly finished his *Dr. Breen,* and yet he felt sure that the coincidence would make *The Atlantic* all the more eager to serialize her tale — after his.[34] In the end his tact did not save him from her candid opinion of his lady physician. "I don't feel that Dr. Breen is a fair example of professional women," she wrote in 1887; "I know she is not for I know the class thoroughly from long personal observation under unusual opportunities." Yet there was comfort in the fact that Howells's misrepresentations were "all the better" for her heroine, who would contrast so "gloriously."[35]

Dr. Breen's reasons for seeking a career were not those that Stanton or Willard or Atherton would have found inspirational. "I wished," she explains, "to be a physician because I was a woman, and because — because — I had failed where other women's hopes are."[36] Female solidarity is not the theme of

34. William Dean Howells to Elizabeth Stuart Phelps, October 28, 1881 (Howells Collection, by permission of the Harvard College Library and W. W. Howells).

35. Elizabeth Stuart Phelps to William Dean Howells, November 2, 1887 (Howells Collection, by permission of the Harvard College Library).

36. William Dean Howells, *Dr. Breen's Practice* (Boston, 1881), p. 43.

Howells's book. He went out of his way to surround Grace Breen with discouraging women: a patient who demands a male physician at the first serious symptom, a sentimentalist full of talk about duty to one's sex who first suggests that Dr. Breen let the mistrustful invalid die, and later, when she turns the case over to Dr. Mulbridge, that she should not miss the opportunity to play Jane Eyre to his Rochester for life.[37]

After volunteering to nurse her misogynistic patient under Mulbridge's direction, Grace Breen comes to see what Howells knew all along, that she was not cut out to be a doctor. Eventually she marries a businessman who decides that she should open a clinic for the children of his operatives when she tires of idleness and is still childless. And it is at this point that Howells steps into his tale to speculate about her marriage. Is the match perfect, in that Grace trusts her husband's judgment implicitly — or has a potentially great woman been sacrificed at the altar? Having posed the question, Howells begs the answer, murmuring only, "it is well perhaps not to be too explicitly in the confidence of one's heroine. After her marriage perhaps it is not even decorous."[38]

Twenty (and thirty) years after *Dr. Breen's Practice,* Howells used the same coy tone in a series of magazine articles to avoid committing himself on the subject of sex roles. These articles typically began on an egalitarian note — girls should be educated like boys; they might resemble their fathers more than their mothers; women certainly should vote — only to end up with Howells speculating in a self-consciously silly voice about the effect the death of chivalry might have on male character (will all men once more be brutes without the refining influence of giving up their seats on trolley cars?)[39]

But it is not necessary to read through thirty years of Howells's squirming to guess that at least part of his egalitarianism was rooted in a desire to force women to acknowledge male burdens, and implicitly, male superiority. Twenty pages before he stepped in to question the moral of Dr. Breen's story, he had given his

37. Howells, *Dr. Breen,* p. 117.
38. *Ibid.,* p. 272.
39. William Dean Howells, "Editor's Easy Chair," *Harper's Monthly* (October 1905), pp. 794–797, and "Editor's Easy Chair," *Harper's Monthly* (February 1918), pp. 450–453.

answer away. Through a combination of Howellsian misunder-
standings and false ideals, it had been necessary for Grace to propose to her husband-to-be. Later, when she berates him for
tormenting her by not speaking out himself, Libby laughs, "You
didn't find it so easy to make love!" "Oh, nothing is easy that men
have to do!" she answered with passionate earnestness. "There
are moments of extreme concession," Howells murmurs as he
closes the curtain, "of magnanimous admission, that come but
once in a lifetime."[40]

Howells's taste for the moments is as marked as Gertrude
Atherton's delight in female sexual triumphs or Elizabeth Stuart
Phelps's relish for crises of decision. And while examples in
Howells's fiction could be catalogued, the only real clues that we
have as to why he liked to extract this kind of confession from his
female characters come from biographical material. Unquestionably, Howells had an extraordinarily difficult adolescence, marked
by hypochondria, insomnia, and intolerable sickness. His father,
at least in Mrs. Howells's eyes, had been a dreamer who need-
lessly jeopardized his family's income with a variety of schemes
and idealisms. She had chosen her oldest child, Joseph, to serve
as a surrogate husband, training him for financial responsibility at
an early age and in turn giving him the prerogatives of an adult.
Joe was the only one allowed to tease her, Howells later recalled;
his own position was more precarious.[41]

The second of eight children, four and a half years younger
than Joe and barely a year older than his closest sister, Howells
remembered growing up in a kind of limbo, allowed to be the
bookish one while his brother was forced to be a little man.
Clearly he had mixed feelings of relief and anxiety about his
exempted status, and his first autobiographical piece, *A Boy's
Town* (1891), is full of descriptions of what real boys were like
— as opposed to girl-boys. Although he insisted that "there were
mighty few girl-boys" in his neighborhood, he made his definitions in such a way that it is hard to imagine just where he

40. Howells, *Dr. Breen,* p. 249.
41. William Dean Howells, *The Years of My Youth* (New York:
Harper and Brothers, 1916), p. 99.

thought he fit in.[42] The cardinal sign of real-boyness in his book was a determination to run away from home, yet Howells could not bear to spend the night at an uncle's house.[43]

Still, for all its psychological horror, *A Boy's Town* is in many respects an idyll, describing a time when Howells (and all America) was young and could be forgiven for having "high hopes of a world that could never come true."[44] The book ends with an unrepentant dream of possessing his mother, of giving up the attempt to be a boy's boy, or a man's man, and remaining an idealizing infant forever. The young Howells is sick, as he sets the scene, half delirious, and his mother is wholly devoted to him, smoothing his pillows, cooking "dainties," petting him. "She is so good and kind and loving that he cannot help having some sense of it all, and feeling how much better she is than anything on earth. His little ruffian world drifts far away from him. He hears the yells and shouts of the boys in the street without a pang of envy or longing; in his weakness, his helplessness, he becomes a gentle and innocent child again; and heaven descends to him out of his mother's heart."[45]

It is intriguing then to turn from this idyll to read what Howells had to say about his mother and his sister in *Years of My Youth* (1916). As he described his adolescence in this second autobiographical volume, the same blindness which could be forgiven in a ten-year-old boy, that bookish self-involvement and faith that one's highest duty was to be true to an inflexible moral code, seemed inexcusable in a young man. And Howells's self-critical mood seems to have been reinforced by his reaction to what fundamentally conservative feminists like Jane Addams were saying about the cruelties of the double standard and the claustrophobia of most women's lives. Certainly he was hardest on himself in this second autobiographical installment when he re-

---

42. William Dean Howells, *A Boy's Town* (New York, 1890), pp. 152, 93, 179.

43. Cady, *Road to Realism,* p. 56. See also Kenneth Lynn, *William Dean Howells: An American Life* (New York: Harcourt, Brace, Jovonovich, 1971), pp. 62, 73.

44. Howells, *Boy's Town,* p. 147.

45. *Ibid.,* p. 236.

flected on his failure to respond sympathetically to the plight of troubled females.

In the first of a number of painful anecdotes, Howells recalled how he tortured a local girl, a seamstress, who had become involved with a prominent man only to be abandoned. Several of the neighbors, including Howells's mother, continued to give the girl work, room, and board and to treat her like one of the family. Howells was twelve and aware of the seamstress's "shame" when he took it upon himself to punish her. "In the cause of social purity," he would not take a dish from her at table, or hand her one, and would not speak to her if he could help it.[46] Finally his mother forced him to change his tune — if not his mind. Certainly he found it as difficult to comprehend his closest sister's thwarted life as to sympathize with the seamstress.

Victoria Howells was the first person to get her brother to talk about his literary ambitions. Nonetheless, he remembered in *Years of My Youth,* he never once had asked her what she wanted to be when *she* grew up. Knowing that she shared his adolescent discontents, he had never paid any attention to her options. Twenty years after Howells left home (while Victoria lived out a self-sacrificing life of domestic usefulness), she sent him a play she had written, a play in which "village motives and village realities [were] treated with a frankness which I still had not the intelligence to value." In *Years of My Youth* Howells took small comfort in the fact that Victoria as a young girl had been allowed to accompany him and his father to Dayton, Ohio, where they spent several months covering the state congressional session and she had had an outing. In retrospect Howells felt that this had probably been the high point of her life.[47]

Perhaps it was Victoria whom Howells most wanted to bring to her knees when he wrote *Dr. Breen's Practice.* He may have hoped to exorcise his guilt over her lifelong confinement by mak-

46. Howells, *Years of My Youth,* p. 42. It is difficult to know for sure whether the seamstress's "shame," her "misfortune," was actually pregnancy. Howells's own sense of propriety kept him from saying anything explicit, but it is hard for me to imagine that the neighbors would have rallied around a merely abandoned girl.

47. Howells, *Years of My Youth,* pp. 124–126.

ing her admit that his had been the harder course, that everything a man did, beginning with the time he had to run away from home, was more painful than a woman's sheltered life. *A Boy's Town* gives us many clues about why it was difficult for Howells to leave the maternal nest; in *Years of My Youth* he tells us how he finally did it. When his fears of exile and death coalesced in a wholly ungrounded terror of getting hydrophobia, he managed to survive by "a psychological juggle; I came to deal with my own state of mind as another would deal with it, and to combat my fears as if they were alien."[48] He conceived of the maturing process in terms of becoming some other, of becoming Joe, perhaps, of wrestling with and subduing his dreaming, yearning, frightened yet hopeful self, and thereby achieving manhood.

It is no wonder that Howells, who at twelve must have already partially internalized this model, had resented and feared the seamstress who was protected by Howells's own mother, sheltered in the bosom of their family and apparently loved all the more for her lack of superego. Mrs. Howells, her son later recalled, had drawn a sharp line between the duties of girls and the responsibilities of boys, a distinction that must have seemed unfair to her son at times like these. One part of Howells wanted more than anything to hear his mother say what Frances Willard's father had — you are my child; you belong with me until you have a safe home of your own.

It is significant that his fiction is so thickly populated with men who for reasons Howells could never quite define were satisfied to live out their lives in small towns, men of uncommon native capacity who did not have to leave home to prove themselves. In *A Boy's Town* he introduced one of these characters as an alter ego, a boy who came to live with the Howellses to learn the printing trade and to become William Howells's boon companion. The two rode together, yearned over tales of heroic adventure together, but in the end Howells went off to Boston while his friend became the editor of a country newspaper. "He was one of those boys who grow into the men who seem commoner in America than elsewhere, and who succeed far beyond our millionaires and

48. *Ibid.*, p. 94.

statesmen in realizing the ideal of America in their nobly simple lives. If his story could be faithfully written out, word for word, deed for deed, it would be far more thrilling than that of Monte Cristo, or any hero of romance."[49]

Howells's chosen heroes were not the railroad kings but those men whose lives were all of a piece, men who had not had to achieve maturity by mitosis. Women as a sex were in the category of the once born, as far as he could tell, and while they frequently failed to achieve adulthood, they still had a special power over the more complicated and compromised males. As a twenty-one-year-old reporter, Howells had been instructed by his editor never to write anything he would be embarrassed to tell a lady, and he had taken the advice to heart.[50] Howells's characteristic method of dealing with female moral superiority was to try to capture it for himself. He loved to tell stories in which he was purer than women; it was the lady authors, not the male realists, who had pushed hardest for literary license; it was he who called for chastity when his hypothetical niece demanded sensationalism in fiction.[51] He would beat the ladies at their own game.

One of Howells's strategies for breaking in on the female monopoly on purity was to assume the persona, while still in early middle age, of the desexed octogenarian whose attitude towards sexuality and romance was one of perpetual bah humbug. A second, and perhaps more comfortable tactic, was to marry, thereby becoming not only the bourgeois family man of Gertrude Atherton's despair, but the owner of a genuine female superego in the person of his wife. Edwin Cady has read Howells's acknowledgements of his debt to Elinor's critical intelligence as the sign that theirs was a marriage made in heaven. But without questioning the happiness of the match, it is not hard to see in Howells's descriptions of what his wife meant to him a certain smugness that he had become whole by capturing and effectively absorbing the female principle for himself. In marrying Elinor he managed not only to reconstruct a home but to reconstruct his

49. Howells, *Boy's Town,* p. 190.

50. Howells, *Years of My Youth,* pp. 145–146.

51. William Dean Howells, "A Niece's Literary Advice to Her Uncle," *Imaginary Interviews* (New York: Harper and Brothers, 1910), pp. 176–183.

personality. He was a man who went out every day and proved himself by wresting a living in the city, and he was a woman, he *was* Elinor, and she was nothing by herself.

In the introduction to a collection of stories entitled *Their Husbands' Wives* (1904), Howells described his own ideal spouse. "The editors," he explained there, "have had peculiarly in mind those wives who perpetuate in the latest woman the ideal of the earliest . . . What is this ideal, then, in a word: But it cannot be put in a word. It can only be suggested in two or three. We ourselves should say it was that of a sort of Impatient Grizzle, who achieves through a fine, rebellious self-sacrifice all the best results of the old Patient One's subjection. It is the wife who has her will only the better to walk in her husband's way."[52] The first story in this collection is "Eve's Diary" by Mark Twain. Twain's Eve, initially horrified by the brutish Adam, is consoled after the fall by her own perfect love for him. "The Garden is lost, but I have found him and am content. He loves me as well as he can. I love him with all the strength of my passionate nature." The tale ends with a tableau, Adam standing at Eve's grave and Twain in a stage whisper hissing, "Adam, Wheresoever she was, *there* was Eden."[53]

The almost superstitious respect with which Howells and Clemens regarded their wives (and each other's wives), their love for these women and their cannibalistic concern to get the ladies' manna for themselves, was worked out in their attitudes toward their elder daughters. Susy Clemens and Winnie Howells both died young. Their mothers, who were rarely well to begin with, never recovered from the shock, and their fathers were devastated.

Susy Clemens lived longer, long enough to experience the horrors adulthood held for a girl who identified with her successful father. In letters to her sister, Susy wrote of her fear of going crazy, of her alternating "horror of being 'stirred up' " by anything and her determination to make herself *"hopeful* and *industrious* . . . It seems to me now that the *only* thing in life is work . . . But who knows, perhaps this is only a spurt. I hope not with all my

52. William Dean Howells, ed., *Their Husbands' Wives* (New York: Harper and Brothers, 1906).

53. Mark Twain, "Eve's Diary," *Their Husbands' Wives*, pp. 23–25.

heart."[54] Susy died of spinal meningitis without ever discovering why or how she should live. Just before her death she had toyed with the idea of becoming a professional mental healer, and Clemens had encouraged her ambitions. But how far this father-authorized experiment had been from giving her a sense of herself as an autonomous adult was revealed in the last days of her life when she sat at the window of her room in Hartford deliriously intoning, "Up go the trolley cars for Mark Twain's daughter. Down go the trolley cars for Mark Twain's daughter."[55]

Clemens apparently was consoled by her filial pride; he never seemed to understand why life was such a problem for Susy. Howells was unquestionably a more responsive, less perverse parent, but many of Winifred Howells's difficulties seem to have grown out of her father's determination to make her into the perfect boy-girl that he had been afraid to become (except in marriage), with the result that she could not face the idea of growing up. It all seemed too complicated and painful. In the tribute he wrote after her death, Howells recalled how often Winnie had "said she would rather be a child," remembering in particular,

> one twilight, while she seemed as yet quite well . . . She was driving home with her mother and me, when something in the talk made us speak with hope of what she might do in literature. She broke suddenly into a wild grief of tears, and sobbed into her hands, and besought us, "Oh, don't expect anything of me — *don't* expect anything!" We comforted her with what was the truth — that we were not ambitious for her, and only glad in the gift which she would know best how to use to the best end — and she was gay again in her gentle way; but the prescience in her appeal struck us with the first chill of the sorrow that advanced fitfully but certainly upon us.[56]

All Howells may have meant to say here was that Winnie seemed to know she was not long for this world, but at other times in his tribute he felt compelled to put his finger on his own

54. Quoted by Edith Salsbury, *Susy and Mark Twain: Family Dialogues* (New York: Harper and Row, 1965), pp. 332, 330, 354.
55. Salsbury, *Susy,* p. 386.
56. William Dean Howells, *Winifred Howells* (privately printed), pp. 7, 10.

mistakes, mistakes that were "bitter to remember; they are wounds that bleed and burn."[57] What tormented him most in retrospect was the way he had insisted that Winnie's adolescent complaints were psychosomatic. He believed she was suffering from the same kind of morbid introspectiveness and hypochondria that had marked his own youth and that she simply needed to pull herself together — or pull herself apart — as he had done years before. When she seemed incapable of following his advice and was in a shockingly emaciated state, Howells, against the wishes of his wife, decided that the best thing for Winnie would be to put her in the hands of his old friend S. Weir Mitchell, the leading alienist of the period, a popular novelist in his own right and a great fan of Howells.

Mitchell described his famous rest cure in *Doctor and Patient,* a book which came out in 1888, the very year the Howellses entrusted Winnie to his care. A notable misogynist, he had a nightmarish vision of women as bleeding, suffering, nervous creatures, whose best friends were their physicians. The worst thing for any neurasthenic female (for so he had defined Winnie, and most of his patients) was to be nursed at home where she could play upon the sympathies of her relatives. His own solution was to place the invalid in a hospital or convalescent home, to deny her access to anyone but a trained nurse and the doctor, to leave strict orders, at least in the worst cases, against reading or writing, and to force feed if necessary.

In November 1888, the Howellses took Winnie to Mitchell's hospital in Philadelphia. By February she showed signs of improvement, and Mitchell sent her to a rest home in the country. At the beginning of March she died.[58] Still, the worst was yet to come. Mitchell, with all the advantages of medical hindsight, decided that Winifred Howells had been suffering from some organic disease and that her pain had been horribly real. On March 7, four days after his daughter's death, Howells wrote to Mitchell: "I must not let your kind letter . . . go unanswered longer. [It] brought us the sad satisfaction of knowing that the end which came so suddenly must have come soon at the best,

57. Howells, *Winifred,* pp. 6–7.

58. Edwin Cady, *The Realist at War* (Syracuse: University of Syracuse Press, 1958), pp. 97–98.

and we are almost happy to be assured that it was not through any error or want of skills, though this is what we believed from the first. The torment that remains is that perhaps the poor child's pain was all along as great as she fancied, if she was so diseased, as she apparently was; and that homesickness was added when she had to have you."[59]

Winnie was the supreme test of Howells's ability to be a man; he would provide for her on a generous scale, he would help her to become a fully competent adult. But instead of rising to meet her future, she fell prey to what he believed was nervous prostration, which he responded to with what was meant to be invigorating firmness. She would know the psychic pain he had known if he had to hire S. Weir Mitchell to inflict it. He would help her to grow up if he had to push her from the nest. And when he did, and she died, Howells had a sickening sense of having misunderstood everything.

Two years after Winnie's death, Howells again wrote to Mitchell, this time to thank him for a book of poems which the doctor had written. "You speak of deepening convictions," he confessed to Mitchell, "but I have none except of absolute helplessness. Sometimes this seems tragic, and then sometimes comic. This helplessness, and the consciousness of a 'wild and whirling' contancy of change in all I think and feel appear at times to be all there is of me."[60] Even before Winnie's death Howells had shown signs of being too interested in complexity and mixed motives to help his readers find a way to live.[61] It is not surprising that there were no Altrurian clubs; at his most utopian he was unable to explain how America could be converted to the new way. An American woman could be brought to see the light by dedicating herself to do her Altrurian husband's will, but what about the men? Howells was not talking about revolution, or even evolution, but about shipwreck. Perhaps Mrs. Stanton and Miss Wil-

59. William Dean Howells to S. Weir Mitchell, March 7, 1889 (Mitchell Papers, by permission of the Charles Patterson Van Pelt Library, University of Pennsylvania and W. W. Howells).

60. William Dean Howells to S. Weir Mitchell, April 2, 1891, (Mitchell Papers, by permission of the Van Pelt Library and W. W. Howells).

61. See Agnes Repplier, "The Decay of Sentiment," *Atlantic Monthly* (July 1887), pp. 67–76, for a particularly trenchant analysis of Howells's failure to inspire his readers.

lard could find something to like in Altruria; Mrs. Stanton no doubt relished the idea of cooperative labor, Miss Willard craved the resurrection of "The Home." Any feminist could have taken wry pleasure in the Altrurian's surprise that American women did not vote. But this was education by negatives with a vengeance, and not feminist realism.

"Life is never the logical and consequent thing we argue from the moral and intellectual premises," Howells wrote ten years after *Altruria* in *The Son of Royal Langbrith.*

> There ought always to be evident reason in it; but such reason as it has is often crossed and obscured by perverse events, which, in our brief perspective, give it the aspect of a helpless craze. Obvious effect does not follow obvious cause; there is sometimes no perceptible cause for the effects we see. The law that we find at work in the material world, is, apparently, absent from the moral world; not, imaginably, because it is without law, but because the law is of such cosmical vastness in its operation that it is only once or twice sensible to any man's experience.[62]

It is a physician, Dr. Anther, who speaks for Howells in *The Son of Royal Langbrith,* a physician who in his understanding of the frailties of womankind resembles S. Weir Mitchell. In a letter to Mitchell dated December 12, 1904, Howells confided, "I like your liking Anther's name which I thought a fortunate invention, and your liking him. Two or three people besides you will feel what I meant in him, and in his resignation to fate, which teaches all of us when we are not too thick-headed — as I sometimes think *I* am. It is a great thing to have interested and pleased you. My public cannot be large."[63]

Howells wrote these words just when Edward Bok was declaring him one of the two most popular authors with the *Ladies' Home Journal* readers.[64] The truth is that he, at least in this let-

62. William Dean Howells, *The Son of Royal Langbrith* (New York: Harper and Brothers, 1904), p. 282.

63. William Dean Howells to S. Weir Mitchell, December 12, 1904 (Mitchell Papers, by permission of the Van Pelt Library and W. W. Howells).

64. Edward Bok, *The Americanization of Edward Bok* (New York: Scribner's, 1923), p. 191.

ter, was writing off his great conservative female audience, just as in *The Son of Royal Langbrith* he wrote off Langbrith's widow (and the love of Dr. Anther's life) as a hopelessly childish, though charming, woman. Mrs. Langbrith was not privy to Anther's colloquies. And Anther, who in a franker age might have been called Dr. Balls, was clearly a man's man. However, when Howells named his physician, he undoubtedly had in mind not only the dictionary definition, but the first of his fictional professional men to express utter bafflement — Atherton in *A Modern Instance*.

When *A Modern Instance* ends, Atherton is heard moaning, "Oh, I don't know! I don't know!" What he does not know is how to advise the androgynous Ben Halleck. Is Halleck free to marry Marcia, whom he loved before her husband's death, or does he owe it to "civilization" to avoid the heinous act? Dr. Anther is sure that if *he* had loved Grace Langbrith while her husband was still alive, he would never have asked for her hand; the union would be irredeemably defiled. It is Mrs. Langbrith who admits to an adulterous affection, but that is somehow all right, for she is so childishly good that Anther-Howells never forces her to cope with moral dilemma.

Atherton's wife, the former Clara Kingsbury, is a different case, as different perhaps from Grace Langbrith as Elinor Howells in 1881 was from Elinor Howells in 1904. By the time Howells wrote *The Son of Royal Langbrith,* Winnie had been dead fifteen years and his wife had become a permanent invalid. Clara, who reappears (unmarried) in *The Rise of Silas Lapham* (1885) and *The Minister's Charge* (1886), does not allow her husband monologues. She is right in there at the end of *A Modern Instance,* counselling mercy for Ben and Marcia. Yet at best she is a parody of the "Impatient Grizzle" of Howells's dreams. Even if Atherton does not know his own mind at the end of the book, he does not have to take his bride's ideas seriously, for, Howells assures us, as soon as Atherton put "his arm around her waist," she was deprived "of her reasoning faculties." In fact, "In the atmosphere of affection which she breathed, [Clara] sometimes feared that her mental powers were really weakening. As a girl she had lived a life full of purposes, which, if somewhat vague, were unquestionably large." She had once had "great interests — art, music, literature — the symphony concerts, Mr. Hunt's classes, the novels of George Eliot, and Mr. Fiske's lectures on the cosmic philosophy; and she had always felt that they expanded and elevated existence. In her moments of question as to the shape which her life had taken since, she tried to think whether the happiness which seemed so little dependent on these things was not beneath the demands of a spirit which was probably immortal and was certainly cultivated."[65]

Clara Kingsbury, whom Howells made more ridiculous each time he introduced her, already (in 1882) had "a very large streak of silliness in her nature." And if she was like the young Elinor Howells in her spunkiness, she was closer to Gertrude Atherton in ideology. "One day," Howells tells us, "when she whimsically complained" of being unable to do "great things" for Atherton, he replied,

> "I'm very glad of that. Let's try to be equal to the little sacrifices we must make for each other; they will be quite enough. Many a woman who would be ready to die for her husband makes him wretched because she won't live for him. Don't despise the day of small things."
>
> "Yes, but when every day seems the day of small things!" she pouted.
>
> "Every day is the day of small things," said Atherton, "with people who are happy. We're never so prosperous as when we can't remember what happened last Monday."[66]

Howells later described *A Modern Instance* as his personal favorite, and it is understandable how the story, particularly its ending, would have appealed to him twenty and thirty years later. The book has been faulted for rambling towards the close — we know that Howells had some sort of breakdown before he wrote the last chapters. Surely this was the first time, and perhaps the last, that Howells's own bafflement came across in his fiction in form as well as philosophy. There was no sleight of hand here, no coy speculation, no sudden death or resigned marriage to tidy up the finish. Howells may have been paying retrospective tribute to the fact that he had builded better than he knew in *A Modern Instance;* or rather, that because he had not quite mastered his

65. William Dean Howells, *A Modern Instance* (Boston, 1881), p. 469.
66. *Ibid.,* p. 469.

craft in 1881, he had been able to say things that were beyond all contrivance.

Contrivance, and this was the lesson of Winifred Howells's short life, was a form of callousness, of imperviousness. Winnie's pain had no doubt initially affected Howells like the pain of the seamstress. Young women had to be punished for frankly acknowledging their weaknesses; all women had to be forced to see things as they really were. They had to stop indulging themselves and reading fairy tales in order to become full citizens in a world of mixed motives and bifurcated selves. Howells appreciated the charms of the perpetually girlish, but he could not forgive them their peculiar strength, their wholeness and self-righteousness, and while he could not hope to absorb all women, he would see that they were enfranchised, that they were educated like boys, that they were in no way exempted from adult responsibilities.

Elizabeth Cady Stanton and Frances Willard and Gertrude Atherton and Elizabeth Stuart Phelps had no particular affection for female invalids. But they were sure that novels full of passion and heroism would stimulate women's ambitions to remake the world. They spoke from their own experience — and Howells spoke from his. Their insistence on coming of age through conversion and commitment was the mirror image of his personal solution. The feminists recognized that many of their sex were egocentric, were cruelly idealistic, and were fatally innocent, but they felt that one of the few ways women could achieve a healthy level of self-esteem was through identification with ideal heroines. Howells recognized that many women were egocentric, cruelly idealistic, and fatally innocent — and half hated them for never growing up and getting away with it. Both the romantic feminists and the realist Howells identified a certain female stereotype as a blight on American civilization at the turn of the century, but where the feminists wanted to convert these parasites into zealots for social change, Howells felt that they first had to be inducted into American life as it really was.

Howells envisioned human development in stages; the adolescent-female stage, the adult-male stage, and the Altrurian stage, in which people would be able to mature without leaving significant pieces of themselves behind. But there were to be no short cuts. Women were not going to be allowed to slip from stage one to stage three; they would have to survive that painful intermediate condition. Even when he was most eloquent about the horrors of capitalism ("the brutal and entirely manmade conditions of the life which prevails throughout the world, ironically calling itself Christendom"), Howells felt that schools for women could not do better than to fit them for full participation in the system, at least "until *their brothers* shall imagine some gentler and juster economy, in which they shall each be chosen wife by a husband worthy of her, and dwell with him in a home of their common creation, safe from want and the fear of want."[67] This was certainly not a feminist scenario, and while Howells's realistic canons were never consciously aimed at sabotaging the woman's movement in America, Elizabeth Cady Stanton, Frances Willard, and Gertrude Atherton were not far wrong when they sensed that Howells was an enemy — or when they insisted that there must be more to life than waiting for your Altrurian.

67. My italics. William Dean Howells, "Editor's Easy Chair," *Harper's Monthly* (November 1901), p. 1007.

JOHN HENRY RALEIGH

History and Its Burdens: The Example of Norman Mailer

History for Mailer has two principal constituents: the American writers of the 1920's and history itself, or Mailer's version of it; and both are burdens for him. His real subjects, as has often been said, are war and history. But the dramatic *modus vivendi* is the portrayal of human suffering; and the insistent question asked is: how much can a man, or a woman in the case of Elena in *The Deer Park,* stand? What sticks in one's memory about *The Naked and the Dead* is the sheer amount of agony, physical, emotional, and mental, that practically all the characters must endure. This same sense of physical and psychic agony, more psychic than physical in his later work, although the physical component never completely disappears, continues on in subsequent work and remains as a central theme of his novels and journalism.

The other side of this particular coin, the positive side if it can be called that, is that it is one's duty or justification always to face directly what one fears the most. The moment in *The Deer Park* when Eitel finally realizes that Elena is stronger than he is comes when he sees that she makes choices not of comfort but of spirit and chance as if purposely to put herself in a more perilous posi-

tion. This same message is made explicit in *An American Dream:*
" 'That which you fear the most is what you must do,' said my
mind. 'Trust the authority of your senses.' "[1]

To all of which as subject matter must be added, since *Advertisements for Myself,* the sufferings and burdens of Mr. Norman
Mailer, sometimes described ironically, sometimes overlaid with
the bravado of his persona as the expression of "the modern
consciousness" but often laid on the line: how he misused and
abused his body, mind, and talent; how the early fame of *The
Naked and the Dead* projected him into a success that he was not
prepared for and could not handle; how the search for the proper
form and subject matter after the initial success (he couldn't, he
says rather plaintively, write *The Naked and the Dead Go to
Japan*) plagued him and has continued to do so; how his successive attempts to write the great American novel have aborted. In
addition, there is the subsequent disillusion with the protest
movements of the sixties, for which he had been one of the chief
spokesmen. Even in *Armies of the Night* the troops are described
as middle-class cancerpushers and drug-gutted flower children,
with Paul Goodman to lead them. At the conclusion of *Of a Fire
on the Moon* the armies of the sixties are anathematized in detail
and epitomized as a collection of outrageously spoiled children.

And through it all, as Mailer has said on several occasions, there
is always present the nice Jewish boy from Brooklyn — something in his adenoids gave it away — a product of "mother love."
Perhaps this is the biggest burden of all, but that is a matter for
biography or psychoanalysis. The subject here is the never-ending
wrestle with the American writers of the past and with the
past itself.

The Burden of American Literature and the
Weight of Hemingway

Mailer has had a historic connection to the two great flowerings of American literature, that of the mid-nineteenth century and, particularly, that of the second two decades of the twentieth. The premier American writer of the nineteenth century who

---

1. *An American Dream* (New York: Dial Press, 1965), p. 203.

stays in his memory and crops up in his work from first to last is Melville. Hearn, his egghead protagonist in *The Naked and the Dead,* had written a senior thesis, and earned a magna, at Harvard for "A Study of the Cosmic Urge in Herman Melville." And, as all readers of the novel must have noticed, Sergeant Croft is Mailer's Captain Ahab and Mt. Anaka is Croft's White Whale. Moreover, the mountain casts its spell on Croft's "crew" in the same supernatural, naturalistic fashion as does the Whale on Ahab's. Finally, as in *Moby Dick,* nature defeats man. In an interview in 1968 Mailer said that he was on a "mystic kick" in writing the novel and that *Moby Dick* was the prime influence upon it. Similarly, he thinks of that great American novel he keeps trying to write as in the *Moby Dick* mold, if, quoting Melville, he has the time, strength, cash, and patience to carry it off.

The closest Mailer has come to a *Moby Dick* is *Of a Fire on the Moon. Moby Dick* was very much on Mailer's mind during the writing, and there are inevitably references to both Ahab and the White Whale, with the lift-off of the great, white, cylindrical Apollo. The basic similarities between *Moby Dick* and *Of a Fire* are clear: the elaborate preparations for the voyage; the voyage itself with men cramped into a small space on a ship covering vast and perilous distances; the object attained (happily in one instance, tragically in the other, and with no helicopter to pick up Ishmael); the frequent technological explanations and disquisitions; and the intermittent metaphysical broodings on the mystery of things. Melville did not know the word *interface,* which according to Mailer was the biggest word at NASA, but if he had, he would have hung upon it and the concept or nonconcept it embodies, many an eloquent sermon on the inherent ambiguities and final enigmas of all things. "Abysses," "edges," "dreams," "dives," "precipices," "questions begetting only further questions" — these are the Melvillian areas, as they are also Mailer's, both in this book and elsewhere. Melville is there in Mailer's world right from the start, and while it is true that in the largest sense *The Naked and the Dead* derives from Dos Passos, with some strong touches of Farrell, Melville remains a kind of presiding spirit and is to remain so for Mailer: the creator of the American epic novel and the supreme American connoisseur of the mysteries of creation, the poet of the shudderings of the cosmos.

The other seminal literary impulse from the American nineteenth century, for which Whitman was the progenitor but which
Mailer attributes to twentieth-century novelists Dreiser and
Wolfe, is the urge to encapsulate all of America between the
covers of one book. In a lecture on American literature published
in *Cannibals and Christians,* Mailer sees this intent as the proper
aim of the serious writer, in spite of the fact that America was a
phenomenon never before described, in fact, never before visible
in history, and that it changed more rapidly than the ability of its
writers to record the changes. Dreiser had come the closest to
success, but no writer had ever written the country's *War and
Peace,* and in mid-century America no one tries any more. In a
sense, then, the movies and TV give us our culture.

It is, however, the American twenties and the novels and the
personalities thereof which are the most real and immediate to
Mailer and which, to his continuing disappointment, he has unsuccessfully tried to connect with, or emulate, or equal, or, in
more grandiose moments, to surpass: Hemingway, Faulkner,
Fitzgerald, Wolfe, Dos Passos, Farrell, Steinbeck.[2] With all their
failures and tragedies, he thinks of that generation as much more
impressive than his own of the forties.

2. Mailer has European favorites as well: in the twentieth century,
principally Malraux, Joyce, Lawrence, and Forster. His most ambitious
Harvard story, "A Calculus of Heaven," was published in Edwin Seaver's
Cross-Section. Since "A Calculus of Heaven" is a war story ending with
two men, the sole survivors of a platoon, facing certain death, Seaver
remarked that the story looked to have been influenced by *Man's Fate.*
Mailer told Seaver he would like to become another Malraux. Retrospec-
tively, he remarked that he has not come remotely close, although no one
else has either. At the beginning of *The Prisoner of Sex,* Mailer says that
in the fall of 1969 there was a rumor in New York that Malraux was
going to receive the Nobel Prize. It was, however, won by Beckett over
Malraux, but Mailer adds that Malraux was his idea of a great writer.
There is an excellent discussion of Lawrence — one of the best, short,
shrewd critiques on the subject — in *The Prisoner of Sex.* Mailer's description of Lawrence's writing at its best, and by extension all good
writing is worth quoting in full: "The confidence is that some of Lawrence's passages have a ring — perhaps it is an echo of that great bell
which may toll whenever the literary miracle occurs and a writer sets
down words to resonate with that sense of peace and proportion it is
tempting to call truth." *The Prisoner of Sex* (Boston: Little, Brown, 1971),
p. 152. Lawrence's preoccupation with sex, the unconscious, the instincts,
his diatribes against modern civilization, all these matters are congenial

Mailer has said he was initially set off on his literary bent while a freshman at Harvard by reading *USA, Studs Lonigan* and *The Grapes of Wrath* between December 1939 and January 1940. Later he went on to Wolfe, Hemingway, Faulkner, and Fitzgerald. He has thus been right from the start and has remained — violence, sex, scatology, obscenity to the contrary notwithstanding — a very "literary" writer, always trying to measure himself by the best literary standards of the past, especially those exemplified by his first teachers, and has continued to feel that he has never caught up with some of those teachers. He sees himself as a sort of perpetual neophyte, a condition that goes some way to explain his thrashings around in various verbal, and nonverbal, modes and mediums. The profane, scatological, lyrical, and beautiful *Why Are We in Vietnam?* is studded with usually obscene but heartfelt tributes to various literary and cultural eminences: Shakespeare, Eliot, Twain, Melville, "Sigismund," "Fyodore Kirkegaarde," among others.

For Mailer the writers of the twenties form an American literary hierarchy with Hemingway, the king, at the top, and slightly

---

to, and have influenced, Mailer. Above all, of course, it is Lawrence's dualism: "yet he was still a great writer, for he contained a cauldron of boiling opposites" (p. 137).

The third most important twentieth-century writer is, naturally, Joyce. Mailer confesses to have read part of *Ulysses* and dabbled at *Finnegans Wake*. But Joyce's impress on twentieth-century writing has been so potent and pervasive that one does not have to have read him at all: he's in the air that subsequent writers breathe — which is precisely the point Mailer makes in *The Deer Park*. Sergius O'Shaugnessy, the neophyte author, shows Eitel a poem that he has written. Eitel immediately perceives the influence of Joyce, but O'Shaugnessy says he has never read him and appears to know only the name. Joyce receives the customary, obscene tribute in *Why Are We in Vietnam?*, Mailer's most Joycean novel. Elsewhere Mailer calls Joyce the only genius of the twentieth century who has written in the English language and makes him, as he does Lawrence, a precursor of the hip and a mystic of the flesh.

In a *Paris Review* interview with Steven Marcus, Mailer claims, quite unexpectedly, to have learned most from E. M. Forster, this apropos one of his own great difficulties: narrative point of view. But any pervasive Forsterian impress is hard to demonstrate. Elsewhere Mailer also mentions Proust and Conrad as among the members of his twentieth-century pantheon. His own preoccupations with time and memory demonstrate the affinities.

Mailer's complete Valhalla includes nineteenth-century writers as well, principally Tolstoy, Dostoevsky, and, of course, Melville.

below him Faulkner, with Fitzgerald considerably lower down. Their impact upon him is seen not so much in any direct influence on his own work, although of course there is some, as in his ambition to be as good as they are but on his own terms. The final problem is that he does not really know what his own terms are or at least what they permanently should be.

As for Fitzgerald, more of him turns up, as might be expected, in *The Deer Park,* Mailer's Hollywood novel. At the end of the book, with Eitel and Lulu carrying on their love affair in a beach house at Malibu and Elena about to begin dancing lessons, we sense echoes of both Fitzgerald's fiction and life. Further, according to Mailer, in the original version of *The Deer Park* (submitted to Rinehart) the narrator, Sergius O'Shaugnessy, sounded like Nick Carraway, sensitive and seemingly well educated and well born. He "roughed" him to make him fit his actual background for the published edition (Putnam). (At the same time he bowdlerized the novel itself, although he denies this.) In general, it is Fitzgerald's tragic sense and the fact that Fitzgerald had lived his own personal tragedy that appeals to Mailer.[3]

Faulkner's influence is asserted by Mailer himself, although it is in toto a pretty cloudy affair. An early story written at Harvard, "Maybe Next Year," was composed after reading *The Sound and the Fury.* It is the interior monologue of a boy, with the voices of his bickering parents whining in the background, undergoing an "initiation" with grownups. The sentences tend to be long; there is much verbal repetition; the time is the thirties; the ambience is grimy; and the boy, self-encased in the armor of his own ego, is growing up. For a college student it is a rather impressive performance, as is all of Mailer's early work, and constitutes a good imitation of Faulkner. Mailer also claims that the Faulkner impress is upon his "ugly duckling," *Barbary Shore* (for which he appears to be an appreciative audience of one), as, for example, in McLeod's monologue to Lovett, and in *The Deer Park,* in Elena's letter to Eitel (I agree with Mailer on the virtues of this epistle — it is a masterpiece). What Mailer appears to mean when attributing these set pieces to Faulkner's influence is that

3. For a more extended treatment of Fitzgerald and Mailer, see Richard Foster, "Mailer and the Fitzgerald Tradition," *Novel* 1 (1968), 219–230.

the mode is the monologue, the themes harrowing, the sentence patterns lengthy, and the rhetoric complex and "unliterary." Mailer also claims that *Barbary Shore* is the first existential novel, unless one says, "correctly," that Faulkner was an existentialist, by which he means a writer whose subjects are "the mysteries of murder, suicide, incest, orgy, orgasm, and Time."[4] The trouble here is that while these subjects emerged naturally and organically from the historic soil upon which Faulkner stood, Mailer is always wildly casting about for them in various settings. Finally, Faulkner as stylist was a signpost pointing the way for aspiring writers. So overpowering had been Hemingway's style, according to Mailer, that one had either to write like him or against him. Faulkner, according to Mailer, had chosen the latter course, as has by and large Mailer: the intricacies, the complexities, the nuances, the massed freight that can be packed into large sentence patterns.

For it is Hemingway who is "Big Papa" both as a writer and as a man, or, more accurately, as mask or persona. Not that Mailer has tried to imitate him, save in some of his apprentice work at Harvard, as "The Greatest Thing in the World," which is redolent of a Hemingway short story in subject matter, characters, setting, and dialogue. Mailer's only mature imitation was vicarious: the imaginary novel reportedly written by the imaginary Sergius O'Shaugnessy, after a sojourn among the bulls and bullfighters of Mexico, turned out to be inevitably imitative of Hemingway, here called "that excellently exiguous mathematician." Mailer claims, however, that the third version (never written) of *The Deer Park,* whose outlines he could discern while reworking the first version into the second, but which he had neither the nerve nor energy to pursue, could have given him a small chance of finding his way into a novel as important as *The Sun Also Rises.*

In any event, Hemingway as writer, as personality, and as moralist-aesthetician-philosopher is pre-eminent: "Many would say — I am one of them — that he has been our greatest writer. It is certain that he created my generation — he told us to be

4. *Advertisements for Myself* (New York: Putnam's Sons, 1959), p. 107.

brave in a bad world and to be ready to die alone."[5] Moreover,
Hemingway had provided the final moral code, beyond ideologies:
if something made you feel good, it was good: the aesthetic
ethic. Mailer even makes the beauty-bravery-grace-under-pressure
moral code of Hemingway a precursor of the "philosophy" of the
hipster, whose lineaments are set forth in "The White Negro."
He traces "the intellectual antecedents" of hipsterism to Lawrence, Miller, and Reich, but then adds it was all in Hemingway anyway.

It is moot whether Hemingway the man or Hemingway the
writer is more important to Mailer. "Manhood," "courage,"
"proving yourself," all these personal Hemingway preoccupations
keep reappearing in Mailer's work, fictional and nonfictional.
Leaving aside the psychological complexities and ambiguities of
these concerns in both cases, one can discern in Mailer's "Hemingway" two themes or lessons about the male character. First,
manhood is never given, has to be earned, once attained is never
held indefinitely, and must continuously be re-earned and retested
(the theme of *An American Dream*). Beyond that it was more
important to be a man than to be a very good writer: so Hemingway had said. And, as Mailer has remarked, Hemingway knew
what he was talking about, for he had had always to wrestle
with his own demons, his father's suicide ever behind him, his
own, however obscurely, ahead of him: he was brave by virtue
of an act of the will and not by nature's beneficence. In any event
Mailer became an *aficionado* of sport and his later work is be-
strewn with athletic simile and metaphor — the "Joe DiMaggio"
syndrome, invented and patented by Ernest Hemingway. This
emulation of manliness is not without its moments of pathos, as
when Mailer wonders what reader credibility would have been
had *A Farewell to Arms* or, better, *Death in the Afternoon* been
written by a man who was five-foot-four, had acne, wore glasses,
spoke in a shrill voice, and was a physical coward. The other lesson of Hemingway the man was the importance to a writer of
becoming a known personality to his time, for the author's
personality could help or hurt the attention a reader gave to
his books.

5. *The Presidential Papers* (New York: Putnam's Sons, 1963), p. 73.

For Hemingway's actual writing, there is not much specific from Mailer save a sense of awe: if anybody can "pin" Tolstoy it is Ernest Hemingway, the champion; something like *A Farewell to Arms* defeats synopsis; and a few other scattered remarks.

Finally, the spell of Hemingway on an American writer has its sepulchral side as well, although Mailer himself does not dilate upon this aspect. As the common saying goes, American writers were doomed to failure and to either early deaths or tragic deaths or both, or, probably worst of all, simply fading away, like old generals. Hemingway lived out the archetype of disaster on a Homeric scale and managed to contrive the most sensational, dramatic, and macabre end. Even in this unhappy end, Hemingway managed to assert his pre-eminence: exit dramatically, literally with a bang. One of Fitzgerald's many memorable axioms was that Hemingway had the authority of success, while he, Fitzgerald, had the authority of failure. But in the ravages and whirligigs of time, it turned out that Hemingway finally wound up with both titles. In a genuinely spectacular and unique fashion Hemingway had managed to put together Eros and Thanatos and to give each its victory: the Napoleon of American fiction with a Waterloo that was, probably, to haunt his successors. At least, it appears to haunt Mailer: "One has still not recovered from Hemingway's death. One may never."[6] It cannot be said of Hemingway that nothing so became his life as his manner of leaving it, at least in the sense that that phrase was originally intended, but it can be said that in death he managed to loom as large as he did in life and to leave a legacy of more beauty and more horror than any other American writer.[7]

A model for an American *War and Peace* carved out of this complex would go something like this: it would encapsulate

6. *The Presidential Papers,* p. 103.
7. There must of course have been many people close to Hemingway who could see what was coming; and Philip Young's book had certainly pointed in the general direction. Malraux, whose own father was likewise a suicide, sums it up as follows: "Hemingway, throughout the curve which begins with the young man in love with an older woman, then with a younger one, and ends — after God knows how many instances of impotence and suicide — with the sixty-year-old colonel in love with a young girl, never ceased to foreshadow his own fate." *Antimemoirs,* trans. Terence Kilmartin (New York: Holt, Rinehart and Winston, 1968), p. 8.

American culture at some profound level; it would encompass the
Melvillian cosmic itch and Faulkner's subject matter; it would be
written in a style more on the side of the Henry James–Faulkner
tradition than on the Mark Twain–Hemingway one; and it would
carry the authority of the work of Hemingway. Dostoevsky would
be present, as would Tolstoy, Joyce, Lawrence, Freud, and Marx.
But, of course, novels are not written in this fashion.

What the complex further shows is that Hemingway, Faulkner,
and company are a hard act to follow, especially in an age where
you are no longer allowed to imitate even yourself. Perhaps the
most formidable ghost of all is Joyce, the permanent "avant-
garde," who said that if he wished, and could abandon his mind
to it and had a secretary or a dictating machine to help him,
he could "*certainly* write any of the novels I have read lately in
seven or eight hours."[8]

A further moral appears to be: don't look back; it will only
discourage you. Or to paraphrase and alter Satchel Paige: don't
look back; the past may be gaining on you. But there are two
final, and contradictory lessons: the only ones worth competing
with are the acknowledged "quality"; and if you can't lick them
or join them, then try to go another way.

History: Journalism and Fiction

Mailer as a historian is interesting not because he is particularly
original, except in his prose style, but because he is symptomatic
of some of the major discontents of the civilization of his time,
and, more importantly, because his sense of history has had
something to do with his career as a novelist. In this respect he
is a rarity among contemporary novelists.

The reconstruction of Mailer the historian from his journalism
and novels in any kind of systematic manner naturally offers its
difficulties. He is not a "philosopher" of history, and it may appear portentous to treat him as such. He is not particularly
learned about the past, as he is the first, cheerfully, to admit. In
Armies of the Night he remarked that he was no Arnold Toyn-

8. This is Joyce speaking about conventional novels in a letter to his
brother Stanislaus from Pola on February 28, 1905. *Letters of James
Joyce,* ed. Richard Ellman (New York: Viking Press, 1966), II, 83.

bee, no Bertrand Russell, not even an Eric Goldman. Further, many of his observations are pat "throw-aways": saying purposefully outrageous things in order to shock, to put up a smoke screen, or to reach truth by way of hyperbole. In addition, far from trying to be consistent, he glories in his inconsistencies. Finally, he is inveterately both consciously and unconsciously dualistic, and he also keeps changing his mind. And much of his history is in his journalism, which he does not take as seriously as his fiction. Mailer has said that he is overrated as a journalist and underrated as a novelist, and I think he is right on both counts.

However, he has set himself up as a prophet and must bear the consequences. Furthermore, he has always, beginning with *The Naked and the Dead,* discoursed ponderously on History (often with capital *H*), and he has tried to play a role, both as commentator and actor, in the history of his own time. In both *Armies of the Night* and *Of a Fire on the Moon,* by which time he is fully into his anal stage, he speaks of the "bottom" of history and of the author either as having his initials carved on history's buttock or his hand on her rump. In a famous phrase a Dickens character exclaimed, "The law, sir, is an ass." With a different intent than Dickens, Mailer might have a character say, "History, sir, is an ass."

Having made all these provisos, I would say it is still possible to reconstruct Mailer's historical *Weltanschauung* with some degree of coherence. Further, it would be possible to do this in great detail, with specific references to the historic roles of Jews, Christians, and other racial-cultural strains, parables about the origins of civilization, and so on. There is not the space for this, and, further, what I am interested in is the form or the rhythm of his historical outlook and its relationship to his novels, rather than the specific content of the history, although some of this must be mentioned.

Having made these provisos about Mailer the historian, I would say first that his concept of history had at one time a Hegelian-Marxist dimension, especially in *The Naked and the Dead* and *Barbary Shore,* the sense of a sweeping, onrushing power that in Marx's famous phrase is made by men although they do not know that they make it — always unique in that it never repeats itself; decipherable only to those who have the key (Marxism); headed for apocalypse or beatitude or perhaps only another form of slavery. The historiography of *The Naked and the Dead* consists largely of baleful glimpses into an ominous future: history was in the grasp of the right; technique had outraced psyche; the natural role of men in the future would be a state of anxiety. These Hegelian rumblings with an Orwellian forecast are hedged at times by statements that prophecy in history is impossible. *Barbary Shore* is awash with past-present-future constellations. The protagonist, an orphan amnesiac, who has in his memory only fragments of a personal past that may or may not have happened, expresses his bewilderment in paradoxes, that is, "No history belonged to me and so all history was mine." "I recovered nothing except to learn that I had no past and was therefore without a future."[9] This innocent, or first man, is set down not in paradise but in a Brooklyn boarding house, there to be bombarded by experience: the various outpourings of an ex-burlesque queen turned landlady; an F.B.I. agent; a somewhat deranged young woman; and above all a Marxist who gives him lectures on reality and uses such terms as "locomotives of history." The concept for the novel was good, but in the execution it is all fairly jejune and at times embarrassing in its earnest portentousness. In Mailer's later career the Hegel-Marx dynamic tends to be replaced by a Henry Adamsesque sense of history as an enormous and progressively accelerating speed-up that is in reality, although we do not recognize this on the surface, a running-down into entropy. Through all of this, like a refrain, is Mailer's favorite aphorism: "It is the actions of men not their sentiments that make history," which is dealt out to Lovett in *Barbary Shore,* Eitel in *The Deer Park,* Sam Slavoda of "The Man Who Studied Yoga" and is repeated by Mailer at the end of *Advertisements for Myself,* where it is characterized as the best sentence he ever wrote.[10]

9. *Barbary Shore* (New York: Rinehart, 1951), p. 4.
10. This is a variation, as Mailer mentions in *Barbary Shore,* on Marx's "Men enter into social and economic relations independent of their wills." Why this sentiment should mean so much to Mailer I do not know, as, of course, it is a historical commonplace. It is the starting point for the disquisitions on history in *War and Peace* in that Tolstoy said you could not begin talking about history until you admitted the primacy of men's actions. But there was much more to be said after that.

To be more specific, I would say that his notion about the actual workings of history has three dimensions: the conscious, the unconscious, and the superconscious. Finally, in every realm a persistent dualism prevails, later to be given its primordial name, Manicheanism. For history, like memory, is simply a record of oppositions.

The conscious element is "what happened in history," what you read about in books, or hear of in lectures, or what in your own lifetime you see with your own eyes or hear with your ears or sense with your own senses.

Like so many Americans today, or modern humans in general, caught up in a variety of ongoing crises, Mailer is obsessed by the present, although it is a present attempted to be seen from a historical perspective. Thus, the references to a remote past are few, fleeting, and almost wholly conventional. History appears to consist of the Middle Ages, the Renaissance, and Mailer's real subject, nineteenth- and twentieth-century America. The Middle Ages has its appeals, for God or, more importantly, the Devil was supposed to have existed, along with witches, warlocks, omens, black masses, and burnings at the stake. An extended medieval fantasy is given to Mailer's favorite character, Marion Faye of *The Deer Park.* Faye is Mailer's Stavrogin or "The Great-Sinner-Saint" whose story Dostoevsky intended to tell in a series of novels he did not live to write. Faye is likewise the protagonist in Mailer's announced but unwritten series on the same subject.[11] In *The Deer Park,* lying in bed with Elena, whom he is trying to tempt to suicide, Faye imagines himself as Father Marion, a diabolical priest who turns Sister Elena into a witch, who in turn is burned at the stake, blessing Father Marion in her last agonies. Seductions, sodomy, sadism, burnings — all these blessings the hypothetical Father Marion bestows on clericals and nonclericals alike. At the day of judgment, face to face with the

11. Mailer's alter ego, Sam Slavoda, the middle-aged, monogamous novelist-manqué of "The Man Who Studied Yoga" is described as also looking, unsuccessfully, for a proper hero, a man immense, of action and contemplation, capable of sin, large enough for good. Equally unsuccessful is Slavoda's search for a proper form for his unwritten novel. "The Man Who Studied Yoga" is analogous to Joyce's "The Dead" in the respect that Slavoda is to Mailer as Gabriel Conroy is to Joyce: the personal might-have-been. I say analogous, for a complete parallel, for obvious reasons, does not hold for Joyce and Mailer.

deity, he wishes damnation on God. In short, in the Middle Ages one could sin on a scale impossible in a secular age. The Renaissance heritage is described as two-sided: on the one hand, a profound and beneficent change in human consciousness, imaginative heroes, and a dynamic myth that every man was potentially extraordinary (a myth, according to Mailer, that struck deepest and persisted longest in America); on the other hand, the institution of a revolution in the uses of reason which has led to scientific vanity and the destruction of nature. Again America is the final and corrupt end product.

Mailer's sense of European history is dim, as he is the first to admit. One of the reasons he had his war novel take place in the Pacific rather than the Atlantic arena was precisely because he thought he could not handle the European past. The nineteenth century signifies Victorianism with attendant hypocrisies and sexual repressions, but, as with the Renaissance, there is an emergent dualism, and the later Mailer emerges as a neo-Victorian, enemy of masturbation, homosexuality, contraception, and champion of sex with guilt, without which it is meaningless.

So we arrive at America, home of the hero (Kennedy, Rojack, and all) and technological totalitarianism. Mailer's notions about the further reaches of American history are few, familar, and usually dualistic, with sometimes one dualism posed as an antithesis to another dualism. For example, the heritage of the Puritans is two-sided. They bequeathed us gloom, sickness (their last contribution in the mid-twentieth century has been cancer), a sense of unworthiness, a belief in the primacy of the will, along with repression, hypocrisy, smugness. But they are also Faustian, draconian, progress oriented, root destroying (in other words fairly enegertic types, if misguided). For they also produced the wasp, for whose energies and powers, lamented in other contexts, *Of a Fire on the Moon* is brimming with admiration. In this book the wasp is wrapped in a Hegelian amplitude: he emerged from history to take us to the stars. And at the Republican convention at Miami (the first) that nominated Nixon, Mailer professed to a feeling that no less than Nixon himself was evidencing a profound historical sense and was therefore moving into the "oceans" of modernity, the worlds of Marx, Spengler, Heidegger, Tolstoy, Dostoevsky, and Kierkegaard. In any event the primary dualism of America is the many-sided power-holding wasps against the many-sided — and they have their own set of antitheses — powerless everyone else, from blacks, to trade unionists, to acid heads, all of whom are usually thought of in a general sense as spontaneous, freedom loving, intuitive, subversive, anarchic: the romantic to the classic of the wasp.

Nineteenth-century America had two principal, and antithetical, constituents: the frontier and the small town. The frontier bequeathment was twofold. First, it explained our lawlessness and our sympathy for the outlaw, especially as the myth of the frontier had been elaborated by the movies in which the outlaw was often worth more than the sheriff — with the corollary that there were no American sacred cows and no American institutions that could not be treated with irreverence. Second, the frontier had been the safety valve. And when the West was filled, the expansion turned inward to constitute an "agitated overexcited, superheated dream life."[12] The idea of a frontier is a key concept for Mailer generally; for Mailer's American history, what it signifies is that modern America must return to its frontier psychology, only this time a psychic frontier where the future is unknown, to walk into the nightmare and become more extraordinary or perish.

The small town also stood for old America, and in the twentieth century it was the last home of the true war party. Like everything else in Mailer's world the small town has two sides. On the one hand, its denizens relished ribaldry and obscenity, and in a defense of the vocabulary of *Why Are We in Vietnam?* Mailer claimed that the language he used was that of the small-town storytellers who, generation after generation, had passed on to one another, in an underground river of obscenity, stories that revealed more surely and truly how things really were in the life of America than did any official document. But at the same time the small town stood for and embodied narrowness, provincialism, caution, and repression. Thus, to put the last antithesis, the unspoken but major internal war in the twentieth century had been between this static entity and the dynamic, orgiastic, explosive, accelerating City.

12. *Presidential Papers*, p. 39.

But the City (by this is meant really New York) is dualistic as well: if it is dynamic and exciting, it is also cruel, insane, destructive, overwhelming. Hearn's soliloquy in *The Naked and the Dead* contains a grandiose celebration of the City, conceived of as the center, the nexus, the alpha and omega, which dwarfs history itself. In *An American Dream,* New York, not so much a physical as a psychic presence, looms over all: "The City was awake. There was a beast in New York, but by times he slept. Other nights New York did not, and this was a night for the beast" (261). The novel is a tissue of coincidences, enough, one thinks, to have made Hardy blanch, and a detective tells Rojack his theory that there is a buried maniac who runs the mind of the City and it is he who sets up the coincidences. A third aspect of the City that is dramatized by *An American Dream* is its labyrinthine complexity. No one of the characters, from Kelly on down, is ever able to get to the bottom of any problem or relationship or, if one thinks one has, a further complexity or an unknown factor is latterly revealed to upset the calculation. Thus, the modern megalopolis: everything is interconnected; no one knows everything; a beast (sometimes somnolent, sometimes awake) and a maniac preside over it all. Beyond that it is suggested that the City is a palpable Manichean empire where the Lord (perhaps weaker) and Lucifer (perhaps stronger) wage their perpetual and unremitting warfare.

It is the America of the forties, fifties, and sixties, the era of his own adult writing life, that is Mailer's chief province. The "I" and the cosmos are never far apart and are to a certain degree interchangeable. This kind of writing, commentary on the present, suffers from all kinds of potential liabilities: the irresistibility of the large and superficial generalization; the potential identification of one's own neuroses or personal unhappiness or triumphs with the life of the times; the generally depressing effect of contemplating the present. Sinclair Lewis, when married to Dorothy Thompson, said that if he sued for divorce, he would name Hitler as the corespondent. "Past, and to come, seems best: things present worst," as Shakespeare put it.

Modern America, according to Mailer, is encompassed by totalitarianism (called by other names in other contexts), a vast central swamp of tasteless, toneless authority. The critique is fairly familiar, and almost endless. Let me suggest only its general flavor.

History. America was dead, having come to life only briefly in World War II and a short time thereafter and, fleetingly, with what the election of Kennedy appeared to have promised; "culture" and any recognizable pattern to events had disappeared, and chance reigned supreme; a time of apocalypse was on the way; "plague," a synonym for cancer, was accelerating exponentially; the past had been wiped out and abandoned; the present was unbearable; the future unthinkable. The present, like a cancer, was eating up the past and the future. Looming over that present was the horror of the war in Vietnam.

Technology. Man was being converted into a machine, and the machine was polluting both nature and human life.

Sex. Homosexuality was on the increase, and even in heterosexual relations the anus rather than the vagina was increasingly the desired destiny of the penis.

The Human Condition. A compound of dread and apathy, anxiety and indifference, nervousness and boredom, daily life is built on two distractions: interruption and annoyance; authentic character has disappeared; the inherited nervous system no longer works; mind and instinct are severed; modern man has become a suicidal schizophrenic, but he represses the suicidal urge and dies from other causes. As Mailer puts it in graphic excrementalism: "The progression was from man to merde, the Twentieth century was the rush of all souls to search out shit, to kiss the Devil, to rescue a molecule of brown from its extinction."[13] But, then, running like a counterpoint, faint and intermittent but real, through

---

13. *Presidential Papers,* p. 276. This brief sketch does not adequately describe Mailer's own peregrinations, for, as usual, he went in two different directions. The first one, later abandoned, professed by many of the young radicals, or dropouts, or bohemians, or what-have-you of the sixties, was to embrace this enormous present, seemingly pastless, and using that catch-all phrase which means everything and nothing, for it is never defined, existentialism, to aver that a new moment in history has arrived and that a new man is aforming, adequate to the needs of the new hour. Historically, according to Mailer, it was Kierkegaard who first saw either that human nature had never been properly understood or that it was in the process of changing. In any event, at this point enters the Hipster-White Negro, the new genus: existentialist, psychopath, saint, lover, with his "burning consciousness" of the present and

the whole jeremiad there is the usual antithesis: affection and
patriotism and a rueful final admission that he cannot fully understand the complex phenomenon that is America. In *Of a Fire on
the Moon* he writes that America was like his wife (his fourth):
he loved both and understood neither. And the older he got the
more "interesting" he found the country itself.

But there is also an unconscious dimension to American history
and American life. World War I constituted a fundamental turning point because it thrust America on a world stage, and at the
same time the national psyche split in two, into a conscious and
unconscious aspect, moving on two rivers, one visible, embodied
in and reflected by national politics, the other invisible and sub-
terranean, containing all the "untapped, ferocious, lonely and romantic desires, that concentration of ecstasy and violence which
is the dream life of the nation."[14] In other words, the last frontier
is underground.

Finally presiding over all history, or accompanying it, is some
kind of superconsciousness (by "super" here, I mean both the
literal sense of "above" and the colloquial sense of "intense"),
a power or cosmic force or stellar struggle or the religio-mythical
mystery that is above mankind yet related to it, although in a
fashion that can never be precisely known, but into which the
human mind has, or thinks it has, intuitions or divinations. "God"

---

his utter disdain for past or future. His ethic consists of instantaneous
gratification and his mecca is apocalyptic orgasm. In him a new character and nervous system has begun to form. Only at the end of the
essay "The White Negro," where *Das Kapital* is invoked in its epic
grandeur as the first of the major *psychologies* to analyze the social scene,
is a bow made in the direction of the past and of human thought with
the hope that in the future some kind of grand and new intellectual synthesis can be formed. In a postscript to the essay, Mailer makes another
traditional bow: the hope that the future will be mindful rather than
mindless when the "radical bridge" is built between Freud and Marx.
By the time of *The Presidential Papers,* however, Mailer had added
Burke to Marx and had become a proponent of the historic connection.
Totalitarianism itself was nothing less than the refusal to face back into
the past. Modern architecture, or modern building practice, endlessly
wiping out the old, was both the reality and the symbol of the "ism"
itself. The hipster gets turned upside down, and living solely in the present is described as living in "no-man's-land."

14. *Presidential Papers,* p. 38.

begins to appear in Mailer's writings in the fifties, and in an interview he unveiled a Manichean cosmology with a god who is not all-powerful but a warring element, against a devil, in a divided universe.

My concern here is not whether such a belief is true or whether Mailer really believes it, but with the uses he makes of what I shall call the Manichean metaphor. Manicheanism, which at one time had claimed St. Augustine as a proponent, is a primordial belief and was at the beginning of what we call the Christian era a chief competitor of Christianity itself in the battle for men's minds and religious allegiances. It has hung on as an underground belief in Western culture, springing to periodic notoriety as a heresy (Joan of Arc was suspected of it; the Albigensians were devotees).[15] There are echoes of it throughout our literature. So stout a rationalist as James Mill once remarked to his son that he would not be surprised, with Christianity falling under the hammers of rationalism and science, to see a resurgence of Manicheanism. What Mill meant is that if one must have a supernatural belief, then Manicheanism made sense to the common sense. Given the nature of the world, it is much easier to accept the idea that God and the Devil, light and darkness, perpetually wrestle for the possession of the universe than that an omnipotent and omniscient and presumably beneficent God presides over it. Especially for certain kinds of creative writers would such a conception have an appeal, that is, that the world is a literal struggle between a force for light and a force for darkness. One can almost sense writers like Dickens (although not Thackeray), Hardy (although not Zola), and even Henry James, in his oblique and civilized way, saying: "Give us back our demons."

Or to put it all another way, in his essay "The Sorcerer and His Magic," Lévi-Strauss says:

15. In a letter to the editor in the *London Times* of September 8, 1972, Mr. Malcolm Muggeridge, who is currently gracing the reading public with his autobiography and his religious lucubrations, is criticized by a correspondent for disseminating Manichean ideas, especially his setting the material and the spiritual in opposition. There is no suggestion, at least from this particular source, that Mr. Muggeridge should be burned at the stake.

we must see magical behaviour as the response to a situation which
is revealed to the mind through emotional manifestations, but
whose essence is intellectual. For only the history of the symbolic
function can allow us to understand the intellectual condition of
man, in which the universe is never charged with sufficient meaning and in which the mind always has more meanings than there
are objects to which to relate them. Torn between two systems of
reference — the signifying and the signified — man asks magical
thinking to provide him with a new system of reference, within
which the thus-far contradictory elements can be integrated."[16]

A universe charged with meaning in a reciprocal relationship
to the human mind — this is magic, and, according to Lévi-
Strauss, its modern equivalent is psychoanalysis; and certain kinds
of literature perform, or attempt to perform, an analogous function. Freud's cosmology, history as the interaction of the three
hypostatized powers, id, ego, and superego, is similarly another
non-supernatural interpretation of history that provides the drama,
the struggle, the personifications, the timelessness for which a
certain kind of imaginative literature craves in order to escape
from literal, conscious history.

Why Are We in Vietnam?

Under the historical categories of consciousness sketched above
Mailer's novels might be grouped as follows: *The Naked
and the Dead* (1948) and *The Deer Park* (1955) in the realm
of conscious history; *Barbary Shore* (1951), conscious but
an attempted foray into the unconscious; *An American Dream*
(1964), conscious but with ventures into the unconscious and,
to a certain degree, the superconscious; and *Why Are We in
Vietnam?* (1967), all three (conscious, unconscious, superconscious). I would not wish to give the impression that I offer this
typology as good, better, best, aesthetically speaking, for I regard
Mailer's finest novels as *The Naked and the Dead* (still the best
American novel of World War II), *The Deer Park* (surely one of

16. Claude Lévi-Strauss, *Structural Anthropology*, trans. Claire Jacob-
son and Brook Grundjist Schoepf (New York: Anchor Books, 1967),
p. 178.

the leading candidates for *the* American novel about Hollywood),
and *Why Are We in Vietnam?* (small, probably unrepeatable,
but Mailer's most original novel and one of the most original
American novels of our time, simultaneously one of the funniest
and one of the most serious).

Why Are We in Vietnam? contains many literary echoes: the
archetypal American novel of the non-Henry James type, that
of Cooper, Melville, Twain, Hemingway, and Faulkner: the
wilderness and the frontier; the two males; the hunt; and the initiation. The use of a contemporary American vernacular derives
from Twain, Hemingway, and, as is often forgotten, T. S. Eliot.
The use of pop culture for serious purposes, the extensive word
play, the artful employment of obscenity and scatology, the creation of a self-coherent cosmos or mythos — all these attributes
suggest Joyce. The intermittent interplay and ambiguities and
jokes about who is telling the story or who is listening to it or if
it is being actually told at all are reminiscent of a whole line of
authors from Sterne to Nabokov.

Why Are We in Vietnam? constitutes many riches in a little
room (the prose alone on either its light side or its serious side
is worth the price of admission.) So I'll confine myself to a brief
account of what I have called the superconscious level, the Manichean metaphor, which is used with considerable ingenuity and
wit. It should be said that such a procedure makes quite an artificial separation since all three levels of the novel cohere. Conscious history is modern America, personified by Texas and its
natives, corporations, funeral parlors, sex and war, along with
disc jockeys, beep-talk, initialization of everything from institutions to people, guns, electronics, celebrities, and so on, all conveyed graphically and at a frenetic pace by the insistent beat of
the prose.[17] As for American symbols, the eagle is described

17. Just as Mailer later said of *The Naked and the Dead* that his unconscious sympathy lay with Croft, so it can be said of *Why Are We in
Vietnam?* that his unconscious instincts and in considerable part, conscious intentions, especially in the creation of D.J. and Tex and even to
a certain degree their parents, are on the side of the Texans. His wonderful, bawdy, hilarious epitome of the spirit of the Alamo is a case in
point: "down in the seed, boy, anybody in the direct line of the heroes
of the Alamo got seed like Mexican jumping beans, cause when all those
Alamo troopers maintained to their positions and didn't piss in no pants

as the cruelest and meanest of scavengers and is shown in a futile action: trying unsuccessfully to dive bomb a wolf. The unconscious level, the back to the frontier motif, is literally enacted by the two young men: they get civilization (shit) out of their system and pass on through dread, through murderous urges, through homosexual urges, to emerge as blood brothers, twin killers, although it is not known whether they are owned by the prince of darkness or the lord of light — the primary theme: "God or the devil takes over in sleep — what simpler explanation you got, M.A. expert type? nothing better to do than put down Mani the Manichee, well, shit on that. D.J. is here to resurrect him" (172).

There are some difficulties in describing a system which has as interworking coordinates, among others, the Brooks Mountains of Alaska, the aurora borealis, the magnetic north pole, the anus, God, the Devil, urine, the colon, bears, wolves, a tape recorder in heaven, electricity, light, crystals and a variety of other human and natural manifestations, not to mention a considerable gallery of human characters (all in pairs; everything in this novel comes in a paired contrast). But there is a central axiom whose meaning is the message and which is announced right at the start: *"no such thing as a totally false perception"* (8). Immediately after this there are references to Edison and electricity and to McLuhan, the message man. Perceptions (which are often wholly true and never totally false), electricity (the mysterious conveyor) and messages: this is what it is all about. The whole universe — which encompasses the human world, the animal world, the natural world, and the supernatural world where the Lord and Lucifer not only wage their own war but extend that war into the other three worlds as well — is a gigantic perception-receiving,

---

and held their shit, tight honourable asshole in the face of certain death, and hung on, why a cloud and vale of love rose up above them in the middle of all this Mexican fire and shit storm . . . and each time one of them got one of Santa Ana's rounds in his virile little old Alamo heart, why the fuck went up to death with a spring of joy, cause his buddies and his far-gone relatives were going to be . . . spiritual beneficiaries, and the spiritual essence of secret zinging semen went across the desert and through the air on the trooper's last breath and gave swinger pricks and springing cunts to some of the best and worst people in Texas. (Which accounts for why it's such a crazy state)." *Why Are We in Vietnam?* (New York: Putnam's Sons, 1967), p. 166.

message-sending system with each part, micro or macro and every stage in between, constantly sending and receiving messages: God or the Devil to humans, and vice versa; man-woman back and forth to woman-man; nature to man and vice versa; man to animal and vice versa; and so on. Even in dreams, especially in dreams — defined as the Magnetic-Electro fief or M.E.F. — humans are sending and receiving messages. For example, all night as North America sleeps, each dreaming head, or "shit head," as Mailer puts it, is sending and receiving messages. These messages, conditioned by God and the Devil, shoot out over the ether all the way up to the Brooks range, God's attic, to that enormous, silent mass of snow and mountains, which is in reality a great parabolic reflector, an avatar, a bowl of resonance, from which the answer to the message comes back to the sender, God and the Devil presumably having had their input once more. But messages run the other way, too. Ruling the North in the name of the Lord and Lucifer is a troika consisting of M.E.F., Mr. Awe, and Herr Dread, collectively called the "Cannibal Emperor of Nature's Psyche" and also the "Sender"; his primary message is, "You're all alone, bud." These are examples of the macrocosm, but there is a microcosm as well, along with an Elizabethan or Blakean sense of correspondences. Thus, for everyone there are two tape recorders: one in each human being, constituting memory; the other kept by God, who, by using the latest scientific methods of storage and retrieval, can reduce a person's whole history to one tiny electronic beep: "but every sound in a symphony is contained in the bong of one gong, just as all Creation is heard and felt in the shriek of a tight wire in one pebble piss-or-pinch orgasm . . . the Lord hears your beep, the total all you, good and bad" (25). Now various ambiguities are introduced into these correspondences. In *An American Dream,* where the cosmology had begun to develop, it is said that the vagina is the province of the Lord and the anus that of Lucifer. In *Why Are We in Vietnam?* the Lord locates his transistors in the anus of humans, and indeed the seat of electricity is said to be the asshole. If this is so, then the Lord must be Satan, but we never know for sure.

In any event all the real messages, bad or good, are nonverbal or subverbal. D.J.'s fullest, finest, most explicit message comes from the eye of a dying bear: a message, an intelligence of some-

thing fine and far away from an eye intelligent, wicked and
merry, "that wild wicked little look of intelligence in the eye,"
saying something like, "Baby, you haven't begun" (147). And
this look of dying Grizz confers many benefits on D.J., including
a psychic transistor in his ear.

The dead center of the universe is in the Brooks range, and
what we find there, along with the Manichean struggle, are the
following attributes: inhuman force ("if the center of things is
insane it is insane with force" [143]); murderousness ("yeah God
was here, and He was real and No man was He, but a beast"
[202], whose message is "Go out and kill — fulfill my will, go
and kill," [203]); and, finally, a central mystery, which can be
approached but never finally penetrated, but whose message appears to be that what it is all about is beauty, woe, and hurt:
"September light, not fading, no, ebbing, it went in steps and
starts like going down a stair from the light to the dark, sun
golden red in its purple and purple red in the black of the trees,
the water was dark green and gold, a sigh came out of the night
as it came on, and D.J. could have wept for a secret was near,
some mystery in the secret of things" (196). The closest he can
come is a perception of: "the sorrow of the North, the great sorrow up here brought by leaves and wind some speechless, electric
gathering of woe, no peace in the North" (196). It is here that
King Moose enters the scene, and in his deep caw is the last part
of the final message: "something gruff in the sharp wounded
heart of things bleeding somewhere in the night, a sound somewhere in that voice in the North which spoke beneath all else to
Ranald Jethroe Jellicoe Jethroe and his friend Gottfried (Son of
Gutsy) 'Texas' Hyde" (197).

In *Why Are We in Vietnam?* the Devil possesses the conscious
world, while in the unconscious and superconscious realms the
power of light and the power of darkness wage their eternal
struggle. At the center, as in all of Mailer's work from first to last,
is the mystery and the piteousness of human suffering, "the sharp
wounded heart of things bleeding somewhere in the night"; and
this is what history appears to be really about: in Hegel's phrase,
"the slaughter-bench at which the happiness of peoples, the wisdom of states, and the virtues of individuals have been sacrificed."

ALAN LEBOWITZ

No Farewell to Arms

The New Criticism, with its standards of verbal and structural order and its ideals of control and impersonality, has been especially harsh on untidy and self-proclaiming writers, many of whom have, of course, been Americans. Some of the most passionate and intensely committed of our writers have used their work, in one way or other, for purposes of self-confrontation and self-exploration, and their efforts to translate complex, half-grasped private matters into coherent public constructs have rarely been entirely successful. But imperfections that may derive from a writer's private connections to his material do not necessarily diminish the real value of his work. Indeed, the resultant flaws are often index to the important human energies behind them, and they offer us rich insight into the very source of literature, that shadowy, original area where author confronts subject in the turmoil and the great uncertainty of creation.

Hemingway is a notable instance. A writer of unquestionable stature and unique influence, his work has surely earned our serious attention. Yet it has often been misread by admirers too eager to find in it aesthetic virtues it demonstrably lacks or else — worse — ignored, or mocked, for its failure to meet standards

that are — or ought to be — considerably more flexible and relative than the standard-bearers would allow. *A Farewell to Arms*
is an interesting case in point. Most of the serious analytic attention the novel has received has tended to read into it a very ques-
tionable coherence of theme and purpose, based on the obvious
narrative movement from war to love. Frederic Henry's "separate
peace" is thus regarded as humanizing and ennobling, a turning
from the dullness and the desiccating cruelties of war toward a
more decent and more positively meaningful life defined by love
and impending fatherhood.

That Henry does not finally achieve such a state is, for some,
evidence of Hemingway's tragic view of life and, for others, of his
basic disbelief in domesticity or his inability to write believably of
women and of sexual relationships generally. The former view involves considerable distortion, as I will try to show, but the latter,
however accurate as judgment, is too easy a dismissal of a work
which ought to command our serious attention if only because it
is the one real love story of a major American writer who did not
otherwise believe in the important therapies of love.

The implicit premise of the title and the physical movement of
the narrative surely indicate that Hemingway's intention was to
write of love as a preferable alternative, if not an antidote, to war.
Frederic Henry's war — modeled, of course, on Hemingway's
own World War I experience in Italy — has in fact turned terribly sour in all respects by the time he abandons it. It is dead-
ening and dehumanizing to all involved in it, both wounding and
boring, and entirely devoid of larger purpose or significance.
Moreover, the desertion itself, the actual farewell, is portrayed as
an expressly cleansing act. Henry passes from war by swimming
a river, and this rite of aquatic passage from the old life to the
new is surely intended to denote a significant progression.

Certain details, however, seriously qualify, even undermine,
the plausible clarity of the outline. Most obviously, Frederic
Henry takes his purifying plunge at gunpoint, compelled by the
threat of an immediate, unjust execution as some kind of spy. The
separate peace he makes is thus provoked by neither moral nor
psychological considerations, but is, in fact, an absolute physical
necessity. If he does not take that transfiguring swim, he dies immediately. Moreover, Henry has himself just anticipated this con-

frontation at the bridge from the other side of the gun, shooting one of two fleeing soldiers picked up on the retreat who attempt to desert his group and flout his authority as ranking officer when he commands their help. It is hard to know quite what to make of this episode, the effect of which is to make Frederic Henry a killer — and so, one may say, a completed soldier — just prior to his actual farewell to arms. It is possible, of course, that Hemingway intended it only to signify the dimension of the war horror that finally drives Frederic Henry across his river. There is, however, no visible irony in the telling, or any indication whatever of any kind of moral response — no subsequent reflection, let alone remorse. Whatever Hemingway's intentions here, a major effect is simply to confirm his hero's prowess with a gun, and willingness to use it in the name of martial logic and authority, before he makes his actual farewell. The episode serves, in other words, as a kind of badge, indicating that the deserter-to-be has known his business to the full, has been a good man with a gun.[1]

Hemingway's use of guns throughout the novel reflects an almost ritualistic connection between weaponry and virility — the gun as phallus — which in itself makes the premise of the narrative disturbingly ambiguous. A farewell to arms obviously ought not to signify any loss of sexual power when its purpose and direction is the active role of heterosexual lover, husband and father. An early encounter with a cowardly deserter elucidates the symbolic context. This man — also, curiously, an Italian soldier with an American connection — attempts to justify his desertion from battle on the grounds that he has a hernia. (The accusation is that it is self-induced.) The opposite of this cowardly, maimed deserter, the warrior with *cojones,* is, of course, a recurrent Hemingway ideal, typified by Robert Jordan, who wears his pistol like a Hollywood cowboy, and by Harry Morgan, a real killer. In almost formulaic contrast, Nick Adams' father is shown pumping an empty shotgun in terrible frustration after backing down before

---

1. Henry is actually only relatively good at killing — and not technically a killer — since he misses one of the two men entirely and does not actually kill the other, though he wounds him mortally. The *coup de grace* is administered by one of his men. This is, I think, only a kind of hedging, a means of achieving the desired effect and still letting Henry off as blamelessly as possible.

a bully's challenge in "The Doctor and the Doctor's Wife," and
Pablo's cowardice in *For Whom the Bell Tolls* earns him a rather
lengthy description as an altered boar (193–194). For Robert
Jordan, sex with Maria is a respite from martial activities. In the
aftermath of that famous moment when the earth shakes from
their lovemaking, she wants to talk about it, but his mind, cleared
of such nonsense, goes immediately to the battle ahead. Frederic
Henry confirms his manliness in comparable fashion on the night
he leaves Catherine Barkley to return to the front for his second
experience of battle. Before they go to a hotel for a last few hours
of love, he insists on buying a new pistol, his old one having been
lost. The scene in the store takes nearly two pages, lovingly and
pointlessly detailed. "Now we're fully armed," he tells her,[2] and
off they go, pausing only to buy Catherine a nightgown, apparently an equivalent female preparation.

A more central and telling detail clarifies all this with immediate pertinence to the novel's title. Reaching the other side of the
river and his new life, Frederic Henry hops a passing freight car
filled with guns, all smelling "cleanly of oil and grease" (239).
Though Henry is cold and wet under the canvas that encloses the
car, the cloistered, tentlike atmosphere is evocative of other such
places of refuge in Hemingway's work, most notably Nick
Adams' "good place," his tent at the Big Two-Hearted River. But
though the sense of new security and the womblike connotations
may well suggest a rebirth into love, the surrounding presence of
the guns is either the oddest and most pointless of ironies or, as I
believe, strong indication that although he has said his farewell to
arms, Henry is still most perfectly at home with, and now most
especially needful of, his guns.

Henry retains his virility throughout. (As Catherine's pregnancy develops he grows a beard, though later, finding a gym-
nasium and someone to box with, he considers shaving it off.)
But he loses the male society that is its inevitable concomitant. On
a train to Stresa, where Catherine is vacationing, he encounters a
group of aviators who point the realities of his new situation in a
moment of considerable, though probably uncalculated, resonance.

2. Ernest Hemingway, *A Farewell to Arms* (New York: Scribner's),
p. 155. Except where otherwise noted, all references to Hemingway's
writings are to the Scribner Library edition.

The aviators, a warrior elite, are silently contemptuous of Henry as a man in civilian clothes young enough to be in uniform. He does not "feel insulted" by them, however, though in "the old days," as he quickly asserts, he "would have insulted them and picked a fight." When they leave the train, Henry is momentarily "glad to be alone," but immediately his thoughts turn to his desertion, and his mood abruptly changes. "I was going to forget the war. I had made a separate peace. I felt damned lonely and was glad when the train got to Stresa" (252). Henry's swagger here, which calls as much attention to his pugnacious past as to his present, belies the declaration of newfound maturity and purpose, asserting, albeit in negative terms, a manliness he obviously feels he has abandoned with his uniform. "Othello with his occupation gone" (266), Catherine calls him, forcing a heavy irony and a rather odd one, considering both Catherine's end and Desdemona's. Henry's sense of shame continues, though never with significant force or psychological consequence. "I feel like a criminal," he says at one point. "I've deserted from the army" (260) — to which Catherine responds, "It's only the Italian army," and takes him off to bed where love can once more work against such feelings. To the end, however, it does so only conditionally and temporarily. The shame repeatedly surfaces in one form or another, as does that loneliness which returns so quickly once the aviators have left him on the train.

A sense of lost male camaraderies attends Frederic Henry steadily during his lonely cloistered life in Switzerland with Catherine. Though the war has soured the previously congenial atmosphere of the officers' mess by Henry's second tour of duty, prior to the retreat and his desertion, the values implicit in the image of a drinking, joking band of warrior-brothers have been steadily upheld. For instance, a fussy, womanish, nondrinking doctor, only a captain, refuses to operate immediately on Henry's wounded knee, insisting for safety's sake on waiting at least six months. Rejecting this diagnosis on the grounds that any good doctor would surely be a major, Henry finds another surgeon, a laughing major with a large moustache who drinks hard, makes bawdy jokes, and, of course, operates immediately. Needless to say, Catherine doesn't like this Dr. Valentini as much as Henry does, and quite sensibly, since his efforts will shortly return Henry to war and to companions just like Dr. Valentini, whereas the effeminate doctor would have kept him in the hospital with her.

The homosexual implication here surely needs no belaboring but requires some mention, since it is a visible factor in *A Farewell to Arms* and not merely implicit in the general configuration of relationships. Dr. Valentini is the counterpart of Henry's closest comrade, Dr. Rinaldi, and between Henry and Rinaldi there is considerable physical affection — much touching and kissing — as well as tenderness, talk of love, tension over Catherine, and casual sexual banter. At any rate, whatever the veiled psychodynamics, the loss of male society is a major factor in Henry's later life with Catherine, a theme to which they constantly advert. "Isn't it grand how we never see anyone?" she says in one such moment. "You don't want to see people, do you darling?" (313). And in another, more pointed moment, she asks, "Wouldn't you like to go on a trip somewhere by yourself, darling, and be with men and ski?" (308). Henry's answer, here as elsewhere, is a simple, unenthusiastic denial, but he is obviously not telling the truth. And, more to the point, neither is Hemingway.

The love of Frederic Henry and Catherine Barkley is empty, puerile, and, above all, appallingly inadequate, but the problem is not simply one of craft. It is not merely that Hemingway can't say what he is trying to say, can't write of women and of love, but rather that his real attitudes, deeply rooted and painfully visible through all his work, go drastically counter to the conscious intentions of his story. *A Farewell to Arms* is in fact an attempted reversal of previous postures and convictions, and therein, I think, lies a special interest. When Hemingway has Frederic Henry deny a desire to "be with men and ski," for instance, he reverses a position taken in a story called "Cross Country Snow" in *In Our Time,* published four years before *A Farewell to Arms,* in which Nick Adams and a friend named George are skiing in the Swiss Alps. The trip, it develops, is their last such, because Nick has married since we saw him last in battle on the Italian front. His new wife is pregnant, and they are shortly to return to America, where the skiing is no good and the atmosphere, Nick says, is "not exactly" hell, but so close to it that he cannot name the differences when asked (146). The act of skiing itself offers Nick a highly energized state of being akin to the physical sensa-

tions of battle, a downward rush which "plucked Nick's mind out
and left him only the wonderful flying, dropping sensation in his
body" (139). Such feelings are Harold Krebs' richest memories
of war in "Soldier's Home" in *In Our Time,* memories of "the
times so long back when he had done the one thing, the only thing
for a man to do, easily and naturally, when he might have done
something else" (90). Krebs, returned from war to his Kansas family, which is dominated by his mother, is one of Hemingway's symbolic sexual impotents, wanting no sexual connection,
feeling no love, his only "girl" his little baseball-playing sister.
Nick's skiing companion is presumably the George of a previous
In Our Time story, "Cat in the Rain," a slight sketch about a married couple trapped by rain in a hotel room in Italy, both deeply
bored with a life apparently characterized by such moments. The
husband reads, speaking only occasionally in tired monosyllables.
The wife's unhappiness is more vivid, triggered by the sight of a
forlorn cat outside in the rain. Hemingway capsules her discontents in a mocking, even insulting, line: "It isn't any fun to be a
poor kitty out in the rain" (120). And he locates her ambitions
squarely in conventional domesticity: "I want to eat at a table
with my own silver and I want candles. And I want it to be spring
and I want to brush my hair out in front of a mirror and I want a
kitty and I want some new clothes" (121). To which her husband
answers, "Oh, shut up and get something to read." The connection to *A Farewell to Arms* is not merely thematic — the sense
of domestic trap and such. Catherine Barkley is nicknamed Cat,
and her impending death is repeatedly symbolized by rain.[3] "I'm
afraid of the rain," she says, "because sometimes I see me dead
in it" (131).

3. Hemingway's use of small-animal pet names for his romantic
heroines is, of course, habitual. Maria in *For Whom the Bell Tolls* is
called Rabbit, and though Hemingway is aware of the sexual innuendo
in the name — playing on it at one point — he seems oblivious to the
implicit insult. Renata in *Across the River and Into the Trees* is affection-
ately called Honey-dog by her lover. The imagery is grotesquely liter-
alized — and the pattern very oddly reversed — in *Islands in the Stream,*
with Thomas Hudson, who has said farewell to three wives and is
now a solitary and at war. Hudson sleeps regularly with his cats, his
favorite being a male called Boy, with whom he shares not just his
bachelor's bed but also the sexual frustrations that go with it. "There's
nothing we can do. You don't know anything to do — do you?" he tells
and asks this loyal, horny Boy, pressing hard against his much-loved
bedmate (193).

Though it can hardly have been calculated, Hemingway's reversion in *A Farewell to Arms* to the materials of these earlier stories is in no way accidental. His attempt to portray romantic love in *A Farewell to Arms* is grounded in a hatred and fear of women and domesticity, and something like a love and need for war, as activity and as society. Both may properly be termed obsessions. The first story in *In Our Time*, "Indian Camp," concerns an Indian who commits suicide because he cannot stand the screams of his wife having a baby in the same room. The second is, in effect, a story about how a man can be driven to suicide. Dr. Adams, Nick's father, backs down before a bully's insults, then goes indoors where he furiously pumps an empty shotgun and is stupidly cajoled by his wife, who seems somehow responsible and is clearly an odious woman. In the next story, Nick breaks off a romance with a girl named Marjorie because "it isn't fun any more" (40), and because, since he has taught her all he knows, she knows as much as he does. This story ends with Nick turning to a male friend, obviously by prearrangement, with whom he spends the next story ("The Three Day Blow") in typical Hemingway activities — drinking, joking, talking of books and baseball, hunting. In "The Battler," Nick meets an old punchdrunk fighter, on the bum with a male companion, whose downfall was in large part caused by a bad marriage. And so on. Women figure more or less unpleasantly, as threatening or overtly hostile forces, in eleven of the fourteen stories, and where they do not, it is because the world is exclusively male or solitary, as in "The Big Two-Hearted River." Moreover, the vignettes, called chapters, which are set between the stories and consistently illuminate by contrast the stories' themes, are almost exclusively about war and bullfighting — the one great equivalent of war, according to Hemingway in *Death in the Afternoon* — and are predictably uninfluenced by women.

The Torrents of Spring, published the year after *In Our Time,* tells the related stories of two more victims of women. Scripps O'Neill is a pathetic, effete figure with literary interests as well as name, who keeps falling in love and marrying at first sight only to feel immediately trapped and discontented, cut off from dreams of achievement and escape. The other, Yogi Johnson, has been wounded in war and is also sexually impotent, until the end, because of a wartime sexual trauma. (He discovered that a beautiful woman, met and loved in Paris, was really a prostitute, and that all the while they were loving, they were being watched by paying customers through a peephole.) These two reappear in *The Sun Also Rises,* Yogi as Jake Barnes, Hemingway's only literal impotent, and Scripps as the romantic Robert Cohn. Trapped by early marriage, then by a bitchy, marriage-minded woman, Cohn makes a first significant self-assertion in his brief affair with Brett Ashley. Brett, however, offers only castration as alternative to his stifling life with Frances, to whom Cohn will return, or so Jake predicts, at the novel's end. Brett unmans him in large ways and small: "When he fell in love with Brett his tennis game went all to pieces. People beat him who had never had a chance with him" (45). On the other hand, Frances shames his manhood and dominates his life. Cohn's situation, in other words, offers him a choice between what might well be called immediate or slow castration. Nor is his dilemma entirely due to his own inadequacies. Romero, Brett's other lover and the novel's only other actively potent male, is also visibly diminished by his relationship with Brett. The boy, as he is called initially, who insists that he will never die, echoing the young Nick Adams of "Indian Camp," earns through Brett the battle scars of manhood. Because of her, the idyllic, almost mythic image he originally projects has been significantly undermined by the end of the novel. In Book III we discover that, like Cohn, Romero finally wanted to marry Brett, wanted her to be faithful and more womanly and to grow her hair long. The aftermath reveals, too, that the heroic bullfighter turned bourgeois lover was once a waiter in Gibraltar, a disclosure which tends to tarnish even further the original pure image of the man. On Romero, as on Cohn, though to a lesser — or less visible — degree, Brett's effect is finally degrading as well as destructive. The ear of the killer bull Bocanegra, magnificently killed by Romero, is given by him to Brett, "who wrapped it in a handkerchief . . . and left both ear and handkerchief, along with a number of Muratti cigarette-stubs, shoved far back in the drawer of the bed-table that stood beside her bed in the Hotel Montoya, in Pamplona" (199).

Only Jake is really saved from her, and this, of course, is because of his impotence. The immediate consequences of Hemingway's decision to make Jake's impotence clinical, rather than symbolic, have been too little appreciated. The ostensible focus on Jake's loss and pain and burden tends to conceal certain clear advantages he derives from his condition — and Hemingway from the stratagem. As a physical actuality, Jake's impotence can have no psychological sources. More important, it serves to insulate him from Brett as sexual predator. By actualizing Jake's condition, Hemingway has effectively protected his hero in two threatened areas. Jake has no unmanly psychosexual terrors in his past and no active woman-troubles in his present. When Hemingway first advances the curious steer-bull analogy that informs the novel's interpersonal relationships, Jake is necessarily to be recognized as one of the steers, who "run around like old maids trying . . . to quiet down the bulls and keep them from breaking their horns . . . or goring each other" (133). The steers are just "trying to make friends," he says, and it is surely as much Jake's condition as his character that allows him his steady friendliness and decency, his role as pacifier and mollifier and confidant. But when Cohn, too, is later named a steer by Mike Campbell, the inescapable implication is that it is Brett, whom Cohn calls Circe, who represents the real bull in this grim, topsy-turvy world, and that what she has done to Cohn is make of him a version of Jake Barnes.[4]

Frederic Henry is not turned swine or steer, nor can Catherine Barkley be called castrating in any obvious sense. She is, in fact, quite the opposite, the self-demeaning and self-sacrificing good game girl of Hemingway's later fictive fantasies. Her sole purpose, appallingly reiterated, is to serve her lover; her sole concern is his entire satisfaction. When she tells him she is pregnant, for instance, it is his upset that worries her, not her own condition. But underlying her habit of service is something of a self-

4. Harold Loeb, the original of Robert Cohn, has recounted the actual events behind the Pamplona festival in his autobiography, *The Way It Was* (New York: Criterion Books, 1959). Loeb's story is especially interesting because it locates Hemingway himself in Jake's place, not-so-secretly leching after a woman named Duff Twitchell — the model for Brett — and kept from her not by impotence, of course, but by the presence of his wife, Hadley.

protecting instinct. In this regard, she resembles Scripps O'Neill's wife in *The Torrents of Spring,* a similarly giving woman whose repeated concern is her ability to "keep" Scripps, to "hold him for her own." The love relationship in *A Farewell to Arms* is terribly fragile, though never dramatically so, and Frederic Henry's constant unvoiced urge is toward escape. Disclosing her pregnancy, Catherine asks Henry if he feels trapped. "You always feel trapped biologically" (145), is his answer, and while she is rightly angered at the word "always," nothing more is made of it. The implication of the word is obviously generic, not personal. Whatever its biological basis, the trap, like that in "Cat in the Rain," is as much domestic as physiological, imprisoning the male partner and keeping him from certain kinds of fun with other men.

When Nick Adams breaks with his first love because "it isn't fun anymore," the specific context, and immediate reference, is fishing. Fishing, hunting, and skiing, like war, their ultimate extension, are male prerogatives as well as Hemingway's ideal activities. When we next see Nick in *In Our Time,* after the revelation that he is returning to America and fatherhood, it is in the happy solitude of the Big Two-Hearted River, and while Hemingway has elsewhere told us (in *A Moveable Feast*) that the war is what Nick is escaping from in that "good place," it seems far more plausible, especially in terms of the sequential narrative biography, that the refuge is rather from the burdens of his new domestic obligations. Jake Barnes and Bill Gorton also find temporary pleasure, and relief from the tensions caused by Brett, trout fishing at the Irati River. But for Frederic Henry, committed to love and threatened by marriage, there is only a short hour's fishing with a hotel barman on Lake Stresa, with not even a strike, let alone a catch. In this context, the role of the company priest is especially noteworthy. At the opening of the novel, before he meets Catherine, Henry is about to go on leave. The situation is set as a kind of morality drama with his bawdy comrades urging him to spend his leave with women and the priest offering the alternative of Abruzzi, his own home, where, he tells Henry, "there is good hunting. You would like the people and though it is cold it is clear and dry. You could stay with my family. My father is a famous hunter" (9). Henry, of course, opts for women, though in restrospect he seems vaguely to recognize a special personal validity to the priest's way. "I had gone to no place where the roads were frozen and hard as iron, where it was clear cold and dry and the snow was dry and powdery and hare-tracks in the snow and the peasants took off their hats and called you Lord and there was good hunting" (13). If Rinaldi represents an inadmissible homosexual alternative, the priest seems to offer a dream of what might have been and what once was — a dream of innocence and, specifically, of celibacy. And we need look no further than the two Africa stories, shortly to be written, for sharp evidence of the fatal dangers that ensue when women are taken hunting by their men.[5]

The notion that a vague ideal of celibacy may underlie this romantic tale of thwarted love is in no way farfetched, however deeply troubling. In Jake Barnes — emblem for an age — Hemingway has already tentatively advanced something very like that possibility. The ending of *The Sun Also Rises* confirms what any reader should have known all along — namely, that had there been no war wound, Jake and Brett would never have been happy together. His impotence simply shields him from the frictions and exacerbations that would have been his lot with Brett. And also because of the impotence, there can be no homosexual innuendo to darken the position. When Jake first sees Brett amidst a group of homosexuals, he can assert conventional virilities, wanting "to swing on one . . . to shatter that superior, simpering composure" (20). And when, on their fishing trip, Bill Gorton speaks of his fondness for Jake, carefully disclaiming that the declaration makes him "a faggot" (116), we know the surface truth of that because, although not sexually virile, Jake himself is obviously no faggot.

5. In these, too, we may see still more clearly the closeness of Hemingway's ostensibly antithetical female types. Margot Macomber, who shoots her husband in the head the instant that he finds his courage and his manhood in the act of hunting, extends the image of the promiscuous, castrating female to its logical conclusion. But the wife in "The Snows of Kilimanjaro," a generous and loving mate to her dying husband, though entirely blameless, is made to seem somehow responsible not merely for his death, but for his wasted life as well. It is also pertinent that in his dying hallucination, Harry is rescued by an aviator friend (male) who flies him to the top of Kilimanjaro, pointedly leaving the wife behind because there is no room for her in the plane.

The glamorous image of the lost generation (the epigraph from Gertrude Stein) has tended to obscure certain resonances in the words themselves, primarily, I would suggest, the irony of the term generation in a story about an impotent in love with a woman whom most readers would probably see as a nymphomaniac. Such a pair is truly lost, and from them is generated nothing, let alone the earth-affirming and life-continuing visions of the epigraph from Ecclesiastes from which the title is taken. Jake is entirely out of that great natural cycle, and happily so if we take Frederic Henry's notion of biological trap as literally as he seems to do. At the end, while Catherine is beginning the labor that will end in her death and his son's, Henry reverts pointedly to the earlier image of entrapment: "And this was the price you paid for sleeping together. This was the end of the trap. This was what people got for loving each other" (330). The meaning seems to be only that labor pains are the price of lovemaking, but Hemingway knows, if his hero doesn't yet, that the real penalty is death. And he should know, too, that if a trap may be said to have an end, that end would be a liberation of one kind or other. For all the dark melodrama, the pretense of tragedy, the focus at the end is on Frederic Henry, alone and unentangled. The trap has sprung on Catherine. For him it is truly trap's end.

Lying in his freight car full of guns and pondering his recently achieved farewell, Henry anticipates his new life thus: "I was not made to think. I was made to eat. My God, yes. Eat and drink and sleep with Catherine" (242). At the end, facing another new life, whatever that might be, he has lost only the third possibility. All the while that Catherine has been laboring and dying, in fact, Frederic Henry has been eating and drinking. Two full meals, rather lengthily described, are set as counterpoint to the hospital terrors. It may of course be plausibly argued that this represents a calculatedly affirmative act, a kind of symbolic endurance — appetite persisting in the face of impending loss — but Henry's obvious pleasures at table are surely inappropriate in the circumstances. The *plat du jour,* veal stew, is gone, and so he is offered *choucroute,* which he rejects because he has already eaten *choucroute* earlier in the day. So he settles for ham and eggs — two orders, because he is very hungry, and several glasses of beer as well. The sexual implications of eating and drinking throughout Hemingway's writings are surely self-evident. I would suggest, though, that food and drink are not merely sexual outlets for Hemingway's characters but are often actually preferred alternatives. Jake Barnes is again the paradigm. At the end of *The Sun Also Rises,* Jake and Brett go to Madrid's best restaurant, where Jake eats an enormous meal with unmistakable pleasure. Brett, who never eats much, we are reminded here, points the obvious: "You like to eat, don't you?" she says. "Yes," Jake answers. "I like to do a lot of things." And when she asks, "What do you like to do?" he repeats, "I like to do a lot of things" (246).

Fishing and bullfights we know to be among Jake's other important pleasures, and probably hunting, too, since he suggests a hunting trip to Africa to Robert Cohn at one point when Cohn is looking to escape from Frances just before he goes off to San Sebastian with Brett. And war has presumably been another. Though we are told little of Jake's war experience, it would seem to have paralleled Frederic Henry's — and Hemingway's — to a point. Though a flier in Italy, and no mere ambulance driver, Jake also spent a time in a hospital in Milan. Like Catherine Barkley, Brett Ashley was an English V.A.D. in that same hospital, although Jake's memories of that time focus on his Italian comrades and a society they formed there, not on Brett. Behind both fictive nurses, of course, is Hemingway's own nurse in Italy, Agnes von Kurowsky, with whom he fell seriously in love — probably for the first time — and who broke off their plans for marriage after his return to Oak Park. The affair with Agnes von Kurowsky is chronicled once before *A Farewell to Arms,* in a slight piece in *In Our Time* called "A Very Short Story" in which the rejected hero — presumably Nick Adams but not named — takes a sophomoric kind of vengeance on the betrayer of his love, contracting "gonorrhea from a sales girl in a loop department store while riding in a taxicab through Lincoln Park" (85). Catherine Barkley's end is certainly more dramatically appropriate, and more seemly, but one might speculate that it represents no less a kind of revenge.

An image of a plausible future for Jake Barnes is offered by an incidental character named Count Mippipopolous, who looks, oddly, rather like the later Hemingway. A man who has been "in seven wars and four revolutions" (60) and who proudly displays

to Brett and Jake old battle scars on his large stomach, Mippipopolous no longer falls in love because, he claims, "I am always in love" (61). When Brett objects, telling him, "you're
dead, that's all," his answer is a forceful, if less than illuminating,
denial: "No, my dear. You're not right. I'm not dead at all"
(61). So far beyond the threat of love he can even enjoy Brett's
company without involvement, Mippipopolous's principal pleasures are good food and drink. The "secret" of enjoyment of
life, he says, lies in getting "to know the values" (60), and "I
get more value for my money in old brandy than in any other
antiquities" (61). Jake himself later echoes the lesson, though
still somewhat questioningly: "Enjoying living was learning to get
your money's worth and knowing when you had it" (148). Mippipopolous represents an ideal of style and of stance, a model of
how to live well on nothing but the world's small offerings, outside, or far beyond, all sexual and familial entanglements. Jake's
pleasurable last meal with Brett would seem to indicate that he
has finally learned the lesson of his mentor. Frederic Henry, too,
has his own exemplary nobleman, a graceful, dignified old man
named Count Greffi, who, though very old, is still able to beat
Henry handily at billiards, all the while calmly sipping fine cham-
pagne. Greffi, though, is an ideal of endurance, a man who has
managed to maintain his style to the end and without belief in
God. To reach that final stage, Frederic Henry would first have
to pass through something like Jake's way of life and then Mippipopolous's, and whatever the terms of the projection, that seems
most plausibly his direction. A man with two first names (at one
point, Hemingway plays on this, reversing them), Frederic Henry
has neither father nor hometown, only a stepfather, otherwise un-
specified, and a grandfather, pertinent only as a source of funds.
Void of past family connections from the outset and having lost
the possibility of future ones at the end, Frederic Henry seems already as true a member of the lost generation as any of the group
in *The Sun Also Rises*. In Paris, one supposes, he will shortly find
his future self, now knowing better than to fall in love again.

Hemingway himself would seem to have learned a comparable
lesson from the writing of *A Farewell to Arms*. His next novel,
To Have and Have Not, opens with a scene of pointless, bloody
carnage — gunmen inexplicably killing each other all over the

place — and has for hero a big-game fisherman and real killer. In *For Whom the Bell Tolls,* Robert Jordan, like Jake Barnes and Frederic Henry a fighter in a foreign war, does not have to give more than his life — as someone jokingly says of Jake — because his fated death allows him to love without fear of consequence. In *For Whom the Bell Tolls,* too, we see the beginnings of the Papa role, another of Hemingway's eventual resolutions of the vexing problems that ensue when warriors love neither wisely nor too well. Though Jordan does not name Maria daughter — as Richard Cantwell will do with Renata in *Across the River and Into the Trees,* and as the older Hemingway apparently did with younger women — he treats her as a child, repeatedly sending her away when anything serious is at hand.[6] The later heroes have something of the flavor of the worldly-wise, serene Count Mippipopolous, but the basic outlook never really changes. Despite a romantic sexual moment in a gondola with his nineteen-year-old Renata, Colonel Cantwell spends most of his time with her talking about the profession of arms and about his own martial past in World War II. He leaves her prematurely to go duck hunting with male friends, a trip on which she is pointedly not invited, though several times she asks to go. His last extensive recollection of their love before he dies is of a street brawl with two young sailors, whom he easily wipes out for whistling at Renata and for disregarding, then insulting, his military rank.

Thomas Hudson, the hero of the posthumously published *Islands in the Stream,* provides a final gloss, grotesquely reenacting the earlier love-war situation, but quite literally reversing its direction. In the midst of World War II, Hudson is briefly reunited in Havana with his first wife — still his only love — a movie star who looks like Hemingway's longtime friend Marlene Dietrich and who resonates with all the nostalgic, loving memories Hemingway expresses for his first wife, Hadley, in *A Moveable Feast.* After they make love, Hudson tells her that their only son, a flier, has just been killed in combat. Almost immediately, Hudson is himself abruptly summoned back to war, where he com-

6. At one point, he even thinks of her as a daughter: "Maria is my true love and my wife. I never had a true love. I never had a wife. She is also my sister, and I never had a sister, and my daughter, and I never will have a daughter" (381).

mands a boat that searches the Caribbean for German submarines — as Hemingway did in the early stages of the war, though the fictive character finds considerably more action than did his maker. In the novel's last section, Hudson is in his boat chasing Germans, the captain of a loyal band of tough, ribald comrades, all with clear affection and respect for him. In this almost painfully familiar context, Hudson one night dreams that the war is over and he is reunited with his first wife and dead son.

> He dreamed that Tom's mother was sleeping with him and she was sleeping on top of him as she liked to do sometimes. He felt all of this and the tangibility of her legs against his legs and her body against his and her breasts against his chest and her mouth was playing against his mouth. Her hair hung down and lay heavy and silky on his eyes and on his cheeks and he turned his lips away from her searching ones and took the hair in his mouth and held it. Then with one hand he moistened the .357 Magnum and slipped it easily and sound asleep where it should be. Then he lay under her weight with her silken hair over his face like a curtain and moved slowly and rhythmically.[7]

The Magnum is actual. (Hudson handles it while "sound asleep.") Its dream uses, however, are obscure and contradictory, for although patently symbolic, "where it should be," the "moistened" gun seems also to represent his fantasied bed partner, to whom (which?) Hudson speaks odd words of love. "Thank you for being so moist and lovely and for pressing on me so hard." But though the real gun and the impalpable ex-wife may have momentarily coalesced for Hudson dreaming, within the dream itself the gun must be abandoned for the lovemaking that follows. "The pistol's in the way of everything," she complains, so he allows her to remove it. Finally, the dream and the lovemaking end simultaneously on a note of mutual destruction. "Will you swing your hair across my face and give me your mouth please and hold me so tight it kills me?" he asks. "Of course," she answers, "And you'll do it for me?"

7. Ernest Hemingway, *Islands in the Stream* (New York: Charles Scribner's, 1970), pp. 343–345.

When Hudson wakes from his grim dream, he feels "the pistol holster between his legs and how it was really and all the hollow-nesses in him were as hollow and there was a new one from the dream." The hollowness and sense of loss are surely very real, but the assumptions on which the dream is based, and all their devas-tating implications, are far too powerful for any therapy but death. Hudson dies in battle, shot from ambush. His dying sensation is of oneness with the power of his boat. The last words he hears are an outright declaration of love from the very tough-est of his tough crew, an ex-marine of whom Thomas Hudson has earlier said, "I would rather have a good Marine, even a ruined Marine, than anything in the world when the chips are down" (403).

In this present time of evil war, presided over by cowboys and football enthusiasts, one surely need not elaborate on the per-tinence of these tangled themes of war and love, these recurrent dreams of violence so clearly based in sexual fears, this omni-pres-ent woman-hate, veneered by frightful lies and false bravadoes. But if Hemingway was, like all of us, a victim of assumptions that go back to our national beginnings, he has also, as a writer, reinforced those assumptions, bodied them in new images, and transmitted them in the myths that for too long now have shaped our attitudes and our lives. And because he has been a writer of singularly powerful influence, his work — great literature or no — demands our most serious and most rigorous attention. To mis-read him is a danger, but to deny him is a loss, depriving us of an important, perhaps crucial, record of ourselves. For good and for ill, in both his strengths and his weaknesses, his power and his terrible fragility, he is our heritage. And if we are ever to exorcise the destructive element in this legacy — or even modulate it — we must confront him fully, with neither mockery nor adulation.

Three

I. A. RICHARDS

Literature for the Unlettered

Politics has often enough been described as the study, the craft, the art or science of the practicable, the possible. The intention behind the claim is commonly flattering, sometimes self-flattery. It is then an excuse, as a rule, for not doing, for not trying to do or even to experiment with, something which if it were to succeed would be useful. And in politics here we should include not only the handling of suasions, guidance of, contest with, public opinion, but all those multitudinous webs of personal ambitions, dependences, rivalries, jealousies, complots, oppositions — which, perhaps inevitably, infest the bureaucratic worlds from school levels on up.

These despondent reflections arise here from wondering why the great new media — radio, tape, TV, cassette availabilities — have not been more variously, more imaginatively, more venturesomely tried out in support of our spiritual inheritance: specifically, as means of helping literature to have more impact upon those deprived of, unprepared for, access to it. Literature we take here in a wide and a critical sense, as utterance of high quality in whatever genre. In sum, why does professional expertise act as though nothing much of this sort were worth attempting? Plenty of enterprise has been shown in other fields, sometimes too much: TV exploitation of mountaineering, for example, has verged on the gladiatorial.

Physically, these media are among the most alerting instances of how the boundaries of the possible, the frontiers of the feasible, have in our own lifetimes been pushed back. Culturally, educationally, they have been among the most humiliating examples of human inability to take advantage of our new powers — "to the relief of man's estate." The disparity between the new resources and our uses of them is a reproach that has throughout their development been regularly pointed out — without effect. The contrast is indeed grotesque: on the occasion celebrating the twenty-fifth anniversary of British broadcasting, the Bishop of Gloucester told of an old Wiltshire farm labourer and his wife listening to their first broadcast. "Their eyes were almost bursting out of their heads with amazement and every now and again the old fellow muttered under his breath: 'The glory o' God, the glory o' God.' " At about that time, I happened myself on an old Welsh shepherd under Snowdon who had just bought a radio. " 'Deed to goodness," he said, "it's grand to hear the pipple coughing and sneezing in Cardiff!"

What might we be offering in place of catarrhal and still more distressing outcomes of atmospheric and cultural smog? Let me risk here some outlines of what might prove practicable: opportunities that have not been explored in the measure that their promise should invite. The appeal in most of them would be to immediate comparison: to the pleasures of trying to see for oneself *which* of presented alternatives one likes best. Many of them rely on that prodigious mutual control between ear and eye which is the source of the power of writing. There on the screen would stand the sentences, clear and steady in print, while the reading voice (or an alternation of voices) tries out challengingly various ways of saying them.

Such games of choosing or of sitting in judgment while choices are made and discussed presuppose, of course, some fairly well developed ability to read in the audience. I do not enter here on what has been, since 1930, my own chief literary interest: the use of the new media (screen, TV, videotape) in the initial learning of reading. Recommendations as to policy and practice in this can be found elsewhere.[1] Neglect of these practicables is the outstanding example of the educators' failure to use our new powers. I will, though, venture a warning. The unrivalled resources of the media for *distraction* can very easily lead to that replacing *instruction*. The essential thing is for the learner to be helped in finding out for himself how to learn. He is not so helped by being Pied Piper'd off elsewhere. The etymons of *divergence, diversion* and *amusement* can convey my warning: Whoever will turn up and ponder *verge, verse,* and *muse* in, say, Eric Partridge's *Origins* will find good reasons to be wary: *amuse* has behind it a cow with its muzzle in the air; *not* feeding; bemused, may we say?

To return to what the media might be doing for moderately literate addresses and participants: How could the screen help them to find out more about what literature is and how it works? To find out more for themselves — not, as with most lectures, just to be told. One of our major troubles is that people have been led to expect *to be taught* — not helped in learning how to learn.

To start with one of the simplest, most easily explored opportunities. In videotape we have an uniquely flexible means for studying the cooperations, the mutual control of ear and eye in reading. Consider how we might be using it to interest more people more fruitfully in how verse may be spoken, and in learning more about its movement. Here the first hazard is, of course, the poet himself. Ever since Socrates had his fun with Ion, the absurdities of poets and rhapsodes as interpreters of their own and of others' poetry have been an unfailing spring of refreshing comedy. There is hardly a move made by Socrates and his gently, tenderly handled victim which is not highly instructive for our purposes here. A good reading of a suitably simplified *Ion* could be a useful way of arousing curiosity about the poet's dealings with his work. From Socrates's "loadstone" theory of inspiration on *to* his conclusion — which he summarizes so astrin-

---

1. See, e.g., my *Speculative Instruments* (1955), Index; *So Much Nearer* (1968), Index; *Design for Escape* (1968), Appendix: all Harcourt Brace Jovanovich, New York. Also, Sheridan Baker, Jacques Barzun, and I. A. Richards, *The Written Word* (Rowley, Mass.: Newbury House Publishers, 1971), pp. 61–85.

gently in the *Apology* — he is raising one of the most awakening of all literary questions. "After the politicians I went to the poets. I took lines from their own writings and asked them what they meant, hoping to learn something from them. Do you know: the truth is, almost anyone who was there could have talked better than they did — even about the very poems they had written themselves. I soon saw that poets don't write from their own wisdom but from what the gods tell them. Poets say great things but don't know what they are saying. They are like oracles in that."[2] Socrates believed in oracles. His ambivalence on inspiration (and his attitude, almost his devotion, to Apollo) make this a very potent whet to interest. The puzzles of the poet's pose or calling are unending. So many of them seem so often, so clumsily and yet so almost willfully, to get in the way of their poetry — reading it unintelligibly, commenting on it without point or with deliberate distraction, substituting mannerisms (personality quirks) for matter, and so on. They might be wanting to play their poetry down and steal the show. I recall remarking once — in introducing Robert Lowell to an *Advocate* audience — that a wise government should make the distribution of poetry very easy but any ascertainment of which poets wrote what impossible. Lowell in reply thought this the worst plan ever. He was for more and better known poets. And let the poetry take care of itself!

Whatever may be the balanced view in this matter, the various readings of verses presented in print upon the screen should not, in general, I think, include that of the poet. Coleridge, at the end of his great penultimate paragraph (in *Biographia Literaria,* chapter XIV) with which we shall be further concerned, speaks, with a feeling that may have had sad experience behind it, of our need to "subordinate . . . our admiration of the poet to our sympathy with the poetry." Given the current cult of celebrity, we do well to remember that "Words it is, not poets, make up poems." Helen Vendler has wittily described poetry-reading audiences as being "like lemmings: moving in obedience to obscure compulsions."[3] What we have to do is to replace these obscure compulsions by a comprehending concern. Readings such that hardly

---

2. Version in Everyman's English from *Why So, Socrates?* etc.
3. *New York Times Book Review,* November 7, 1971, p. 1.

a soul in the hall can take in from the public address system what the words are do not let "sympathy with poetry" have much chance.

But while avoiding the poet we need not have recourse to the actor. A good reading of a poem should not, ordinarily, be a dramatic performance. It is fine for Ion to tell Socrates that "reciting a tale of pity, my eyes are filled with tears; when it's a tale of terror, my hair stands up on end and my heart goes leaping." This entertains Socrates and helps him to his joke. "Why, Ion, what are we to make of a man like that . . . Shrinking back in fear though standing up before 20,000 friendly people!" But in general, and for deeply interesting reasons, actors are rarely good readers. And when the words are on view to show us perfectly which they are, there can arise especially a conflict of roles. A reader's duty is to suggest how the lines should be *read* (and understood). An actor's business is to represent an *action*. His training has been for that. But, though we may agree, we should not forget that producers are unlikely to think so. They will believe that the poetry needs pepping up with a performance and that a posturing figure before a color movie of the spring shores of Coniston Lake will be the way to put Wordsworth's "Daffodils" across. We can hardly say too strongly that to bring poetry to the unlettered we must allow the poetry to speak for itself — not bury it beneath adventitious trimmings. We should be exponents — not exhibitionists or undertakers — and, above all, beware of showmanship.

Suitable readers, I suggest, should be varied in their styles. It will do no harm if some of them are what judges will regard as bad: irrelevant or exaggerated in their intonations; astray in their interpretations, accidental in their stressings and pausings; misleading in their rhythm. Most listeners are still oddly insensitive and overtolerant as to the handling of the reading voice. Anyone familiar with the resources of musical criticism must be struck by the absence, as yet, of any comparable means of discriminating between readings aloud. It is as if no one thought that such differentiations could matter. Here, good opportunities to compare can do much; faultinesses can bring out by contrast what was unnoticed before. But if ability in comparing is to increase, we should have the better as well as the worse before us.

It is obvious in all this how great can be the advantages of cassette-carried presentations. Most differences being studied require *repeated* experience before they yield full fruit. We should be realizing that technology is now offering us immensely improved means of developing the very discriminations which can be expected to do most people most good. We are not yet benefitting from them, and we will not without far more reflective and systematic experimentation than has yet been proposed or planned, much less attempted.

Two arts — the art of reading poetry and the reciprocal art of listening with discrimination to such reading — can now be developed as never before. They depend upon recognition of the *reading voice* as our prime and indispensable instrument for exploring and comparing meanings. And we have to recognize, too, the equally indispensable cooperative work of the written notation, of print, in the study of meanings. Those who have proposed the dropping of reading-writing from education know too little both about how meanings have developed and how men have become more human. These thinkers are — it should be said forcibly — inadequately prepared for the role they have assumed.[4]

With cultivation of reading-listening go such minor matters as line arrangement, insets as rime markers, and the visual layout of stanza form. The physical conditions of the screen itself can bring these up: long lines must be broken for it as they need not be on the page. Where they are divided and how placed can make differences which belong with our understanding of line movement. So, too, with alternative punctuations and the use of capitals and italics. An unpunctuated sonnet started off what followed from William Empson's *Seven Types of Ambiguity*. Simpler problems suitable for the less lettered abound. The point is not so much that a shifted comma can distort a meaning. That is the casualty aspect. It is that punctuation affords exercise in percipience.

Still more can comparison of phrasings, of different ways of saying what may profess to be the same thing. I choose, as an illustration, a change which has much significance in its own right. It is the "slight alteration" (he calls it that) made by Coleridge in

4. These extremities of folly are well described by Sheridan Baker and Jacques Barzun in *The Written Word*.

quoting at the end of that same chapter XIV from Sir John
Davies's *Nosce Teipsum* (1599). As an illustration it is too challenging to be representative of the games of comparing for the
unlettered that we are considering. I use it here because I have
noticed that suitably simple examples are often disregarded, as
mere school exercises, by many who have the talents needed for
designing such games.

Coleridge prefaces his quotation with " 'Doubtless,' as Sir John
Davies observes of the soul (and his words may with slight alter-
ation be applied, and even more appropriately, to the poetic
IMAGINATION),"

> Doubtless this could not be, but that she turns
>   Bodies to spirit by sublimation strange,
> As fire converts to fire the things it turns,
>   As we our food into our nature change.

In the fourth line Davies wrote "meat." Perhaps Coleridge (no
great carnivore) just remembered the more universal rather than
the more robust Elizabethan term. We may recall Walter De la
Mare's line: "Whatever Miss T. eats turns into Miss T." In the
next stanza Coleridge made no change except in the spelling. I
will use the original:

> From their grosse *matter* she abstracts the *formes,*
>   And drawes a kind of *Quintessence* from things;
> Which to her proper nature she transformes,
>   To beare them light on her celestiall wings:

Now come the alterations:

> This doth she when from things *particular*
>   She doth abstract the *universall kinds,*
> Which bodilesse and immateriall are,
>   And can be lodg'd but onely in our minds:

> Thus does she when from individual states
>   She doth abstract the universal kinds;
> Which then re-clothed in divers names and fates
>   Steal access through our senses to our minds.

"Divers" is one of Davies's favorite words; the next stanza opens with, "And thus from divers accidents and acts," which may have prompted "divers names and fates" and the "Thus" above.

There are obviously points that might be long debated in these changes without any convincing evidence appearing as to whether we should make much or make little of them. We may hold that "individual states" as against "things particular" converts a bare reference to Platonic doctrine into a lively invitation to speculate: *individual:* "not to be split up," "living and acting as wholes"; *states:* "conditions (as in the solid, liquid, and gaseous states)" with something of the political meaning of the city state: My mind to me a kingdom is? Again, we may think that "then re-clothed in divers names and fates" is a very bold transformation, a sublimation indeed, bringing in the great questions so much discussed under the heading, imageless thought. Those "universall kinds" in Davies are only negatively contrasted with "things particular" and thus (were other passages in *Nosce Teipsum* left out of account) in some danger of becoming inconveyable. In Coleridge they are given fresh embodiment (in the teeth of "bodilesse and immateriall") and appareled in changed "names and fates": "new symbols and altered consequence." It is by these transformed habiliments that Coleridge's universals are enabled to "Steal access through our senses to our minds." We may think this "Steal" the most significant and intriguing of his adjustments. Are "our senses" here "necessary channels"? Or are they rather protections, normally preventing access of the Ideas to our minds — needing to be outwitted by the Imagination, as by a smuggler slipping through the coastguards? Coleridge's "slight alteration" may here seem virtually to be defying Davies's prohibition. It may, however, merely be reembodying meanings of phrase after phrase: "synthetic and magical power," "gentle and unnoticed controul" in the account of the Imagination that has just been given.

It may help with what follows to quote from the remarks prefixed to Nahum Tate's edition (1697) of *Nosce Teipsum*. "Written by an ingenius and learned Divine," these comments on the principal poetic composition of Queen Elizabeth's attorney-general may quite well have had their influence on Coleridge's famous paragraph: "in this, as in a mirror (that will not flatter) we see how the soul arbitrates in the understanding on the various reports of sense, and all the changes of imagination: how compliant the will is to her dictates, and obeys her as a queen does her king: at the same time acknowledging a subjection, and yet retaining a majesty: how the passions move at her command, like a well-disciplined army; from which regular composure of the faculties, all operating in their proper time and place, there arises a complacency upon the whole soul, that infinitely transcends all other pleasures." Would that the attorney generals of our times could show us as much or solemnize so high a marriage of their Bible and their Plato! We do not enough remember that Lady Jane Grey thought hunting and other female sport but a shadow compared with the pleasure there is to be found in Plato.

As I have remarked, this illustration may ask for a too minute and exacting analysis to be offered to the participants we have in mind. It is too recondite. But it does bring out an important point. The aim of a suitable exercise is not just to explain (or dissolve) difficulties but to heighten awareness of what is happening and thus improve our ability to look into and select from among meanings.

More appropriate for our less qualified students would be comparison of the *Ion* with what is said of "the poet described in ideal perfection" in the paragraph leading up to the quotation from *Nosce Teipsum*. Let us try what a controlled paraphrase can do with it, remembering that there can be many such versions using varying degrees of focus. But first, let us see what this "controul" (to use Coleridge's spelling) may be.

We well know what high intricacies of stanza form, meter and rime-scheme can do to the process of composition, and what a variety of less *and* more adequate solutions each problem that the poem sets itself can call up. As the conditions being imposed grow stricter, selective attention is heightened. With so many possibilities barred out, those that remain undergo closer study. Much of this is a balancing between alternates — thematic, lexical, syntactic, phonologic. The effect is to make all the items being balanced grow more distinct. The grounds for rejecting some of them enter in and develop those for preferring others. Every

writer who has indulged in elaborate verse knows how many proposals come up which would never otherwise have occurred to
him and how many mutual bearings among the meanings that
have joined in the game have to be discerned and taken account
of. A degree of awareness of all the aspects of these choices can
be induced which is beyond anything aroused in an unrestricted
free verbal flow. He learns, too, what an exchange of mutual serv-
ices the phonologic, the syntactic, the lexical, and the thematic
levels maintain.

With, commonly, a dropping of the phonologic components,
all this is true — in considerable measure — in controlled paraphrase. The control may take the form of restriction to some
specified word-list, or avoidance of some set of constructions, or
a limitation of sentence length: such are some of the analogues to
meter and rime in the writing of verse. These barriers, too, cause
more proposals to come up for judgment, raise the degree of
attention that has to be given to the competing alternates, compel
deeper searchings of the successive problems, and lead to a wider
awareness of what the phrasings under examination can mean.
The analogies between controlled paraphrase and verse writing
are indeed remarkable. The stricter the conditions of the task, the
more penetrating the task — up to a certain point. Then, as the
going gets too hard, the strain imposed by the rules of the game
becomes excessive, and the job to be done loses precedence.

Let us test these observations out on the Coleridge paragraph.
The control here used is that of an adapted Basic English,
Everyman's English.

Original	*Everyman's*
The poet, described in ideal perfection,	The *poet,* if we may say what he is and does at his best, and though no writer of verse may ever, in fact, come up to such a level,
brings the whole soul of man into activity,	puts every power of man's mind and heart into operation
with the subordination of its faculties to each other according to their relative worth and dignity.	with every one of them taking that part in the common work in which it is specially able and has value and authority.

He diffuses a tone and spirit of unity,	He makes the work seem and feel, all through, as though everything in it is needed by, gives support to and takes support from, the rest (is what it is so that the rest may be what it is),
that blends, and (as it were) fuses, each into each,	he puts things together (as though made liquid by great heat: so that they become no longer, in themselves or in their effects, what they would be if separated)
by that synthetic and magical power,	by that uniting power for which
to which I would exclusively appropriate the name of Imagination.	I would keep the word "Imagination."

We may pause here to recall that this "subordination of the soul's faculties to each another according to their relative worth and dignity" is what is displayed at such length in the *Republic* in terms of the analogy of the three parts of the soul — knowledge, spirit,[5] appetite — with the three components of the state — guardians, guards, workers. As in the key stanza of Donne's "The Ecstasy,"

> So must pure lovers soules descend
> T'affections and to faculties
> Which sense may reach and apprehend,
> Else a great Prince in prison lies,

The affections and the faculties here are the intermediaries (the sentiments or feelings, as we might call them) through which alone that which should rule — the great Prince — can control

---

5. "The will (the Platonic θυμός) which is the sustaining, coercive, ministerial power, the functions of which in the individual correspond to the officers of war and police in the ideal Republic of Plato." *The Statesman's Manual*, Appendix B.

that which should be ruled. Knowledge cannot by itself reach down to sense (appetite, desire), nor sense reach up to knowledge, without the aid of spirit. Coleridge's account here is a description of Sophrosyne (Temperance). His marked insistence on control may well be a reply to Socrates's mocking account of Ion as being beside himself as though possessed. It will be noted that he returns to the theme of due subordination to be achieved through the "magical and synthetic power, IMAGINATION."

This power, first put in action by the will and understanding,	This power is first moved to its work by conscious purpose and a knowledge of what it is doing,
and retained under their irremissive, though gentle and unnoticed control . . .	and it is kept under their control throughout — though smoothly and without seeming to be so kept.
reveals itself in the balance or reconcilement of opposite or discordant qualities:	The Imagination is seen to be at work through the way in which it makes forces or conditions which, as a rule, are not able to work together, or are even against one another, give one another room for free play and even get on well together like friends. For
of sameness with difference;	example: it makes things able to be the same and at the same time different:
of the general with the concrete;	be clear examples of general laws and still be no less fully themselves in every least detail;
the sense of novelty and freshness with old and familiar objects;	through it things we have had about us for a long time, and have become used to, seem new — as if then for the first time seen;

a more than usual state of emo- / feelings become stronger and
tion with more than usual order; / freer than in most of our living,
though their behavior to one
another is better; the mind being
like a self-ruling, well-ruled
state;

judgment ever awake and steady / the purpose and the ways to it
self-possession with enthusiasm / are ever in view and the self
and feeling profound or vehe- / keeps itself in control however
ment; / high or deep or strong the
waves of feeling may be;

and while it blends and har- / and while it adjusts to one an-
monizes the natural and the / other what is natural and what
artificial, still subordinates art / is made by art, still keeps the
to nature; / writer's design from becoming
anything more than the servant
of natural forces;

the manner to the matter; / makes "how a thing is said" be
ruled by "what has to be said";

and our admiration of the poet / and puts our interest in what is
to our sympathy with the poetry. / being made before our respect
for or question about the man
who made it.

So far we have been considering means — by use of the reading voice and by controlled paraphrase — for improving interpretation of short relatively detachable pieces of verse and prose.
(It will have been noted, I hope, that the aim has not been the
attainment of any substitutable version but the development of a
more than usual intensity of inquiry into the original. What Coleridge described in the poet, that — with "slight alteration" — I
have been applying to the reading of sentences.) Let us now pass
to a larger question: how can we help people hardly at all acquainted with literature as the continuing embodiment of tradition? And especially with the great enduring sources of our
possibilities of thought, feeling, sentiment and will, the springs, in
fact, of whatever may flow through us?

Probably the most useful suggestion here is offered by the

group of metaphors active with *spring:* leap, fountain, season (re-
beginning), moving, impelling cause, force, motive — the incho-
ative, or, to use one of Coleridge's favorite words, *initiative.*
There are many subjects, fields of interest and study, in which one
sequence, one order, is manifestly and demonstrably more pro-
pitious, more likely to lead into sustained advance than any other,
it being that order in which what comes *first* is both, in itself, most
intelligible and awakening, and most helpful in making the following steps intelligible. This is so, for example, in the learning of
reading and of a second language (and perhaps — though no one
yet knows — of the mother tongue itself, and possibly of all
learning). There is, at least, good reason to think that what is
true of these prime studies may prove as true of a controlled initial exploration into our tradition. But, of course, if this best
order is to be made effective we must find ways of handing the
initiative to the learner himself. Nothing resembling any survey
course in the history of literature is being here proposed.

What we must do instead is to prepare special versions of the
first great works: the launchings of our culture, the master springs,
and arrange them in the sequences that — with due support from
the reading voice — prove most awakening. I repeat this word
as a reminder that in Shelley's Cave of Inspiration (*Prometheus
Unbound,* III, iii, 113), itself a replaying of the Cave of
the Nymphs (*Odyssey,* XIII) and not without an echo of *The
Republic* (514): "in the midst / A fountain leaps with an awakening sound." What we should be doing in this initiation into literature is devising opportunities for inspiration. In a very deep
sense we should be attempting a re-minding.

These special versions — some of them, the *Iliad* and the earliest sources in the Old Testament, for example, will be of literature which predates writing — must, of course, be designed with
due care, with the sort of varied awarenesses, preveniences, and
concern, that we expect in say, heart or brain surgery, or from
those who stand behind space-vehicle launchings. For what is at
stake in these experiments in cultural engineering is plainly of
incomparably greater importance than any individual's continuance as living or than the timing of a scientific advance. It is the
quality of the human future that they will endeavor to improve
and protect. That this is so must, I believe, be admitted by all
who know what a great book is. What we offer in this initiation

must be rightly chosen and shaped. So, too, must the conduct of
the voices which read them. As to just how the choices are to be
made, the versions be written, and the inspiration proved, we may
fairly appeal to what has been recently learned of the role
of experimentation on an adequate scale in other explorations —
spatial and biological, for example.

What we will, practically, have most to beware of is — to
recur to the theme of my opening paragraph — gain-seeking, dis-
tractive ballyhoo. And here is what Partridge in *Origins* has to say
about this word.

> *bally,* coll euphemism for expletive *bloody,* owes something to the
> boisterous village of Ballyhooly (in County Cork) whence AE coll
> *ballyhoo,* noisy preliminary publicity, whence AE *hooey,* bunkum.
> See BUNCOMBE.

> *buncombe,* insincere speech — hence insincere talk, hence non-
> sense; in C20 usu *bunkum,* whence, byabbr, *bunk*: Buncombe, that
> county in North Carolina which was represented (1819–21) by
> Felix Walker; persisting in long-winded speech, he said that his
> electors expected him to 'make a speech for Buncombe' (Webster.)

As the current term puts it: *Madison Avenue.* If that were somehow avoided (those that know most about the media will be most
doubtful here) a hooey-free enterprise matching in rectitude and
scale of effort the sending of a probe to Jupiter could set going
what is needed: a planet-widespread awareness of human nature
deep enough to keep man from wrecking himself.

Upon what literature might be most helpful it is possible to be
fairly specific in exemplification. Any attempt as yet to lay out a
full program would be premature, but some main principles of a
due selection are evident enough. The two great confluents of our
culture (its taproots, if you like), the Hellenic and the Hebraic,
must be represented, each with its major internal tensions, since
these give to each its own unique propelling drive and create between them their perpetual conflict, collaboration, and mutual
control: "the balance or reconcilement of opposite or discord-
ant qualities."

For the Hellenic stream the major internal tension is that between the *Iliad* and the Socratic dialogues, between, we might say,
Achilles and Socrates as hero-models for man. In countless ways

Homer, "the educator of Greece," embodies the opposites of the designs Plato offers for the individual (man or woman) and for the State. Plato's models, as Werner Jaeger shows so amply in his *Paideia,* amount to the invention (or discovery, if you prefer) of conception, capable of growth and propagation, of what the human endeavor should be. It is a conception that has stood in strong contrast to those obtaining in other cultures, over which it is today extending its transforming rule so widely. Plato's design is opposed to the Homeric world — as plus is to minus, and, for that reason, deeply dependent. Without Homer to depart from there could have been no Plato. And within and behind Plato's models much that is Homeric lives on. Nations, for example, remain appallingly Achillean.

We may note, as closely relevant to our purpose, that the Homeric-Platonic opposition corresponds with, and is largely resultant from, the transformation of a preliterate culture into one that has become extraordinarily responsive to writing. Eric Havelock (in his *Preface to Plato*) has well described these changes — with a discernment and realization of their consequences which is, as compared with the opinions of Marshall McLuhan, again as plus is to minus. A reflective reader of Plato is, beside an Ion, a system of vastly extended capacities. Nonetheless, the new culture can encompass the Homeric order, though its judgment of that will be different. As I write far more than half the human population are trying to accomplish an analogous transition. What proportion of them are failing, and thereby being left mentally nowhere, no one knows. It is most probably huge. They are attempting to pass from inevitably polluted and decaying preliterate cultures to some sort of substitute carried less by living example and custom than by radio and TV commercials and by cinema — media which are at present providing what amount to travesties, gross wrenchings of derivatives from the Hellenic tradition. And, nearer home than Africa, it is with this dauntingly crucial transition — from preliteracy to the ads, from sets of mores conveyed mainly by word of mouth and parental example to what TV, cinema, and pulp offer in its place — that our new megalopolitan populations are supposed to *cope.* (Here again, the etymon is not encouraging: *cope,* v [to deal adequately with] ME *coupen:* OF *couper, colper,* to hit, strike, from *coup,* a blow, [powerful]

stroke . . . from LL *colaphus,* a kick, a cuff or a punch. *Origins.*)
And many bemused citizens wonder why the crime rate is rising.
A. F.B.I.-recorded 80 percent increase in reported rapes in the
first six months of 1971 in Washington, D.C., is surely a sufficient
portent. The traditional, large, personal channels have been
broken, and the assaulters now have less than nothing (only
minus exemplars) to guide them. (My pen, which seems sometimes to be trying to help with its *lapsus calami* interventions, has
been writing *unletted* when I intended *unlettered!* Its point, I take
it, is that WRAGG is not in custody.)

The other great confluent (indeed more often the major stream)
of what was our culture — the Hebraic — is, for very mixed reasons, less easily outlined. Countless Bibles hide in hotel drawers
and spread-eaglewise adorn lecterns in places of worship; but
what impact their contents still have grows ever harder to assess.
Nor is it in the least an easier matter to judge the values, past or
present, of most items in their content. Blake ventured the view
that "The strongest poison ever known / Came from *Caesar's
Laurel crown."* There have been some who have held that *"Jacob
on his own"* might be a wiser suggestion. And many other odd
examples are exalted in Holy Writ. Much in it has been regard-
lessly distorted by doctrinal concern. Hardly any of its multi-
farious ingredients have not been mercilessly misused: forced by
contending parties to serve opposing purposes and given by
superbly equipped scholars quite incompatible interpretations.
Nonetheless — and this is why Coleridge called it *The Statesman's Manual* — there is no literature and no enchiridion from
which more that most deeply matters has been, and perhaps still
can be, learned. And this can be admitted even by those ready to
charge the Bible for much that has been atrocious in the conduct
of its adherents. Not all lessons are beneficial. Attempts to restore
some knowledge of the Bible through intelligent reading via the
media must reckon not only with its fearsome powers but with
much further probable misuse. The protection is that no literature
better shows how equally compelling opposed views of it can be.

For example, the greatest confluent of the Old Testament, the
Book of Job, consists of a verse drama enclosed in a folk-tale
prose frame. First-order authorities have upheld every possible
theory of the relations — chronologic, thematic, dramatic, theo-

logic — of the poem to its frame. All that is agreed upon by all is that both are preeminent: each unmatched in its kind by anything else in the literatures of the world. There has been, however, growing agreement among scholars of the last century or so that these two masterpieces are irreconcilably incompatible in the extremest degree. There is a victim, named Job, in both; but these victims are radically opposed in character; one proverbially patient, the other rebellious beyond limit. Moreover, their circumstances and their afflictions are very different and neither knows anything about the other's situation or sufferings. Further, their afflictors are as diverse as the victims: a supersheik in the folk tale; a cosmic creator in the poem. Lastly, the endings the two offer are as apart as any can be. None of all which has, however, prevented the Book of Job from being presented and received by pastors and their flocks as a single harmonious work through over a score of changing centuries. And this strange state of affairs, in varying measure, is the case with much else in the literatures comprised in both testaments.

We would be mistaken, though, I suggest, were we to conclude that such uncertainty makes the greatest works in the Bible unsuited for study by the unlettered, if we can contrive, through reading via the media, to return them (unruined) to the general consciousness. The truth, as I see it, is that we have nothing to take their place. And nothing that can make their successors so intelligible. The Bible, however understood, has been the source in them of too much — excellences and defects alike — for any to read them discerningly without it.

And, we must recall, we must restore and retain the inexhaustible interinanimations (Donne's word) of the Hellenic and Hebraic confluences: the interplay of themes common to both, though with what differences of handling. To consider the brothers' account of injustice at the outset of book two of the *Republic* along with Job's arraignment of existence is to be offered a peculiarly entire view of the central problem of living. It is a preparation, to be gained in no other way, for seeing it as later masters, as Shakespeare and Donne, Marvell and Milton, Wordsworth and Arnold have seen it, and for facing it as we ourselves must meet it. Squanderers of inestimable energies, let us devote some of them to opening such opportunities to all.

CLARA CLAIBORNE PARK

Rejoicing to Concur with the Common Reader: The Uses of Literature in the Community College

> As a general rule, people, even the
> wicked, are much more naïve and
> simplehearted than we suppose. And we
> ourselves are too.
>
> Fyodor Dostoevsky,
> *The Brothers Karamazov*

> Until I came to college there wasn't a
> lamp in the house you could read by.
>
> Community College sophomore

The first literature I taught in a community college was in an old-fashioned great books course. Its reading list was frankly copied from that of a course at that time required of all sophomores at the University of Massachusetts. Our own college was only in its second year of operation, and it was both easy and helpful to suit our courses to the institution many of our students hoped to transfer to. Accordingly, I began with Homer, the Oedipus plays, the dialogues in which Plato tells of Socrates's trial and death. It was after this Greek exposure, while we were reading the *Inferno,* that an incident occurred that has come to embody for me the special quality of teaching literature in a community college.

The student was not one who often talked in class, although he

225

was not especially diffident. He was a well-set-up young man from a farm family who liked to hunt and who did his school work the best he could, which was not well. He expressed himself in short, simple units of meaning — some of them were sentences and some were not — and he could spell most of the words he knew. When he was assigned something to read, he slowly read it, and occasionally, as today, he said something about it. "Mrs. Park. We've read what Homer says about the afterlife, and what Plato says, and now we're reading what Dante says and they're all different. Mrs. Park, *which of them is true?*"

I smile, of course. I suppress, just in time, the condescending laugh, the easy play to the class's few sophisticates, who are already laughing surreptitiously. They are good students; they ask a lot of questions; I depend on them and they know it. They have reliable academic instincts, which are at the moment informing them that this is not one of the questions one asks. But the open seriousness on this boy's face encourages reflection. Who, in this class, is reading as Plato and Dante would have expected to be read? Who is asking the right questions? I and my sophisticates, or this D-level student whom I have just time to realize I shall put down at my peril? Did I really mean my students to assent to the proposition that nothing need be true where everything is interesting?

I have never taught literature in an elite college, but I went to one. This experience could not have taken place there. Such naïveté as surfaces in the kind of college I went to is generally false. The real kind subsists, of course. But elite students hide it even from each other; they almost never expose it to their teachers. What I have learned from teaching in a community college is this: that real naïveté is precious, and that it sets up changing expectations, and changing opportunities, for the teaching of literature.

Echoing in this incident are most of the things that make teaching in a community college different from teaching at Harvard. It is obvious that class background matters here, and that in most ways it is going to translate itself into what we advantaged ones call "cultural disadvantage." (Roughly two-thirds of our freshmen, categorized according to the usual sociological criteria, are working class and lower class; most of the rest are lower-middle class.) It is obvious that the culturally disadvantaged will be culturally naïve. It is obvious that the nonhomogeneity of the class, the presence of the few sophisticates, presents a complex situation, and perhaps it is obvious that it is a promising one. It is less obvious — until one has repeatedly experienced it, when it comes to seem self-evident — that the culturally naïve have an intense interest in eschatology, in what Ivan Karamazov called "the eternal questions." It is less obvious that they — not all of them, but a surprising number — see their teacher as a wise person who can help them understand important things. It is perhaps least obvious that they should expect that literature can bring them important things, that what they read can matter in the way that other elements in their surroundings matter: that it can offer them something they can use. A simple assumption, simply made: that literature has uses, like other things in life. It is a loaded simplicity. One can almost imagine it turning cultural disadvantage to cultural advantage.

In graduate school I had a young professor — he is now a respected old one — who argued passionately against censorship. He did not argue that it was wrong (no doubt he took that for granted) but that it was unnecessary. Why should society censor literature, since literature did not influence action? Which of you, he asked his students, would actually go out and do something because of something you read? I remember feeling doubtful, but I do not recall that any of us objected.

It is probably clear that this discussion took place twenty-five years ago. The New Criticism was then in fact new, the work of art self-contained and sovereign, the artist's life and his intentions irrelevant, and the intentions and lives of us readers as well. The idea that literature affected action was represented by the crudities of the Soviet police and the remembered Nazis, and the unsophisticated directness of the Renaissance critics whom, as a matter of fact, we were then studying. They lived a long time ago, before the "rise of the historical attitude" and of that other convenient distancing mechanism, the minute concern with language. Ideas persist, however, and those who were trained twenty-five years ago are influential teachers today. Ellen Cantarow, in "The Radicalizing of a Teacher of Literature," attributes a similar complex of attitudes to her professors:

At Wellesley what I read moved me deeply; in so many words I was told that my feelings didn't matter, that it was "form" that did. What I read often moved me to reflect on my own experience; I was told essentially that literature was timeless, above the petty details of any one person's daily living. I loved literature; when I reached graduate school I was given to understand that loving literature had nothing to do with literary professionalism. I dimly felt that literature must give life exaltation, specific moral sense; I was told that Western civilization dictated the values of pure form, of "universality."[1]

Was it really that bad? Hard to believe; she can't have been taught exclusively by mandarins. Nevertheless, a 1971 Harvard Ph.D. experienced seven years of some of the finest English teaching in the country and came out feeling like that. Is it possible that she would have been better off if she had started off in a community college? There the simplicity of our students, combined with our own survival instincts, must contradict each of these assumptions. Years before we began hearing it from blacks and movement theorists, our students instructed us in the guiding assumption of this collection: that literature has uses, and that these are at the heart of its interest and excitement.

They did not teach us that it has revolutionary uses. That will not surprise anyone who has had experience of students from the lower and lower-middle class. (Perhaps urban blacks are different.) Revolutionary ideas are abstractions, and the attitude that has brought most of these students to sit in our classrooms is not abstract; it is, rather, "What's in this for me?" Literature for them will offer understanding of personal processes and events before it offers involvement in society or rebellion against it. Teaching in a community college can be peculiarly discouraging to the radical teacher, who if he is sensitive becomes aware that he is listening to his own voice rather than his students' and pulling them in a direction they do not wish to go. The uses of literature are for them, as they were for Cantarow before she was radicalized, primarily personal.

The directness of its personal application can be disconcerting as well as instructive. After the publication of *The Sorrows of*

1. *Change* (May 1972).

Young Werther there was a wave of suicides; that is one of the curiosities of literary history that one knows without believing it. We do not take these deaths into any real account when we hear about them in our course, The Romantic Movement: they are felt as somewhat ridiculous, if they are felt at all, unconvincing as the suicides in *Zuleika Dobson*. What shouldn't have occurred can't have. Contemporary distancing mechanisms work better than that; contemporary readers know the difference between life and literature.

Yet in my community college, within a fortnight of finishing *The Myth of Sisyphus,* the finale to a rather dryly taught introductory philosophy course, one very capable student passed in a blank final, two dropped out of school, one attempted suicide, accounting for 25 percent of the total class enrollment. If you take it seriously, the absurdity of all human effort is a profoundly disturbing idea. The moral of this is not, I suppose, that we should drop Camus from the reading list and substitute Bill Haywood's autobiography, which though more optimistic, seems to have bored Ms. Cantarow's students, but that we should prepare ourselves for the power that literature may have among students whom familiarity has not rendered immune to ideas found in books.

How would we teach literature if we were in fact convinced not only that for one reason or another it mattered in our own lives, the lives of a highly educated elite, but that it can matter in the lives of students? Most of the changing functions of literature in mass education follow from this question. If new claims are made on literature in a community college, they are new only in the sense that they are made by, or on behalf of, a population who before this made few claims on literature at all. In fact, these claims are very old, so old that perhaps it is time to recognize that disuse has made them new again. What the culturally disadvantaged expect of literature, when they expect anything at all, is very like what the culturally advantaged used to expect in the days of Sidney and Johnson and Arnold, and learned to stop expecting only in the very recent past. Un-self-conscious and old-fashioned readers, they expect "just representations of general nature," which will help them understand their own lives and the world more truly.

It is easy to romanticize the community college student. I can already feel my tone turning Wordsworthian, with a corresponding loss in credibility. A class at a community college does not, of course, consist entirely or even preponderantly of students to whom literature matters. Many have never thought about literature at all, have read only what they were forced to in high school, hear rock music but don't listen to the words. Most of them have come to college expecting that what goes on there will help them to get a better job than they would otherwise. They are for the most part willing to believe that the English requirement will contribute to this end. Reading and writing may be unpracticed activities, but they are what you do in school, and for the first time these students are in school because they've chosen to come. If they don't like it they'll drop out; they haven't come to rebel, or question fundamentally the value of education, which, like literature, is an abstraction of a kind they don't think about. But they will impose their assumptions, which in their simplicity have a certain self-fulfilling quality: since these students are here because they think something's in it for them, literature rises — or sinks — to the occasion.

It is hardly necessary to state that the community college is not an English teacher's paradise and would not be even if pay scales, course loads, student-teacher ratios, and fringe benefits were comparable to those at good four-year colleges. The opportunities afforded by working with students new to literature are balanced by frustrations. Simplicity is, if not always, often the more attractive face of what it is hard not to call stupidity, although we who are involved in mass education commonly find gentler words. There are plenty of times when our students' limitations make us feel we have spent the day being nibbled to death by ducks. In brief, we teach literature to students whose CEEB verbals range from 300 all the way up, but which cluster between 400 and 500. Any one of us is capable of writing an essay on the deceptiveness of board scores, embellished with an impressive group of sketches from life. Nevertheless, college board verbals reliably predict a number of discouraging facts: that a large, though variable, number of our students will read slowly and inaccurately, that their writing will be labored, crude, and incorrect, and that without our help, and probably not even with it, they will neither make nor understand the distinctions and freighted allusions which are the life of language. They are aware of few of the public events of the present or the past. Their interests are narrow, although if it is opportunity and not choice which has narrowed them, they may broaden with a rapidity which astonishes the teacher and may terrify the student, who feels himself changing into someone he can hardly recognize. For community college students have a final handicap, which both measures their receptivity and checks it: for them, education is a perilous undertaking. It will not, as it does for second-generation college students, confirm them in the assured performance of roles they know and understand. It will act to change them and thus to separate them from the life in which they have been at home.

It is exactly those to whom the new experiences mean most who are most vulnerable to what is happening to them and most aware of what they have to lose. Marjorie Fallows, who teaches sociology at my college, has collected a number of statements of such students, "threatened," in her words, "by the loss of the familiar without having acquired the confidence that they can adapt to the unfamiliar."[2] "I didn't have any idea college was going to be like this. I thought you just went to college and stayed the same, except for having a diploma, but it wrenches you away from a lot of familiar things and people." Or, "I wish I could talk with my parents about what I'm doing in college. Perhaps they're not interested, but it's more like they're afraid of what I'm learning. They have a pretty rigid view of the world, and they aren't articulate. So we don't talk, because it would end up in a fight or in somebody's being hurt. Some of the kids have had to break completely with their parents but I'm trying not to do that. I still love them, even though I don't want to be like them." Or, "My back is to the wall and I'm scared because I'm out of my depth, and not just academically. This is a whole new world for me. I don't talk the same language, even. I was top in my class in vocational high school, and I think I'm bright enough to have done college work, but something's getting in the way. I don't belong. If I'm not in class some day, you'll know I couldn't take it any longer."

2. "The Junior College Social Experiment: The Relationship Between Social Status and Academic Success," *Commonweal*, October 7, 1966.

These people know something is happening to them. They are changing so fast it hurts, like the growth that Günter Grass's Tin Drummer experienced as his midget's body wrenched its way into maturity. Some of them flee the experience and drop back into the familiar — the attrition rate at community colleges is very large. But many will see it through and allow themselves to become different people.

How would we teach literature if we were in fact convinced that what we were doing could make a person different? Most of us do believe, I think, that education changes people, although we believe it with that kind of sickly hesitance we accord to ideas which we want so much to be true that we feel we must consider them false. Such compulsive cynicism is shaken again and again in a community college. By the time a dozen human lives have taken right-angle turns before your eyes, you begin to believe your job is worth doing. Where you are, hope has been institutionalized. Being at this college can make all the difference to this student. Not that we don't think Harvard makes a difference. But behind this conviction (which most of us who went to Harvard would affirm) is the consciousness that if it hadn't been Harvard it would have been Amherst, and if it hadn't been Amherst it would have been Reed or Carleton, or if we'd been less lucky, a state university, and that though each of these would have moved us differently, we would have gone on to a life in which approximately the same set of possibilities lay open. The community college alters possibilities — not only the objective options before a student, but his whole sense of what is possible for him. His life will be spent differently because he happened to come to college.

"Happened" is the word; adventitiousness is the point. For this population, coming to college is not inevitable, it is a function of cheapness, nearness, convenience, unimpressiveness — qualities which add up to physical, economic, but above all emotional availability. A student comes in from a thin Irish welfare childhood, from vocational school and the service; he hopes to rise to be a salesman. Silent and invisible in the back rows of his classes, he begins to metamorphose. For months, only the librarian notices him, sitting in the library reading *Masterplots*. Too diffident to consult his teachers on how to nurture his new excitement, he seeks out his own ways of catching up, surfacing a year later transformed from a marginal to an exceptional student — of, of all things, literature. But changed possibilities need not be measured by intellectual values and academic futures (this man married a black woman and has just taken his M.A.T. at the University of Illinois). Another student comes in expecting to follow an admired father into the roofing business. What he learns wrenches daily his acceptance of Archie Bunker's values. He goes exploring at the University of Massachusetts, passes beyond irritation and contempt to understand his father more fully, graduates, to return home to the roofing business, but with three cartons of books and a mind enlarged and excited so that he can follow it as a respected occupation, not resent it as a prison. Such capsule histories, though accurate, betray the rich particularity of these students' lives, and thus their quality of miracle. In the community college we assist continually at such miracles (whether we assist in the French or the English sense one never knows). I could fill this essay with such accounts, most of them less credible than these two, which were chosen particularly because neither of these students seemed in any way distinguished when we first encountered him.[3]

The needs of people like this affect how we use literature, when we find out how deeply they are going to use it. "I must have read that poem fifty times," the first student told me. "I *am* J. Alfred Prufrock." And Eliot's image of inadequacy and isolation stayed with him, to help him confront and surmount his own. The second student *was* Achilles — or whatever other splendid image of self-destructive pride we happened to be studying. Achilles was right to stand up for his honor and his prize, for what he'd earned and had coming to him. Archie Bunker knows that. But he was wrong, too, and he found it out by suffering. It's a complex world we have to live in.

What are teachers to do with this realization, at first resisted as arrogant and rejected as incredible: that they participate in a

3. It is less misleading than it appears to talk of students who go on to four-year institutions after the community college's two years. Of those who finish the two-year course at our college about two-thirds transfer, some to elite colleges they would not otherwise have reached. The ranking graduate of Amherst's class of 1972 had transferred from Berkshire Community College.

process that changes lives? How come to terms with this new role: that of persons of influence, whose students will take seriously not only what we have told them to read but what we say about it, and about them? "Nobody expected me to go to college, and I didn't expect to go. Then the community college opened up and about five of us began tossing around the idea of whether to go or not. We finally flipped a coin. It was college or the service. College won out, but we expected to flunk out pretty quick. All my friends did flunk out. I'm the only one left. But something happened to me here. One of my teachers wrote on a paper, 'You have a good clear mind — use it!' It made me sit back and think."

Given such students, then, what and how do we teach? But things are more complicated than that. We are not simply given such students. We are given many such. Yet a community college is not more homogeneous than the ivy league, but less so. Where I teach, students are mostly white, mostly young, mostly conservative though mostly Democratic, mostly Irish, Italian, Polish or French Canadian if they come from the city, mostly wasp if they come from the hills about, in which case they aren't very waspish.[4] Most share the values that are commonly traduced by the term "Middle American." Yet the class profile is characterized by the obtrusiveness of its variations from this norm, in age, in intelligence, in social and cultural background. Many of our most rewarding students are people who have returned in middle life to enjoy the education that has suddenly become available within commuting distance.[5] Most of these, though not all, are women; they include ex-salesgirls, ex-secretaries, and executives' wives who married young. Among the working-class students, most commonly the ex-servicemen, are autodidacts whose commitment to high culture is more intense than their teachers' and who press us for classical languages and Pound. There are failed preppies and dropouts from prestige colleges. There are even ordinary,

4. Leonard Kriegel's "When Blue-Collar Students Go to College" (*Saturday Review,* July 22, 1972) gives an excellent picture of our students. His experience is based on Brooklyn, while mine is of a small-city college drawing from a large rural area. It doesn't seem to matter.
5. "Enjoy" is the word. For an excellent presentation of the special qualities of these returned students, see Thomas J. Cottle's "College at Middle Age," *Change* (Summer 1972).

capable high school graduates. Such students contribute a rich variety of assumptions and experience; what do they need from us, and what can they use from literature? They would seem to have little in common, but there is one characteristic they share: a near-crippling sense of inadequacy. We have few confident students. That the "below average" will come in with a sense of failure is obvious (the Illinois M.A.T. was one of these). But even the "average" have no high opinion of themselves. Progressive admissions deans may remind us that the 500 college board score is set to predict the capacity to do college work, but these students have had to do not with progressive admissions deans (who in any case would overlook their undistinguished scores only for unusual reasons), but with a high school milieu in which kids with 600's can complain that they are not good enough for a good college. Few of these average students have been treated in school as if they were either interesting or important. The older students fear they have lost whatever academic ability they had and can never compete with "all these bright young minds," while the autodidacts and the conspicuously talented are, paradoxically, the most uncertain of all.

Of course, we can only grope to meet these needs. For some, one accepts the imprecise answer, encourages the vague adumbration. For others, the relaxation of standards confirms their own self-doubt, and what they most need is that insistence on excellence which testifies to intellectual respect. What all need is continuing support for that sense of possibility which their life histories have not supported.

It is all very personal — their relationship to us, ours to them, both of ours to literature. I can write case histories because I know what happens to my students after they leave, and I know because they come back, or write, and tell me. I learn about them through how they respond to what they read, and how they respond teaches me new things about literature. An intelligent and perceptive student of mine titled her paper on the Odyssey "Telemachus and My Boy Friend." The teacher who finds this intrinsically ludicrous will be out of place in a community college. He may comfort himself with irony and steady his nerves with put-downs, but to no avail. None of us can beat it; most of us join it. When we do we find our understanding enriched as we learn from our students to read Homer as the Greeks did, as a paradigm of human experience. "Soldiers shall never spend their idle hours more profitably than with his studious and industrious perusal . . . Counsellors have never better oracles than his lines: fathers have no morals so profitable for their children as his counsels . . . husbands, wives, lovers, friends, and allies having in him mirrors for all their duties." The Greeks and the Elizabethans, who were not stupider than ourselves: so Chapman, in his Preface to Homer.

We in the community college have little choice but to emulate that antique simplicity. We hold on to subtlety, or try to, to precision, to elegance, to linguistic astonishment. We can never predict which students may unexpectedly be ready to respond to language and to form. These, too, are necessary to survival, for our own sakes and because the autodidacts and prestige dropouts, out to prove themselves superior to their surroundings, will not be easy on a teacher they feel is talking down to them, or who has the misfortune to be slower than they. But not all literary virtues need be displayed with equal prominence. Our students can use synthesis better than analysis — or rather, all close reading must be clearly in the service of synthesis. (Ponder this comment: "I really enjoyed listening to you tear those poems to pieces." That was an analysis that succeeded.)

The praise of simplicity may even expand to include the praise of superficiality; it is Goethe who reminds us that art deals with life's surfaces. A simple insistence on the importance of what happens, of event and character, is not only reassuring to weak students, but one of the most valuable things we can give our intellectual elite, who tend to try to prove their status by interpretive ingenuity. Consider Eric Bentley's warning: "In principle the drama presents human relationships — the things men do to each other — and nothing else. Other things are not presented on stage, but if 'there' at all, are merely implied. In *King Lear,* much is *implied* about Nature and the gods, but *presented* on stage are a king and his subjects, a father and his children. Dramatic criticism emphasizes the implications at its peril. Had those been the writer's chief interest, he would not have chosen the dramatic form."[6] Accepting this, we will have more patience with students who have difficulty dealing with abstractions. Reading for the

6. *The Life of the Drama* (New York: Atheneum, 1964), p. 63.

human event will get us farther than reading for Significance or Symbol, in the community college, and perhaps elsewhere. The realm of Minute Particulars, where our students are at home, is the realm of the imagination.

Saul Bellow suggests that "deep reading . . . has become dangerous to literature . . . Things are not what they seem . . . Coal holes represent the Underworld. Soda Crackers are the Host . . . The busy mind can hardly miss at this game, and every player is a winner. Does Bloom dust Stephen's clothes, and brush off the wood shavings? They are no ordinary shavings, but the shavings from Stephen's cross . . . Is modern literature Scripture? Is criticism Talmud, theology? . . . Let the soda crackers be soda crackers and the wood shavings, wood shavings. They are mysterious enough as it is."[7] Bellow complains that "it's hard in our time to be as innocent as one would like." Teaching in a community college helps a great deal.

Simplicity need not mean narrowness. The work of art leads out from its personal meanings, from "Telemachus and My Boy Friend" to the great theme of growth and initiation. Abstractions are neither inaccessible nor uninteresting when they inhere in the human event.[8] Through Hamlet and Edmund students can *feel* that new philosophy calls all in doubt, even if they don't *know* it. I was teaching *Dr. Faustus* the day the astronauts first went up. We had just read, "But his dominion that exceeds in this / Stretches as far as does the mind of man." That class was not mired in the particular; we felt the winds of the Renaissance blowing. What had changed since Dante, so that the devil and not God now offered knowledge? Why was he now an interesting and sympathetic companion, when Dante had found him less worth talking to than the most ordinary Florentine in Hell? Is knowledge good in itself? Why might it be forbidden? Have we a right or a duty to follow it wherever it leads? "A sound magician is a mighty god"; how do men play god? Marlowe damns Faustus; should he? Should space be explored, life created in the laboratory?

7. "Deep Readers of the World, Beware!" *New York Times Book Review*, February 15, 1959.
8. The uses of literature in the community college are not confined, of course, to English courses. Fiction is prominent on sociology and psychology reading lists.

Our students have not gone stale on the eternal questions. They will wrangle for hours over the tension between God's foreknowledge and man's free will as *Paradise Lost* takes on an immediacy I never suspected when I was studying for my comprehensives. Teaching them we practice perforce what George Steiner calls "the old criticism," as we try to convey the warmth of ideas, the ways in which they inform personality and are formed by it. "Engendered in admiration," concerned with moral purpose, "above all philosophical in range and temper," the job of the old criticism is (here Steiner quotes R. P. Blackmur) "putting the audience into a responsive relationship with the work of art . . . the job of the intermediary."[9] And Steiner's summation is a guideline for teaching in a community college: "Not to judge or to anatomize, but to mediate." What works in a community college — and the word *work* should make us think of yeast as well as of successful operation — is what Alfred Harbage sees in Shakespeare crossing every frontier: "the pervasive tone of human solicitude."[10]

Harbage is discussing the attraction of Shakespeare for non-English-speaking readers; Steiner is beginning a book on two authors he can read only in translation, conscious that the play of their language is closed to him and yet that they still fill him with things he needs to say. A teacher new to us and fresh from a good Ph.D. program remarked that he'd never before seen teachers enthusiastic about a humanities course; didn't we feel that the fact of translation hampered our resouces? These reflections lead to a principle which most of us will accept only with pain: to the degree that the meaning of a work inheres so tightly in the language that it would not survive translation, that text will not work in the usual community college class. That is what those low board scores *mean*. Many of our students cannot read a complex text with comprehension unless they look up more words than most of us have to when we read French — only they think they know their own language and are not at home with dictionaries. They are not sure enough of denotation, let alone connotation, to pick up verbal irony. They have trouble pronouncing

9. *Tolstoy or Dostoevsky* (New York: Knopf, 1959), p. 6; *The Lion and the Honeycomb* (New York: Harcourt Brace, 1955), pp. 185f.
10. "Shakespeare East and West," *Harvard Today* (May 1972), p. 4.

long words or finding their way through complicated sentences, though they will respond to eloquence if well mediated — that is, read well aloud. Their weaknesses, and strengths, call for some redefinition of what is difficult reading. Jane Austen and Henry James are harder than Milton or Goethe.

Language and class combine to make this true. I taught *Emma* that first year, blindly following the university's reading list for Masterpieces of Western Lit. For the first time, protests surfaced: why are we reading *this?* They had just finished *Faust* without complaining. But *Faust,* and *Lear,* and *Paradise Lost* had not excluded them as *Emma* did, where every character in whose life they were expected to interest themselves was a person for whom they could guess that they and theirs would not have existed even as fully as one of Shakespeare's clowns.

In order to teach Jane Austen or Henry James successfully, one would have to mediate a whole class system. (Howells goes much better.) Asked to name his "least favorite successful writer," Anthony Burgess named E. M. Forster. "People like Virginia Woolf and E. M. Forster belong to a kind of society which I can't understand, I can't possibly touch, and fundamentally loathe. I find it makes my flesh creep to even consider touching any member of that class. It's as physical as that. I can't help it, can't justify it, but there it is; it's just another world."[11] Our students, less self-confident and in a society less savagely class ridden, are more tolerant. They just "can't relate." Of course they can't. Would we give *Howards End* to Leonard Bast?

Yet — taking plenty of time — I have taught *A Passage to India* with success. And this tells us something not entirely obvious about the uses of literature in the community college: the far away, like the long ago, may be easier, not harder, to relate to. Where differences in manners are extreme they can be confronted and recognized, leaving the attention free for deeper similarities. Remoteness in space and time need not confer emotional distance. Where all seems strange, accidents of manner subside into place. Our students may dismiss Emma as a snob, and miss the touching vulnerability of Salinger's Esmé, but no one dismisses Antigone, though she is a king's daughter. They

11. Interviewed by Michael Newman, *Book World,* March 21, 1971.

will identify with King Oedipus and Prince Hamlet. If they are not hurried or badgered with information on epic conventions, they will recognize in Hector not the aristocratic warrior of a legend they didn't know existed, but a steadfast exponent of middle-American values such as the literature of their own time refuses to accord them, a responsible citizen who loves his wife and baby and who fights when his country asks him to, even when he knows it's wrong. Which is to suggest that truisms about beginning with the students' own experience can be easily misapplied. Most of the books we call "great" — in a phrase more dated even than "the New Criticism" — are less bewildering to the average community college student than *Naked Lunch* or *Armies of the Night.*

This is perhaps no more than to say that old-fashioned readers respond to old-fashioned books. And immersion in the old-fashioned encourages old-fashioned pronouncements; as one of my students once told me, we read the classics for their universality and because they have stood the test of time. In the community college they are one solution (only one) to the problems posed by class variety. Great books, as I found out one by one, teaching that first, arbitrary list, are gut books, perennial archetypes of human effort and desire, survivors that have offered something for everybody. One student tells another, "You wouldn't *believe* what happens to that guy Oedipus." Another takes his *Odyssey* home and his father, just retired off the assembly line, finds it the best story he's ever read. *The Iliad,* that morally and emotionally most complex of works, has a special intelligibility for athletes and Vietnam veterans. Dante holds the class elite; they respond to the ordered beauty of his passionate vision, they are interested in medieval and renaissance attitudes, they are satisfied to be reading a classic. They may also learn something from the simple souls who can entertain the possibility that what he says is true.

There will be no Brechtian distancing in the classroom; students transparently identify with what they read. When they can recognize themselves in a character, class and language hinder no longer. Esmé and Emma may be dismissed, but identification with Prufrock can be so strong among lower-class students as to cause a problem in interpretation: they may argue, on the

strength of the one-night cheap hotels, that Prufrock's elegant
attire is all a charade and that he is a social as well as an emotional outsider. Identification can make Joyce and Milton accessible. I took over *Portrait of the Artist* for that first reading list
before I had reread it, and when I did I was appalled at what I had
done. How could I expect insecure students, many of them of
marginal competence, to sympathize with this arrogant young
intellectual, hermetically sealed inside his egotism, his mind full
of words they wouldn't recognize and allusions they would never
trace? But they did; they were Catholic, or had been, ethnic,
young, self-centered — if not all of them all of these, still enough.
They understood the book much better than I had at their age.
They helped me read it better, too; their sympathy taught me a
little mercy.

Other surprises cause us to reevaluate our ideas of literary
relevance. Oedipus's is an archetypal predicament (though our
students perceive Sophocles's archetype, not Freud's). Bartleby,
like Prufrock, hits home. But who could predict the pull of Milton's Satan? Yet when one of my apparently most impervious
students came in at last to talk, it was because after days of Satan
in his pride, we had come to the place in Book IV where the sight
of Adam and Eve "imparadis'd in one another's arms" strips him
emotionally naked, to see "undelighted all delight." "I feel like
that," said this student. "It's like I was sitting on the top floor of
a house" (students often translate a poet's image into their own;
I feel less confident than I used to about stopping them) "and
I'm looking out and there's this bunch of children playing, and I
can't feel anything at all."

This student was brilliant, and deeply disturbed; two years
later he was diagnosed as schizophrenic. But the next year the
same passage brought in a student neither brilliant nor crazy,
just conscious of a split between home and the future, who found
that Milton's ambivalence toward an angel's rebellion expressed
his own awareness of what it cost to challenge values that were
still part of him. Our students know better than those more privileged that life pulls in contradictory ways. Though the poverty of
their linguistic means makes verbal irony inaccessible to most of
them, they can respond perceptively and intensely to ambiguities
of content.

From such revelatory encounters we learn new powers of the works we teach. We may shy away from this particular use of literature, as a diagnostic indicator of psychic turbulence. But it is thrust upon us. We can hardly be unaware that literature can bring the hidden to light; gut books expose the guts. When this happens, students look for somebody to talk to. If their approach to literature is personal, and ours has reflected it, they are likely to end up talking to us. They have a lot to talk about. The strains of social mobility are an evident source of distress, but there are many others. The conspicuously talented show most signs of psychic tension. For the truly gifted, the community college has functioned as a kind of sieve, selecting those and only those who are in some sort of need. Our society is open enough, as most European societies are not, so that a brilliant person who has handled his life sensibly rarely ends up in a third-rate educational institution. Accordingly, when a fine mind turns up in one of our classes it is usually after a series of emotional shipwrecks and disastrous choices which have left him as much in need of support as the most marginal academic loser.

The involuntary functioning of the English teacher as a mental health paraprofessional is only the extreme consequence of accepting the proposition that literature leads to life. Taking literature personally means teaching personally, and if you do that, the problem — quite insoluble — becomes simply where to stop. Community college students need their teachers even more than students do elsewhere. A commuting college cuts out the usual opportunities for bull sessions, particularly since most community college students have jobs. A two-year college with a large enrollment is hard to make friends in. It is harder still for the gifted, who are thinly spread; unless the teacher becomes a kind of matchmaker, they may never find each other. So the English teacher, who has been encouraging genuineness of response since the first papers in freshman composition, reaps the predictable harvest. When the student needs a friend, a mentor, a guru, an example of a newly conceivable life style, the English teacher is on hand. He's in a false position, granted; he never prepared for this in graduate school. He can decline the honor. But if he accepts it — well, we are back where we started, in arrogance and terror, accepting the responsibility of making a difference to somebody's life. Such experiences make a difference to one's own.

That sentence sounds like the end. Yet I am driven to say more about the exceptions, who need mediation less and friendship more. One of them reads Wittgenstein and introduces me to Santayana. One memorizes all thirty-two Beethoven sonatas. One brushes up his Latin by reading Gauss. I want to tell their preposterous, unimaginable stories. That I should need so much to bring them in shows I have not told the whole truth. I have made our work sound too satisfying and ourselves too satisfied, and I have not shown how often we fail. We react with irritation to our students and ourselves, with frustration at being able to teach only a little of what we know, with rage at the ignorance that meets us daily, the stubbornness, the laziness, the times when the response is beside the point or there is no response at all. So, isolated, we return to the exceptions in their isolation, with whom we have a symbiotic relationship of desperate mutual need. With them, the uses of literature are no different from what they are in any other college. Only of course they are, for in another college we could do without each other. For them, on stolen and uncompensated time, with corresponding intensity, we teach according to their needs and ours. Spenserian allegory, Victorian poetry, *Ulysses,* Greek — the list is as unpredictable as they are. Intellectual history is important to them; so are words. With them we can study "that absolute correspondence of the term to its import" which Pater says is the condition of all good art, and feel that we are really teaching literature. But if we push through to the end of the "Essay on Style," that most elegant articulation of the claims of form, we may be startled to find that there, of all places, the claims of substance are reestablished: "Given the conditions I have tried to explain as constituting good art; — then, if it be devoted further to the increase of men's happiness, to the redemption of the oppressed, or the enlargement of our sympathies with each other, or to such presentment of new or old truth about ourselves and our relation to the world as may enoble and fortify us in our sojourn here, or immediately, as with Dante, to the glory of God, it will also be great art." Great art or not, that's the kind of thing we can use in the community college. At which point the claims of the exceptional and of the merely human come back together and we are back in the classroom making the best of things, trying to use literature simply but not stupidly, rejoicing to concur with the common reader.

Reading and Writing in a College with Open Admissions

"Would you rather read essays or short stories in our class?" I asked.

"Well . . . What would you say is the difference exactly between a short story and an essay?"

The woman speaking to me was twenty-four, a Puerto Rican living on the edge of the East Village in Manhattan, in her first year at the City College of New York. She wasn't quibbling or asking for a complex definition. "Would you say . . . exactly" meant that she was embarrassed to ask the question directly. She *didn't know,* and she wanted to know.

"I don't like reading; I never liked it in school. I like drag racing my car. Sometimes I like TV. *The Godfather,* that was a good book. It really shows how things are. But otherwise I don't like reading."

This student had been closed off from me and cold to others in his class during the beginning days of the semester. Sharply dressed, he was from Queens, the son of Italian immigrants. We were standing by his carefully polished sports car on Broadway at 134th Street. This was the first time he had spoken openly to me: he wanted to get things straight between us.

A writer for *Muhammad Speaks,* the Black Muslim newspaper, also in his first year at City College, explained to me why he wanted to be exempted from any course which included literature and the discussion of ideas.

"Our people come to a school like this only to learn technical skills. We have our own values; we know what we want to do. The school will be useful to us for one thing only: to give us the skills to do what we want to do."

"A university education will help us to find a better job," a student wrote in concluding an English department placement exam for the fall of 1972. "It will help us to have a comfortable life."

The student body at City College has changed in the last eight years. Before 1965 admission was based on a student's ranking within his high school class or on a high score on a state-wide achievement exam. From 1965 on, exceptions were made, through a program called SEEK, for residents — mostly black and Puerto Rican — of certain low-income areas of the city. In 1970 change on a grander scale began: the Open Admissions program gave every graduate of a New York high school the right to enter one of the colleges of the City University. During the two years following, City College has admitted more Open Admissions students than any other senior college within the university. A majority of this new population are whites from ethnic, nonprofessional neighborhoods. It includes SEEK students and other deprived people. One out of five speak another language better than English: these are primarily Chinese, Puerto Ricans, Haitians, East Europeans. In 1971–72 Open Admissions accounted for about half of the entering freshman class.

The only "English" required for graduation from the college is a sequence of three semester courses, called Basic Writing 1, 2, 3. (There are extra sections for students who have little experience with the language.) Students are placed within or exempted entirely from this sequence by an exam. There is no further requirement in humanities except a certain number of "core courses," which may be in art, history, music, philosophy as well as in language or literature. If a student's placement exam suggests that he cannot do college-level writing, the college asks the Basic Writing program to enable him to do it.

Those of us who are teaching in this program have found that there is little we can transfer directly from the time-honored curriculum of freshman composition, sophomore survey, English electives. The college makes a simple demand: that students be able to write acceptable exams and term papers. But many students feel no *a priori* commitment to this task — or to English literature, or to a general education of any kind. To many, the disciplines of writing well seem boring, or culturally biased, or insuperably difficult. As teachers we have needed to find out who our students are and what kinds of meaning the use of language can have for them. We have needed to develop our own ideas of what should happen in class, whenever they went beyond the college's demand. And we have needed to determine whether reading has any role in achieving these goals. Should we assign books? What kinds? No teacher I know has reached final answers to these two questions. The most this article can do is to record some experiences and experiments.

Did Adam and Eve feel the need to write, to read? Sometimes, facing my sections in Basic Writing 1 and 2 (largely Open Admissions students), I've felt that I was trying to tempt innocent people into an activity which will involve unmeasured suffering and, finally, only self-knowledge as a reward. I must choose my writing and reading assignments with painful shrewdness. First and more painful: I must shed my preconceptions which would make me unacceptable or useless to these students.

Some preconceptions: (1) An assumption that some writing is undeniably worth reading. It's clear that the traditional English syllabus is parochial, that often black and immigrant and foreign literature may be more valuable for students, even that no one writer — Shakespeare or Eldridge Cleaver — is essential to everyone's education. For years teachers in the Basic Writing program have assessed books by varied measurements — excellence, simplicity, relevance, revolutionary spirit, seriousness, humorousness. Yet it's still hard for me to grasp the reality of the feeling I encounter often among students, that maybe *nothing* is worth reading. There are explanations: bad school experiences, TV, no books at home, anger at white or American culture, general alienation. But explanations don't help. "I don't like reading" means this to the teacher: I can't count on students reading material which doesn't sell itself, and fairly quickly.

(2) An assumption that most words have a meaning for the student, roughly the same meaning they have for me. During my first semester at the college I was distressed that almost everyone in a Basic Writing 1 class disliked Orwell's "Shooting an Elephant." Later in the term, by accident, I discovered that most students had not understood *despotic, coolie, dominion, futility* and some other words central to the essay. Therefore they had concluded that Orwell was a poor writer, boring. Once a student who had recently immigrated from Hong Kong showed me a page of Dreiser he had prepared for class discussion with the help of his dictionary: tiny characters were drawn above more than thirty words. To a class which included several Chinese, a Korean, and an Afghan, a fellow teacher assigned Dylan Thomas's "Reminiscences of Childhood." Discussion faltered on the passage in which Thomas watches ships "steaming away into wonder and India, magic and China." The Orientals were mystified. What did these four destinations have to do with each other?

(3) An assumption that tone and manner, as well as words, will communicate. "I think that Swift was insane," a second-semester student wrote. "He wanted people to eat children."

(4) An assumption that students are seeing what is written on the page. Surveys show that half the first-graders in the country have perceptual problems. Normally college freshmen have had these corrected; others have been tracked out of reading in school and are rejected by colleges. But Open Admissions is giving some of these junked students a chance. One tense, frowning boy told me that he read very slowly and couldn't write. For two months he did no written work. Finally I persuaded him to go to a clinic, where he discovered that he saw p's as b's, m's as w's, and read most words backwards. Other students, most often those taught by word-recognition methods, find it impossible to figure out the sound or meaning of any polysyllable except the few they meet daily.

Assumptions like these can make a course worthless to a student: they can deaden class hours and taint assignments which will be left undone. But gradually, as I understand the effect of such assumptions more clearly, I can begin to free myself from them in two ways. In any page or book which I consider valuable enough to assign, I can require myself to find an approach usable by people who are unfamiliar with this kind of reading. And at the same time I can be putting my preconceived opinion that this page or that book is valuable to a severe test: the responses of people who don't share my preconception.

It's a simple if uncomfortable task to describe some kinds of reading which have *not* worked out in my classes. During the first SEEK years, students were given a book allowance of $15 per course. In a fit of enthusiasm I assigned twelve paperbacks for one semester. It was a chance to give students the beginning of a personal library — books which, even if we did not get to them in class, had such human resonance that students would discover it for themselves. Hemingway, Kafka, Gandhi, Baldwin, Camus, Fanon. Most of the books went untouched, as I discovered next term in the used section of the bookstore on Amsterdam Avenue. Likewise anthologies, even well made ones like *Black Voices* or *Six Centuries of English Poetry,* have not worked well in my classes. I may have communicated my own ambivalence about using anthologies, especially the fat-priced "college text" species. But also I sense that any writing in large quantities frightens or annoys most Basic Writing students. They don't want it sold to them wholesale.

Some of my favorite books have been failures. I got nowhere with *Dubliners* in a first-semester class. I wanted to avoid belaboring the stories with too many explanations, but students couldn't penetrate the allusions and dialect on their own. I didn't realize how much time was necessary to make the language of the book available. Rilke's *Letters to a Young Poet* reached one out of a class of sixteen students; the others discarded it as turgid or precious. Perhaps the problem was the same as with *Dubliners:* the books were too sympathetic and familiar to me. I didn't make it possible for outsiders to approach the world in which they exist.

In one class, looking for Puerto Rican material, I assigned Piri

Thomas's *Down These Mean Streets*. What little discussion the
book aroused was hostile: the author's street language seemed
contrived. During the next semester a black girl from the class
greeted me on the campus. "We're doing real college work in my
English course this term," she said. "We're reading *Antigone!*"
In another class, during the year in which half of the college was
occupied by the Black and Puerto Rican Students' Coalition, I
assigned a passage from Sorel's *On Revolution*. By day and night,
sentinels, including some class members, were standing guard on
the boulders overlooking St. Nicholas Terrace. Yet Sorel drew the
least capable, most boring writing of the term. His statements
were probably too abstract; certainly his references to European
society were too obscure. But there is another explanation for
some of the resistance which the book met, I think: even students
committed to change do not want to drop all other books for
literature of the barricades.

I have come to question "relevance" — in any simple, where-
things-are-at-man sense — as much as every other simple subject
criterion for choosing assignments. If a teacher can show that he
recognizes blackness, foreignness, deprivation of students and that
he is aware of the literatures of these conditions, students don't
want him to consider them limited to their home territory. Students fear condescension or segregated education. "Don't take it
easy in class," I was told by a leader of the black protesters oc-
cupying the Harlem lot intended for a new government building.
"If you've got something to teach, give it to us. I want to learn to
use words. Can you give me that?"

To list reading assignments which have failed is easy; to list
some which have been successful is more difficult. I've found no
magic books, no secrets that always work. But I have experienced
moments when a student or a whole class were caught up by
something they read. These moments have become touchstones
for me.

In *Sister Carrie* there is a chapter which describes the train trip
which Carrie takes away from the small town where she has lived
all her life into the enormous city of Chicago. Carrie is full of
excited feelings, sensing that "large forces" are taking control of
her life. About this passage a Chinese boy, an engineering student,
wrote, "This kind of feeling has existed in my mind for long

periods of time. One day my mind will explode and life will be different for me. I will be free to go any place I want and I will explore them with my mind." Dreiser's description may have reminded this student of leaving cramped Hong Kong slums; I know that he was bothered by a conflict between respect for and rebellion against his parents. Whatever the causes, this piece of writing enabled him to confront his own experience and his feelings about it.

Because of similar responses from students, one book has been used in Basic Writing courses at City College so often that it has almost become a set text, Richard Wright's *Black Boy*. The popularity of the book does not depend on the fact that it is "black literature": since the merger of SEEK and Open Admissions it has still been used repeatedly. It is valuable, I think, because the fears and hopes of a comprehensible person are presented in available language. For the same reason Baldwin, Cleaver, and some other black writers appear frequently on Basic Writing booklists. They speak of common experiences and feelings in plain, forceful language. Their books, like *Sister Carrie,* make it possible for students to identify aspects of their own humanity, to know more about what it's like to be alive and to be themselves.

Another way in which Basic Writing students get involved with reading has come to me as a surprise — almost against my will. "There's only one book I care much about: it's Lao-tse," said a student in his mid-twenties whom I had been unable to interest in anything for several weeks. He was an East European who had spent five years in an Italian refugee camp before reaching New York. Recently his father had left the family, and he was under pressure to drop out of college to support his mother. "I'd like to write about Lao-tse's ideas of how to live, and to compare them with the way I've met the crises in my own life . . ." One day after class a Venezuelan student who practiced karate every afternoon flagged me down with a piece of notebook paper. "This poem I really like; I carry it with me always." Sweat made his handwriting difficult to read:

> If you can keep your head when all about you
> Are losing theirs and blaming it on you,
> If you can trust yourself when all men doubt you,
> But make allowance for their doubting too . . .

Both of these students were trying to define a moral stance, a way to live in the world.

The Puerto Rican girl who began my course by asking what a short story was, ended it by writing a long essay on *Sons and Lovers*. She wanted to read a novel, and I had told her about Lawrence only after she rejected a number of other authors — I had thought that length, dialect, and the descriptive passages in Lawrence would throw her off. "I'm interested in sex," she said, "in how women relate to men." After four drafts, her essay became a perceptive study of Gertrude, Miriam, and Clara as measured by her own understanding of the nature of women.

The desire of each of these students, the admirers of Lawrence, Kipling, Lao-tse, to explore the practical and ethical issues of their lives in reading makes one uneasy. Doesn't it lead to over-simplifying? to Kiplingesque platitudes, or to moralizing? Yet such approaches to literature clearly are important to students, perhaps most of all to students with the practical difficulties that many Open Admissions students have. And if they are helped past superficial moralizing, to the moral core of a piece of writing — what it says about living — such readings should be significant ones. Wouldn't Lawrence, given his choice of an ideal reader, pick one who was interested in sex?

A third way in which books seem to reach Basic Writing students is through their immediate texture and form — and through the students' fascination at seeing how someone else does this complex act, writing, which they are being required to do themselves every college day. A student whose family had immigrated to this country from Madrid insisted on patterning his own autobiographical essay on Dylan Thomas's "Reminiscences." It was a magnificent style, he felt; he would go and do likewise. The effect on his vocabulary and syntax, a tangle of involute clauses and tentacular images, was disastrous. But he had begun to observe, to manipulate, and to care about the language.

Many students in my classes never experience this awakening to language. The formality of printed pages, the weight of thick books in which one is assigned unending passages can be humiliating or discouraging. But copiers and ditto machines make it possible to use short, compassable pieces of writing, which one can underline and scribble on. One class began to talk about language for the first time when I brought in a poem about the loss of identity of Puerto Ricans in New York copied out of a Young Lords' magazine. The same sort of discovery occurred in the class of another teacher when she introduced lyrics from "Eleanor Rigby." For various purposes, I've handed out passages of Lewis Carroll, cummings, Shakespeare, A. S. Neill, Krishnamurti, Freud, even pages including excerpts from several writers to beg comparisons. Dittoed sheets seem to make subject matter as well as techniques more challengeable, available for either criticism or emulation.

In establishing the mysterious connection between students on the one hand and the rewards and disciplines of writing on the other, one sort of literature almost always works. Its effectiveness is one of the few near-certainties of my experience at the college. This is writing done by the students themselves. One of my classes, lively but somewhat aimless in its first six weeks of meeting, included the *Muhammad Speaks* reporter who had wanted to exempt himself from any exchange of ideas. Halfway through the term he read a story he had written about an injustice suffered by an immigrant family in New York. When the story ended the class sat in silence for a moment, then burst into applause. One student accused the writer of plagiarism. Others defended him. From that session onward the class became a serious workshop, producing a 150-page anthology of stories by the end of term. Students who have shown no interest in other writing frequently begin to praise, criticize, and write themselves when they see the work of classmates. For this inspiration to occur, polished or brilliant writing isn't necessary; rather it seems to happen when someone reads a paper in which he has tried hard to put down personal experience or insights. Then, for another individual or sometimes for a whole class, the connection between one's own life and words written on a page will be made.

Faced by a new class of twenty Basic Writing students, expected to assign reading and to turn out competent writers, I feel no more confidence than I did when I began to teach at City College five years ago. Sure-fire syllabi elude me, and I continue to have students who wander into my classroom and out again unaffected except by some anxiety about sentence fragments. But I have developed a conception of what *ought* to happen to students in these classes.

Students should read in a way which helps them to identify and understand their own thoughts, feelings, and experiences. My bias in assigning reading, in which I differ from many effective teachers in the Basic Writing program, is toward materials which are not primarily logical argument or scientific explanation but which contain personal revelation: autobiography, personal essays, poetry, fiction, students' own writing. Most other departments in the college train students to deal with fact. And few people enrolled in Basic Writing classes have made a connection in high school or at home between printed pages and their own experience. Since many major in engineering and nursing, they are unlikely to make this connection later. Whatever reading causes it to be made is good reading. Such reading must be accessible, not because it is simplified or sensationally relevant, but because with enough class discussion it can speak to the human condition. The number of pages covered doesn't matter. What matters is that a student understands a piece of genuine writing deeply and relates it to his own life.

If this experience occurs in reading, it should lead the student to a desire to explore further by doing his own writing. For Basic Writing students especially, because they lack familiarity with the connection between written words and themselves, writing should constantly be related to reading. They should be writing out their responses to material read. More important, they should be writing about their own ideas, hopes, hatreds, memories in any way their reading suggests. Since these students have as many (or more) fears about writing as the rest of us, the teacher may have to midwife their productions. A colleague in the Basic Writing program has described this process: "Then the teacher must give the student (who, like the teacher, has been running from himself most of his life) an avenue toward self-confrontation. He must shape composition assignments which lead the student to re-examine himself and his life, and he must respect — and respond to — what the student writes, not as an artifact to be judged and analyzed, but as a communication from one human being to another."[1] Is such a teacher a bleeding heart? It's important to real-

1. From an unpublished article which has influenced many of my ideas about Basic Writing, by Leslie Guster of the Department of English, City College of New York.

ize that many Basic Writing students have never trusted a teacher; most have never before done writing in which they were personally involved. One exception was a sensitive Puerto Rican man who showed me a twenty-page journal written for his high school teacher in which he described the difficulties of a love affair. The punctuation was corrected on the first three pages; there were no other marks of any kind until the end. The last page was inscribed: "85. Miss Roth."

Finally, if the student has begun to risk putting his own concerns onto paper and has been caught by the excitement of the process, he will move toward the discipline of using words well. He will be willing to consider the problems of diction, of effective sentences, of clear order. Then he will turn back to reading, to see what other people have done and what methods they have used. I can begin to load him with choice excerpts which show what precision writers have used, and with shelves of classics to show what grand designs they have attempted. He may even come to search, like Matthew Arnold, for all "the best that is known and thought in the world." He will have begun to read for himself.

Of course, I never completely trust this progression which I have outlined, because I don't trust my own ability to begin it or to keep it on course for every student. So I do red-penciling of grammar from the beginning of the first semester, and I push students into reading a new book who I know have not personally encountered the last. But I do feel sure that for most Basic Writing students, who come with little commitment to or experience with either writing or literature, it is a mistake to begin at the end of this progression. I can't begin with a list of important classics, or genres, or contemporary works, or favorites of my own which I expect students to master. The appreciation of literature must be part of a process which includes personal writing for most of these students, because they must gain an initial experience of the value of words in helping to define their own being and becoming. They must have time to discuss and write — and the sort of readings which can kindle this experience. Otherwise they may give up on language as a way to approach life. To find these readings and to make them accessible is the first problem.

ADRIENNE RICH

Teaching Language in Open Admissions:
A Look at the Context

My first romantic notion of teaching came, I think, from reading
Emlyn Williams' play *The Corn Is Green,* sometime in my teens.
As I reconstruct it now, a schoolteacher in a Welsh mining village
is reading her pupils' essays one night and comes upon a paper
which, for all its misspellings and dialect constructions, seems to
be the work of a nascent poet. Turning up in the midst of the undistinguished efforts of her other pupils, this essay startles the
teacher. She calls in the boy who wrote it, goes over it with him,
talks with him about his life, his hopes, and offers to tutor him
privately, without fees. Together, as the play goes on, they work
their way through rhetoric, mathematics, Shakespeare, Latin,
Greek. The boy gets turned on by the classics, is clearly intended
to be, if not a poet, at least a scholar. Birth and family background had destined him for a life in the coal mines; but now
another path opens up. Toward the end of the play we see him
being coached for the entrance examinations for Oxford. I believe
crisis strikes when it looks as if he has gotten one of the village
girls pregnant and may have to marry her, thus cutting short a

257

career of dazzling promise before it has begun. I don't recall the outcome, but I suspect that the unwed mother is hushed up and packed away (I would be more interested to see the play rewritten today as *her* story) and the boy goes off to Oxford, with every hope of making it to donhood within the decade.

Perhaps this represents a secret fantasy of many teachers: the ill-scrawled essay, turned up among so many others, which has the mark of genius, reveals a diamond in the coalbin. And looking at the first batch of freshman papers every semester can be like a trip to the mailbox — there is always the possibility of something turning up that will illuminate the weeks ahead. But behind the larger fantasy lie assumptions which I have only gradually come to recognize; and the recognition has to do with a profound change in my conceptions of teaching and learning.

Before I started teaching at City College I had known only elitist institutions: Harvard and Radcliffe as an undergraduate, Swarthmore as a visiting poet, Columbia as teacher in a graduate poetry workshop that included some of the best young poets in the city. I applied for the job at City in 1968 because Robert Cumming had described the SEEK program to me after Martin Luther King was shot, and the motivation was complex. It had to do with white liberal guilt, of course; and a political decision to use my energies in work with "disadvantaged" (black and Puerto Rican) students. But it also had to do with a need to involve myself with the real life of the city, which had arrested me from the first weeks I began living here.

In 1966 John Lindsay had been able, however obtusely, to coin the phrase "Fun City" without actually intending it as a sick joke. By 1968, the uncollected garbage lay bulging in plastic sacks on the north side of Washington Square, as it had lain longer north of 110th Street; the city had learned to endure the subway strikes, sanitation strikes, cab strikes, power and water shortages; the policeman on the corner had become a threatening figure to many whites as he had long been to blacks; the public school teachers and the parents of their pupils had been in pitched battle. On the Upper West Side poor people were being evicted from tenements which were then tinned-up and left empty, awaiting unscheduled demolition to make room for middle-income housing, for which funds were as yet unavailable; and a squatter movement of considerable political consciousness was emerging in defiance of this uprooting.

There seemed to be three ways in which the white middle class could live in New York: the paranoiac, the solipsistic, and a third, which I am more hesitant to define. By the mid-sixties paranoia was visible and audible: streets of brownstones whose occupants had hired an armed guard for the block and posted notices accordingly; conversations on park benches in which public safety had replaced private health as a topic of concern; conversion of all personal anxieties into fear of the mugger (and the mugger was real, no doubt about it). Paranoia could become a life style, a science, an art, with the active collaboration of reality. Solipsism I encountered first and most concretely in a conversation with an older European intellectual who told me he liked living in New York (on the East Side) because Madison Avenue reminded him of Paris. It was, and still is, possible to live, if you can afford it, on one of those small islands where the streets are kept clean and the pushers and nodders invisible, to travel by cab, deplore the state of the rest of the city, but remain essentially aloof from its causes and effects. It seems about as boring as most forms of solipsism, since to maintain itself it must remain thick-skinned and ignorant.

But there was, and is, another relationship with the city which I can only begin by calling love. The city as object of love, a love not unmixed with horror and anger, the city as Baudelaire and Rilke had previsioned it, or William Blake for that matter, death in life, but a death emblematic of the death that is epidemic in modern society, and a life more edged, more costly, more charged with knowledge, than life elsewhere. Love as one knows it sometimes with a person with whom one is locked in struggle, energy draining but also energy replenishing, as when one is fighting for life, in oneself or someone else. Here was this damaged, self-destructive organism, preying and preyed upon. The streets were rich with human possibility and vicious with human denial (it is breathtaking to walk through a street in East Harlem, passing among the lithe, alert, childish bodies and attuned, observant, childish faces, playing in the spray of a hydrant, and to know that addiction awaits every brain and body in that block as a potential

killer). In all its historic, overcrowded and sweated poverty, the
Lower East Side at the turn of the century had never known this:
the odds for the poor, today, are weighted by heroin, a fact which
the middle classes ignored until it breathed on their own children's lives as well.

In order to live in the city, I needed to ally myself, in some
concrete, practical, if limited way, with the possibilities. So I went
up to Convent Avenue and 133d Street and was interviewed for
a teaching job, hired as a poet-teacher. At that time a number of
writers, including the late Paul Blackburn, Robert Cumming,
Toni Cade Bambara, David Henderson, June Jordan, were being
hired to teach writing in the SEEK program to black and Puerto
Rican freshmen entering from substandard ghetto high schools,
where the prevailing assumption had been that they were of in-
ferior intelligence. (More of these schools later.) Many dropped
out (a lower percentage than the national college dropout rate,
however); many stuck it out through several semesters of remedial English, math, reading, to enter the mainstream of the
college. (208 SEEK students — or 35 to 40 percent — have
since graduated from City College; 24 are now in graduate
school. *None* of these students would have come near higher education under the regular admissions programs of the City University; high school guidance counselors have traditionally written
off such students as incapable of academic work. Most could not
survive economically in college without the stipends which the
SEEK program provides.)

My job, that first year, was to "turn the students on" to writing
by whatever means I wanted — poetry, free association, music,
politics, drama, fiction — to acclimate them to the act of writing,
while a grammar teacher, with whom I worked closely outside of
class, taught sentence structure, the necessary mechanics. A year
later this course was given up as too expensive, since it involved
two teachers. My choice was to enlarge my scope to include
grammar and mechanics or to find a niche elsewhere and teach
verse writing. I stayed on to teach, and learn, grammar — among
other things.

The early experience in SEEK was, as I look back on it, both
unnerving and seductive. Even those who were (unlike me) experienced teachers of remedial English were working on new

frontiers, trying new methods. Some of the most rudimentary questions we confronted were: how do you make standard English verb endings available to a dialect-speaker? how do you teach English prepositional forms to a Spanish-language student? what are the arguments for and against "Black English"? the English of academic papers and theses? Is standard English simply a weapon of colonization? Many of our students wrote in the vernacular with force and wit; others were unable to say what they wanted on paper in or out of the vernacular. We were dealing not simply with dialect and syntax but with the imagery of lives, the anger and flare of urban youth — how could this be *used,* strengthened, without the lies of artificial polish? How does one teach order, coherency, the structure of ideas while respecting the student's experience of his thinking and perceiving? Some students who could barely sweat out a paragraph delivered (and sometimes conned us with) dazzling raps in the classroom: how could we help this oral gift transfer itself onto paper? The classes were small — fifteen at most; the staff, at that time, likewise; we spent hours in conference with individual students, hours meeting together and with counselors, trying to teach ourselves how to teach and asking ourselves what we ought to be teaching.

So these were classes, not simply in writing, not simply in literature, certainly not just in the correction of sentence fragments or the redemptive power of the semicolon; though we did, and do, work on all these. One teacher gave a minicourse in genres; one in drama as literature; teachers have used their favorite books from *Alice in Wonderland* to Martin Buber's *The Knowledge of Man;* I myself have wandered all over the map of my own reading: D. H. Lawrence, W. E. B. DuBois, LeRoi Jones, Plato, Orwell, Ibsen, poets from W. C. Williams to Audre Lorde. Sometimes books are used as a way of learning to look at literature, sometimes as a provocation for the students' own writing, sometimes both. At City College all basic writing teachers have been free to choose the books they would assign (always keeping within the limits of the SEEK book allowance and considering the fact that non-SEEK students have no book allowance at all, though their financial need may be as acute.) There has never been a set curriculum or a required reading list; we have poached off each others' booklists, methods, essay topics, grammar teaching exercises, and anything else that we hoped would "work" for us.[1]

Most of us felt that students learn to write by discovering the validity and variety of their own experience; and in the late 1960's, as the black classics began to flood the bookstores, we drew on the black novelists, poets, and polemicists as the natural path to this discovery for SEEK students. Black teachers were, of course, a path; and there were some who seemed able to combine the work of consciousness-raising with the study of Sophocles, Kafka, and other pillars of the discipline oddly enough known as "English." For many white teachers, the black writers were a relatively new discovery: the clear, translucent prose of Douglass, the sonorities of *The Souls of Black Folk,* the melancholy sensuousness of Toomer's poem-novel *Cane.* In this discovery of a previously submerged culture we were learning from and with our students as rarely happens in the university, though it is happening anew in the area of women's studies. We were not merely exploring a literature and a history which had gone half-mentioned in our white educations (particularly true for those over thirty); we were not merely having to confront in talk with our students and in their writings, as well as the books we read, the bitter reality of Western racism: we also found ourselves reading almost any piece of Western literature through our students' eyes, imagining how this voice, these assumptions, would sound to us if we were they. "We learned from the students" — banal cliché, one that sounds pious and patronizing by now; yet the fact remains that our white liberal assumptions *were* shaken, our vision of both the city and the university changed, our relationship to language itself made both deeper and more painful.[2]

---

1. What I have found deadly and defeating is the anthology designed for multiethnic classes in freshman English. I once ordered one because the book stipends had been cut and I was trying to save the students money. I ended up using one Allen Ginsberg poem, two by LeRoi Jones, and asking the students to write essays provoked by the photographs in the anthology. The college anthology, in general, as nonbook, with its exhaustive and painfully literal notes, directives, questions and "guides for study," is like TV showing of a film—cut, chopped up, and interspersed with commercials: a flagrant mutilation by mass technological culture.

2. Friends of mine who taught the returning GI's after World War II have mentioned somewhat similar reactions: students who had seen and done too much already to be patient with elegant platitudes or with the we're-all-gentlemen-of-leisure posture which has been a sickness of the humanities.

Of course the students responded to black literature; I heard searching and acute discussions of Jones's poem "The Liar" or Wright's "The Man Who Lived Underground" from young men and women who were in college on sufferance in the eyes of the educational establishment; I've heard similar discussions of *Sons and Lovers* or the *Republic*. Writing this, I am conscious of how obvious it all seems and how unnecessary it now might appear to demonstrate by little anecdotes that ghetto students can handle sophisticated literature and ideas. But in 1968, 1969, we were still trying to prove this — we and our students felt that the burden of proof was on us. When the Black and Puerto Rican Student Community seized the South Campus of C.C.N.Y. in April 1969, and a team of students sat down with the president of the college and a team of faculty members to negotiate, one heard much about the faculty group's surprised respect for the students' articulateness, reasoning power, and skill in handling statistics — for the students were negotiating in exchange for withdrawal from South Campus an admissions policy which would go far beyond SEEK in its inclusiveness.

Those of us who had been involved earlier with ghetto students felt that we had known their strength all along: an impatient cutting through of the phony, a capacity for tenacious struggle with language and syntax and difficult ideas, a growing capacity for political analysis which helped counter the low expectations their teachers had always had of them and which many had had of themselves; and more, their knowledge of the naked facts of society, which academia has always, even in its public urban form, managed to veil in ivy or fantasy. Some were indeed chronologically older than the average college student; many, though eighteen or twenty years old, had had responsibility for themselves and their families for years. They came to college with a greater insight into the actual workings of the city and of American racial oppression than most of their teachers or their elite contemporaries. They had held dirty jobs, borne children, negotiated for Spanish-speaking parents with an English-speaking world of clinics, agencies, lawyers, and landlords, had their sixth senses nurtured in the streets, or had made the transition from southern sharehold or Puerto Rican countryside to Bedford-Stuyvesant or the *barrio* and knew the ways of two worlds. And they were becoming, each new wave of them, more lucidly conscious of the politics of their situation, the context within which their lives were being led.

It is tempting to romanticize, at the distance of midsummer 1972, what the experience of SEEK — and by extension, of all remedial freshman programs under Open Admissions — was (and is) for the students themselves. The Coleman Report and the Moynihan Report have left echoes and vibrations of stereotypical thinking which perhaps only a first-hand knowledge of the New York City schools can really silence. Teaching at City I came to know the intellectual poverty and human waste of the public school system through the marks it had left on students — and not on black and Puerto Rican students only, as the advent of Open Admissions was to show. For a plain look at the politics and practices of this system, I recommend Ellen Lurie's *How To Change the Schools*, a handbook for parent activists which enumerates the conditions she and other parents, black, Puerto Rican and white, came to know intimately in their struggles to secure their children's right to learn and to be treated with dignity. The book is a photograph of the decay, racism, and abusiveness they confronted, written not as muckraking journalism but as a practical tool for others like themselves. I have read little else, including the most lyrically indignant prose of radical educators, that gives so precise and devastating a picture of the life that New York's children are expected to lead in the name of schooling. She writes of "bewildered angry teen-agers, who have discovered that they are in classes for mentally retarded students, simply because they cannot speak English," of teachers and principals who "behaved as though every white middle-class child was gifted and was college material, and every black and Puerto Rican (and sometimes Irish and Italian) working-class child was slow, disadvantaged, and unable to learn anything but the most rudimentary facts." She notes that "81 elementary schools in the state (out of a total of 3,634) had more than 70 per cent of their students below minimum competence, and *65 of these were New York City public schools!*" Her findings and statistics make it clear that tracking begins at kindergarten (chiefly on the basis of skin color and language) and that nonwhite and working-class children are assumed to have a maximum potential which fits them only for the so-called general diploma, hence are not taught, as are their middle-class contemporaries, the math or languages or writing skills needed to pass college entrance examinations or even to do academic-diploma high school work.[3] I have singled out these particular points for citation because they have to do directly with our students' self-expectations and the enforced limitation of their horizons years before they come to college. But much else has colored their educational past: the drug pushers at the school gates, the obsolete texts, the punitive conception of the teacher's role, the ugliness, filth, and decay of the buildings, the demoralization even of good teachers working under such conditions. (Add to this Nat Hentoff's recent reporting, in *The Village Voice,* of the use of tranquilizing drugs on children who are considered hyperactive or who present "behavior problems" at an early age.)

To come out of scenes like these schools and be offered "a chance" to compete as an equal in the world of academic credentials, the white-collar world, the world beyond the minimum wage or welfare, is less romantic for the student than for those who view the process from a distance. The student who leaves the campus at three or four o'clock after a day of classes, goes to work as a waitress, or clerk, or hash slinger, or guard, comes home at ten or eleven o'clock to a crowded apartment with TV audible in every corner — what does it feel like to this student to be reading, say, Byron's "Don Juan" or Jane Austen for a class the next day? Our students may spend two or three hours in the subway going to and from college and jobs, longer if the subway system is more deplorable than usual. To read in the New York subway at rush hour is impossible; it is virtually impossible to think.

How does one compare this experience of college with that of the Columbia student down at 116th Street in his quadrangle of gray stone dormitories, marble steps, flowered borders, wide spaces of time and architecture in which to talk and think? Or that of the Berkeley student with his eucalyptus grove and tree-lined streets of bookstores and cafés? The Princeton or Vassar

3. Ellen Lurie, *How To Change the Schools* (New York: Random House, 1970). See pp. 31, 32, 40–48.

student devoting four years to the life of the mind in Gothic serenity? Do "motivation" and "intellectual competency" mean the same for these students as for the City College undergraduate on that overcrowded campus where in winter there is often no place to sit between classes, with two inadequate bookstores largely filled with required texts, two cafeterias and a snackbar that are overpriced, dreary, and unconducive to lingering, with the incessant pressure of time and money driving at him to rush, to get through, to amass the needed credits somehow, to drop out, to stay on with gritted teeth? Out of a graduating class at Swarthmore or Oberlin and one at C.C.N.Y., which students have demonstrated their ability and commitment, and how do we assume we can measure such things?

Sometimes as I walk up 133d Street, past the glass-strewn doorways of P.S. 161, the graffiti-sprayed walls of tenements, the uncollected garbage, through the iron gates of South Campus and up the driveway to the prefab hut which houses the English department, I think wryly of John Donne's pronouncement that "the University is a Paradise; rivers of Knowledge are there; Arts and Sciences flow from thence." I think that few of our students have this Athenian notion of what college is going to be for them; their first introduction to it is a many hours' wait in line at registration, which only reveals that the courses they have been advised or wanted to take are filled, or conflict in hours with a needed job; then more hours at the cramped, heavily guarded bookstore; then, perhaps, a semester in courses which they never chose, or in which the pace and allusions of a lecturer are daunting or which may meet at opposite ends of an elongated campus stretching for six city blocks and spilling over into a former warehouse on Broadway. Many have written of their first days at C.C.N.Y.: "I only knew it was different from high school." What was different, perhaps, was the green grass of early September with groups of young people in dashikis and geles, jeans and tie-dye, moving about with the unquenchable animation of the first days of the fall semester; the encounter with some teachers who seem to respect them as individuals; something at any rate less bleak, less violent, less mean-spirited, than the halls of Benjamin Franklin or Evander Child or some other school with the line painted down the center of the corridor and a penalty for taking the short cut across that line. In all that my students have written about their high schools, I have found bitterness, resentment, satire, black humor; never any word of nostalgia for the school, though sometimes a word of affection for a teacher "who really tried."

The point is that, as Mina Shaughnessy, the director of the Basic Writing Program at City, has written: "the first stage of Open Admissions involves *openly admitting* that education has failed for too many students."[4] Professor Shaughnessy writes in her most recent report of the increase in remedial courses of white, ethnic students (about two-thirds of the Open Admissions freshmen who have below-80 high school averages) and of the discernible fact, a revelation to many, that these white students "have experienced the failure of the public schools in different ways from the black and Puerto Rican students." Another City College colleague, Leonard Kriegel, writes of this newest population: "Like most blue-collar children, they had lived within the confines of an educational system without ever having questioned that system. They were used to being stamped and categorized. Rating systems, grades, obligations to improve, these had beset them all their lives . . . They had few expectations from the world-at-large. When they were depressed, they had no real idea of what was getting them down, and they would have dismissed as absurd the idea that they could make demands. They accepted the myths of America as those myths had been presented to them."[5]

Meeting some of the so-called ethnic students in class for the first time in September 1970, I began to realize that: there *are* still poor Jews in New York City; they teach English better to native speakers of Greek on the island of Cyprus than they do

4. Mina P. Shaughnessy, "Open Admissions — A Second Report" in *The City College Department of English Newsletter,* vol. II no. 1. (January 1972).

5. "When Blue-Collar Students Go to College," in *The Saturday Review,* July 22, 1972. The article is excerpted from the book, *Working Through: A Teacher's Journal in the Urban University* (New York: Saturday Review Press, 1972). Kriegel is describing students at Long Island University of a decade ago; but much that he says is descriptive of students who are now entering colleges like C.C.N.Y. under Open Admissions.

to native speakers of Spanish on the island of Manhattan; the Chinese student with acute English-language difficulties is considered "nonexpressive" and channeled into the physical sciences before anyone has a chance to find out whether he is a potential historian, political theorist, or psychologist; and (an intuition, more difficult to prove) white, ethnic working-class young women seem to have problems of self-reliance and of taking their lives seriously that young black women as a group do not seem to share.

There is also a danger that, paradoxically or not, the white middle-class teacher may find it easier to identify with the strongly motivated, obviously oppressed, politically conscious black student than with the students of whom Kriegel has written. Perhaps a different set of prejudices exists: if you're white, why aren't you more hip, more achieving, why are you bored and alienated, why don't you *care* more? Again, one has to keep clearly in mind the real lessons of the schools — both public and parochial — which reward conformity, passivity, and correct answers and penalize, as Ellen Lurie says, the troublesome question "as trouble-making," the lively, independent, active child as "disruptive," curiosity as misbehavior. (Because of the reinforcement received all around them in society and at home, white female students seem particularly vulnerable to these judgments.) In many ways the damage is more insidious because the white students have as yet no real political analysis going for them; only the knowledge that they are not as successful in high school as white students are supposed to be.

Confronted with these individuals, this city, these life situations, these strengths, these damages, there are some harsh questions that have to be raised about the uses of literature. I think of myself as a teacher of language: that is, as someone for whom language has implied freedom, who is trying to aid others to free themselves through the written word, and above all through learning to write it for themselves. I cannot know for them what it is they need to free, or what words they need to write; I can only try with them to get an approximation of the story they want to tell. I have always assumed, and I do still assume, that people come into the freedom of language through reading, before writing; that the differences of tone, rhythm, vocabulary, intention, encountered over years of reading are, whatever else they may be, suggestive of many different possible modes of being. But my daily life as a teacher confronts me with young men and women who have had language and literature *used against* them, to keep them in their place, to mystify, to bully, to make them feel powerless. Courses in great books or speedreading are not an answer when it is the meaning of literature itself that is in question. As Sartre says: "the literary object has no other substance than the reader's subjectivity; Raskolnikov's waiting is *my* waiting which I lend him . . . His hatred of the police magistrate who questions him is my hatred, which has been solicited and wheedled out of me by signs . . . Thus, the writer appeals to the reader's freedom to collaborate in the production of his work."[6] But what if it is these very signs, or ones like them, that have been used to limit the reader's freedom or to convince him of his unworthiness to "collaborate in the production of the work"?

I have no illuminating answers to such questions. I am sure we must revise, and are revising, our notion of the "classic," which has come to be used as a term of unquestioning idolatry instead of in the meaning which Sartre gives it: a book written by someone who "did not have to decide with each work what the meaning and value of literature were, since its meaning and value were fixed by tradition."[7] And I know that the action from the other side, of becoming that person who puts signs on paper and invokes the collaboration of a reader, encounters a corresponding check: in order to write I have to believe that there is something willing to collaborate subjectively, as opposed to a grading machine out to get me for mistakes in spelling and grammer. (Perhaps for this reason, many students first show the writing they are actually capable of in an uncorrected journal rather than in a "theme" written "for class.") The whole question of *trust* as a basis for the act of reading or writing has only opened up since we began trying to educate those who have every reason to mistrust literary cul-

6. Jean-Paul Sartre, *What Is Literature?* (New York: Harper Colophon Books, 1965), pp. 39–40.
7. *Ibid.*, p. 85.

ture. For young adults trying to write seriously for the first time in their lives, the question "Whom can I trust?" must be an underlying boundary to be crossed before real writing can occur. We who are part of literary culture come up against such a question only when we find ourselves writing on some frontier of self-determination, as when writers from an oppressed group *within* literary culture, such as black intellectuals, or, most recently, women, begin to describe and analyze themselves as they cease to identify with the dominant culture. Those who fall into this category ought to be able to draw on it in entering into the experience of the young adult for whom writing itself — as reading — has been part of the not-me rather than one of the natural activities of the self.

At this point the question of method legitimately arises: How to do it? how develop a working situation in the classroom where trust becomes a reality, where the student is writing with belief in his own validity, and reading with belief that what he reads has validity for him. The question is legitimate — How to do it? — but I am not sure that a description of strategies and exercises, readings, and writing topics can be, however successful they have proven for one teacher. When I read such material, I may find it stimulating and heartening as it indicates the varieties of concern and struggle going on in other classrooms, but I end by feeling it is useless to me. X is not myself and X's students are not my students, nor are my students of this fall the same as my students of last spring. A couple of years ago I decided to teach *Sons and Lovers,* because of my own love of Lawrence, my sense that the novel touches on facts of existence crucial to people in their late teens, and my belief that it deals with certain aspects of family life, sexuality, work, anger, and jealousy which carried over to many cultures. Before the students began to read, I started talking about the time and place of the novel, the life of the mines, the process of industrialization and pollution visible in the slag heaps; and I gave the students (this was an almost all-black class) a few examples of the dialect they would encounter in the early chapters. Several students challenged the novel sight unseen: it had nothing to do with them, it was about English people in another era, why should they expect to find it meaningful to them, and so forth. I told them I had asked them to read it because I believed it was meaningful for them; if it was not, we could talk and write about why not and how not. The following week I reached the classroom door to find several students already there, energetically arguing about the Morels, who was to blame in the marriage, Mrs. Morel's snobbery, Morel's drinking and violence — taking sides, justifying, attacking. The class never began; it simply continued as other students arrived. Many had not yet read the novel, or had barely looked at it; these became curious and interested in the conversation and did go back and read it because they felt it must have something to have generated so much heat. That time, I felt some essential connections had been made, which carried us through several weeks of talking and writing about and out of *Sons and Lovers,* trying to define our relationships to its people and theirs to each other. A year or so later I enthusiastically started working with *Sons and Lovers* again, with a class of largely ethnic students — Jewish, Greek, Chinese, Italian, German, with a few Puerto Ricans and blacks. No one initially challenged the novel, but no one was particularly interested — or, perhaps, as I told myself, it impinged too dangerously on materials that this group was not about to deal with, such as violence in the family, nascent sexual feelings, conflicting feelings about a parent. Was this really true? I don't know; it is easy to play sociologist and make generalizations. Perhaps, simply, a different chemistry was at work, in me and in the students. (During the time that had passed my own relationship to the novel had changed; I found myself increasingly interested in the figures of Clara and Baxter Dawes, less so in Miriam and Mrs. Morel.) The point is that for the first class, or for many of them, I think a trust came to be established in the novel genre as a possible means of finding out more about themselves; for the second class, the novel was an assignment, to be done under duress, read superficially, its connections with themselves avoided wherever possible.

Finally, as to trust: I think that, simple as it may seem, it is worth saying: a fundamental belief in the students is more important than anything else. We all know of those studies in education where the teacher's previously induced expectations dramatically affect the learning that goes on during the semester. This fundamental belief is not a sentimental matter: it is a very demanding matter of realistically conceiving the student where he or she is, and at the same time never losing sight of where he or she *can* be. Conditions at a huge, urban, overcrowded, noisy, and pollution-soaked institution can become almost physically overwhelming at times, for the students and for the staff: sometimes apathy, accidia, anomie seem to stare from the faces in an overheated basement classroom, like the faces in a subway car, and I sympathize with the rush to get out the moment the bell rings. This, too, is our context — not merely the students' past and my past, but this present moment we share. I (and I don't think I am alone in this) become angry with myself for my ineffectualness, angry at the students for their apparent resistance or their acceptance of mediocrity, angriest at the social conditions which dictate that we have to try to repair and extend the fabric of language under conditions which tend to coarsen our apprehensions of everything. Often, however, this anger, if not driven in on ourselves, or converted to despair, can become an illuminating force: the terms of the struggle for equal opportunity are chalked on the blackboard: this is what the students have been up against all their lives.

I wrote at the beginning of this article that my early assumptions about teaching had changed. I think that what has held me at City is not the notion of the diamond in the coalbin, the one or two students in a class whose eyes meet mine with a look of knowing they were born for this struggle with words and meanings; not the poet who has turned up more than once, the real poet, like Aaron Swan or Lloyd Campbell, both of whom I met in my first two years of teaching; though such encounters are a privilege in the classroom as anywhere. What has held me, and what I think holds many who teach basic writing, are the hidden veins of possibility running through students who don't know (and strongly doubt) that this is what they were born for, but who may find it out to their own amazement, students who, grim with self-depreciation and prophecies of their own failure or tight with a fear they cannot express, can be lured into sticking it out to some moment of breakthrough, when they discover that they have ideas that are valuable, even original, and can express those ideas on paper. What fascinates and gives hope in a time of slashed budgets, enlarging class size, and national depression is the possibility that many of these young men and women may be gaining the kind of critical perspective on their lives and the skill to bear witness that they have never before had in our country's history.

At the bedrock level of my thinking about this is the sense that language is power, and that, as Simone Weil says, those who suffer from injustice most are the least able to articulate their suffering, and that the silent majority, if released into language, would not be content with a perpetuation of the conditions which have betrayed them. But this notion hangs on a special conception of what it means to be released into language: not simply learning the jargon of an elite, fitting unexceptionably into the status quo, but learning that language can be used as a means of changing reality.[8] What interests me in teaching is less the emergence of the occasional genius than the overall finding of language by those who did not have it and by those who have been used and abused to the extent that they lacked it.

The question can be validly raised: Is the existing public (or private) educational system, school, or university the place where such a relationship to language can be developed? Aren't those structures already too determined, haven't they too great a stake in keeping things as they are? My response would be, yes, but this is where the *students* are. On the one hand, we need alternate education; on the other, we need to reach those students for whom unorthodox education simply means too much risk. In a disintegrating society, the orthodox educational system reflects disintegration. However, I believe it is more than simply reformist to try to use that system — while it still exists in all its flagrant deficiencies — to use it to provide essential tools and weapons for those who may live on into a new integration. Language is such a weapon, and what goes with language: reflection, criticism, renaming, creation. The fact that our language itself is tainted by the quality of our society means that in teaching we need to be acutely conscious of the kind of tool we want our students to have available, to understand how it has been used against them, and to do all we can to insure that language will not someday be used by them to keep others silent and powerless.

8. Compare Paolo Freire: "Only beings who can reflect upon the fact that they are determined are capable of freeing themselves." *Cultural Action for Freedom,* Monograph Series #1 (Cambridge, Mass.: Harvard Educational Review and Center for the Study of Development and Social Change, 1970).

JOHN PAUL RUSSO

Meaning and Language Training:
The Richards Theory and Method

"Do children learn better with a beginning method that stresses meaning or with one that stresses learning the code?"[1] This question underlies Jeanne S. Chall's important contribution to the knowledge of language training in her *Learning to Read: The Great Debate*. Like the majority of educators in America, she favors the latter approach, learning the code. Let us throughout this essay simply call it decoding. Learning to decode the code is the principle behind most of the methods upon which our education in grammar schools and high schools is largely based. We are taught systems of decoding for many reasons, to advance more quickly, to get a better job, to read for pleasure, to be able to speak and spell correctly. It is not to disparage gains made in educational theory and practice to carry out just these functions that I. A. Richards has set himself so consistently against the basic principle on which their method is founded. He takes exception to Chall's and many another's declared or assumed preference for decoding. He has during the past forty years developed

1. Jeanne S. Chall, *Learning to Read: The Great Debate* (New York: McGraw-Hill, 1967), p. 75.

methods of his own founded on a concept of meaning. This essay will be concerned with his criticism of contemporary reading and language programs, the theory of meaning behind his own methods, and a brief exposition of some cardinal points of these methods in practice. According to Richards, in most cases, what applies to training in beginning reading and writing applies equally well for training in a second language. And so his criticism, theory, and method may be taken to concern language training in a very broad sense, including his program for world literacy.[2]

I suggest reading again the opening question of this essay. Richards uses it as a point of departure in criticizing the work of Chall and the drift of contemporary language training. He finds three chief difficulties with this question: (a) what is meant by stress and emphasis, (b) what does learning the code entail, and (c) what should be understood by meaning. "Stress" and "emphasis," first, suggest foggy thinking and not the kind of rational assessment that should go into such a crucial step in education. These words point to "presence in relative amounts," "quantitative proportions among ingredients in a mixture," or "forces in a composition." Between the interaction of meaning and decoding one should not expect to encounter friendly partners where decoding takes the lead and meaning comes tagging along behind. "And is not our problem much more one of achieving valid insight, or a testable theory, as to how 'meaning' and 'learning the code' interact, as to how each takes part in the development of the other."[3] Chall's treatment of this subject does not meet the need for more precise concepts of meaning, the code, and their interplay.

2. No attempt will be made to treat Richards's work historically. Expositions of the development of his theory and programs as described by himself may be found in *Basic English and Its Uses* (New York: Norton, 1943), and his essays in *The Written Word* (Rowley, Mass.: Newbury House, 1971). For a brief summary of individual works, see my "Bibliography" forthcoming in a *festschrift* on the occasion of Richards's eightieth birthday. An inventory of records, films, tapes, etc., of his language training programs developed with Christine M. Gibson and the staff is in the process of being prepared by Language Research, Inc., Cambridge, Massachusetts.

3. Review of Jeanne S. Chall, *Learning to Read: The Great Debate*, *Harvard Educational Review* (Spring 1969), 359.

Richards's second difficulty with the opening question is, what does "learning the code" really mean. Semaphore, Morse code, even computer programming, may be learned without any thought to the messages sent by them. But understanding depends upon knowing where codes are succeeding or failing. Decoding as the educational objective does not distinguish between the illusion of thinking step by step and thinking itself. Too often methods of language training treat the learner as a communication model for decoding as efficiently as possible, without distortion. In this way the mind does not take advantage of what Coleridge called its "modes of intellectual energy," its own active powers, and the development of the mind's growing knowledge of the use (and through the use) of these powers is frequently the animus behind the learner's eagerness to learn itself. Learning the code implies the processing of units of information. We have an apt parallel from contemporary communication theory. The theory has made advances by representing "the various elements involved as mathematical entities" and information as a "measure of one's freedom of choice in selecting messages." But the semantic aspects of communication are "irrelevant to the engineering problem."[4] The processes of thought, however, involve the words (the sign) and that toward which they point (the signified). Meaning is imbedded in the relation between sign and signified; it may hover beyond the signified itself in lines like "There is a willow grows askant the brook," or "But no, I was out for stars, / I would not come in." At the level of beginning reading as well as in the study of poetry, and in order to begin aright the study of poetry, both units, code and meaning, must be shown to be involved, dependent, and of use, and much more than of use, in explicating each other. A student who cannot distinguish easily between information and meaning may end by distorting the information in the process of decoding it. He must ask how the word is shifting its meaning in its new context from meanings it had in other remembered contexts *or* from its dictionary defini-

4. Claude E. Shannon and Warren Weaver, *The Mathematical Theory of Communication* (Urbana: University of Illinois Press, 1948), pp. 99, 3. See I. A. Richards, "The Future of Poetry," *The Screens and other Poems* (New York: Harcourt Brace, 1960), pp. 109–111; and "Toward a Theory of Comprehending," in *Speculative Instruments* (Chicago: University of Chicago Press, 1955).

tion; whether the word is being used for lack of a better one and thus is more likely to be mistaken; whether a literal or a figurative sense is implied, and so forth.

A third difficulty lies in Richards's questioning of the source and destination of the code. We assume that there is a direct path, from the intake of letters, words, utterances, up to the fluent use of the language. Aren't we, in learning a code, at the same time learning a Code? And since we most certainly are, then ought we not to be very careful in knowing just what Code we want to teach, one that teaches the mind how to use its powers self-critically, morally, usefully. We are not the source of *the* Code in this larger sense; it lies in convention, tradition, nature. As Wordsworth writes in *The Prelude:*

> Hard task to analyse a soul, in which
> Not only general habits and desires,
> But each most obvious and particular thought,
> Not in a mystical and idle sense,
> But in the words of reason deeply weigh'd
> Hath no beginning.

In teaching a language Richards believes one could and should teach thinking, common sense, and even a world position, "Where should man go?"[5] For just as we are not the source, we are not the destination of the Code. Our language used wisely carries forward through us, its interpretants, our moral and intellectual spirit. To this spirit, best preserved in poetry and philosophy, succeeding generations must, Richards says in "The Future of Poetry," make their own contribution.[6] Humanity advances, remarked Goethe, man remains the same.

The last difficulty with the opening question is the concept of "meaning." An adequate theory of meaning does not operate in beginning or second language programs. Richards sees many reasons why from the start, in learning a second form of notation

5. B. A. Boucher and J. P. Russo, "I. A. Richards: An Interview," *Harvard Advocate* (December 1969), 7.
6. "The Future of Poetry," p. 112.

(script), or a second language, the learner should be able to take advantage of powers he had already harnessed when he learned the earlier form of symbology, speech. The control of ear and tongue involved a mastery of two channels; adding a third and fourth (reading and writing) should proceed along lines that involved the most successful elements in the mastery of the first two, a point to which I shall return below. "We shall learn," writes Coleridge, "to value earnestly and with a practical seriousness a mean, already prepared for us by nature and society, of teaching the young mind to think well and wisely by the same unremembered process and with the same never forgotten results, as those by which it is taught to speak and converse."[7] These words, Richards reminds us, are set within his criticism of Wordsworth, who is praised for his "perfect appropriateness of words to their meaning."

Through the study of meaning a child may learn far better than through decoding how to think on his own, to develop the habit of self-criticism, discernment, a more creative use of his imagination, a mode of understanding and checking his own thinking and that of others. To clarify the problem, Richards uses a diagram of a triangle with the three factors, the spoken word, the written word, and meaning, at the corners, and the relations between the three factors symbolized by the sides. Thus, the relations between the spoken and written word (the decoding of symbols into sounds) are labeled c. The relations between the written word and meaning (the interpretation of written words) are labeled b. The great debate of which Chall and others write has largely been given over to b and c, whereas "emphasis" should fall on a, the relation between the spoken word and meaning.[8] The purpose of linguistic exercises is to see just "how the meaning of a word or sentence varies with the setting"; to understand that what "any feature in any utterance is (or can do) comes to it from its relations to the possible alternates"; and to recognize that "to the ear a spoken sentence is more like a fluctuant,

7. *Biographia Literaria,* chap. XXII. Quoted in Richards's review of Chall's work; see note 3.
8. Review of Chall, p. 360.

resonant pulse of our inner history, gone by almost before it is completed."[9]

Meaning is the cornerstone of Richards's theory of language training. The development of this theory goes back to 1918 when his long collaboration with the Cambridge polymath C. K. Ogden began. Their early collaboration culminated with the publication of *The Meaning of Meaning* in 1923, much of which had been published earlier in Ogden's *Cambridge Magazine*. Its descriptive subtitle ran: "A Study of the Influence of Language upon Thought and the Science of Symbolism." In years following they went their separate ways, Richards developing his theory into a theory and method of literary criticism (*Principles of Literary Criticism,* 1924, and *Practical Criticism,* 1929), Ogden designing Basic English, a systematically simplified version of English based on 850 key words. In the 1930's Richards's experience in teaching English in China led him from literary criticism to creating introductory courses in reading. The design of Basic English was ready at hand. Much in the way of teaching it remained to be done. Richards would invent methods for teaching it (*Basic in Teaching: East and West,* 1935, *Basic English and Its Uses,* 1943, the "Language Through Pictures" series, 1945–), for showing how it could be used to refine one's mental faculties (*Basic Rules of Reason,* 1933, *How to Read a Page,* 1942), for using it for translating important works of literature for newcomers to the language (*Plato's Republic,* 1942, *The Wrath of Achilles,* 1950, *Why so, Socrates?* [Plato's dialogues on the death of Socrates] 1964), and for adapting it to developing media (record, slide, film, tape, television, cassette). The publicity that Winston Churchill gave to Basic English in his speech at Harvard in September 1942 carried the movement forward, although methods of teaching

9. "What Is Involved in the Interpretation of Meaning?" *Reading and Pupil Development: Proceedings of the Conference on Reading Held at the University of Chicago* (Chicago: University of Chicago Press, 1940), II, 51; "Functions of and Factors in Language," forthcoming in *Journal of Literary Semantics,* 1; "Literature, Oral-Aural and Optical," a talk delivered over BBC radio, 5 Oct. 1947 (unpublished), p. 1; the reader is also referred to "Stock Responses and Irrelevant Associations," *Practical Criticism: A Study of Literary Judgment* (London: Kegan Paul, 1929).

Basic had not advanced far enough to take much advantage of this publicity. With this brief historical introduction we turn to the theory.

Messages are generated by contexts. They are the living instances of meaning issuing from a context of interconnecting signs or words. But a word derives its meaning not only within the context of a specific utterance. It has its meaning from all its past places in specific contexts; a word's context is a "certain recurrent pattern of past events, and to say that its meaning depends on its context would be to point to the process by which it has acquired its meaning."[10] The dictionary provides the routine definitions of its meaning in its most frequent contexts. We must keep both of these senses of context in mind. Both form the principle of "sentence in situation" which guides Richards's reading programs.

To interpret the meaning of a context one must have a variety of parallels from one's past experience in order to "guide one's choice and construct the meaning." Similarly, in teaching reading, the sequence of sentences in situations must be prepared so that each new step can be taken by means of knowledge previously gained. Wrong or distorted interpretation by the learner derives from three main causes: either we lack the appropriate parallels in our experience, or we cannot or will not let them help and guide us. "Meaning" itself may be used as an example to understand meaning. Is not the commonest parallel that exists for basic understanding a parallel between it and sense perception? In an essay written for a conference on reading at the University of Chicago and published in 1940, Richards uses the example of a penny lying on the floor. It is seen as a certain shape, size, distance, angle to the eye, and so forth. These characteristics belong to it at the moment we perceive it to be a penny. We *see* a round penny. "We equally see (in a slightly changed sense of 'see') a certain elliptical patch of color and interpret that patch as a sign of a penny." That sign and its whole sign-field *means* penny to us. The same holds true for the print in a book. Through the black marks "we see what the sentence means just as we see the penny through the elliptical brown patch which is the sign of the penny." In both cases we are dependent on the sign and the whole sign-

10. I. A. Richards, *Interpretation in Teaching* (New York: Harcourt Brace, 1938), p. ix.

field in which it is set. The same brown ellipse might be a manhole cover fifty yards away. The same black marks in another paragraph might be a very different remark. Furthermore, until we experiment we suppose that "with the brown patch, its shape at least — the degree of its ellipticity — will be constant, that this is fixed by the angle of its tilt." But this is not so. "If we have reasons to believe that the thing is 'really round,' we see the ellipse as more nearly circular than it is. The pressure of the context, the influences of the sign-field, distort it for us." The reasons come through the sign-field from experience with similar sign-fields in the past. The sign-field alters perception of the sign. If we look through a tube that permits us to see simply the brown ellipse, we cut out the distortion, but also our means of interpreting the signs. Size, shape, distance, angle are lost. "We no longer perceive a penny but merely have a sign-vehicle waiting for a sign-field to link it up with past parallels through which we may interpret it."[11]

The same parallel may be made for language. The words that surround a word are a part of the sign-field. In a purely visual sense, at the bottom of hierarchies of meaning, they can lead a reader and a proofreader into error. In the sign-field of meaning, too, the word is reined in by a context, the context is reined in by the word. By itself a word (which is not an utterance) has too many meanings, and hence no meaning. The dictionary provides the most routine list of the commonest definitions *(de fine)* taken from the contexts in which it has been "found." Context pressures the meanings of words in one or another direction. But contexts themselves build from immediately preceding contexts and are altered by immediately succeeding contexts, and so forth, backwards and forwards, from sentence to paragraph, and so on. (Richards would later employ the computer *feedback* and invent the term *feedforward* to label just these operations.) Thus, if "we have reasons to believe that a man is talking about *X,* we are already prepared for the distortions of words in that direction." For this reason the study of misinterpretation makes up half of Richards's work in language training. We recall that half of *Practical Criticism* was comprised of misinterpretations of thirteen

11. "What Is Involved," pp. 49–50.

poems and Richards's commentary on their cause. "To find out why something was mis-read is illuminating and confirms human reason, human capacity for paralleling."[12]

Language about language, it has been said, must share in the ambiguities of language. In approaching meaning we need critical instruments that will enable the new reader to see what sorts of work language is doing in a given context. When Richards was designing reading programs he already had at his disposal the results of years of research in psychology and criticism. In *The Meaning of Meaning,* for example, he and Ogden together formulated, among other functions of language, the concepts of symbolic and emotive language. Though often found together, these two functions of linguistic work, if you will, were found to have specific properties: symbolic (later "referential") language applied to strict scientific prose. If the question, "Is this true or false in the ordinary scientific sense?" was at all relevant, then the language was symbolic. The term *emotive* was applied to the language that was used to evoke emotions, attitudes, to employ ideas whose principle function was to arouse a state of mind, richly complex and yet reaching toward equilibrium. Later, in *Practical Criticism,* refining the theory, he distinguished among four functions of language: the sense of the words (picking up the earlier symbolic use), feeling (from the earlier emotive use), tone (the attitude or point of view of the speaker to his audience), and overall intention, in which blends a whole that could be "different" from the parts. Finally, his experience in designing reading programs led him to increase the number of functions from four to seven; even an eighth has been considered. There is nothing at all magical about the numbers. As he pointed out in a recent lecture, one may define as many functions of linguistic work as one likes provided that each function may be clearly distinguished from all the others (Roman Jakobson, in fact, distinguishes six). The seven functions Richards defines in *Speculative Instruments* (1955) are:[13]

12. *Ibid.,* p. 50.
13. "Toward a Theory of Comprehending." Many of these functions are adumbrated in *The Meaning of Meaning* (1923), 2nd ed. (New York: Harcourt Brace, 1927), pp. 10–11.

1. Pointing to: what is the subject under discussion in the context.
2. Saying about: what is being said about the subject.
3. Presenting: is the utterance realizing itself or not in its effect on the addressee.
4. Valuing: how do the addresser and addressee value what is being said.
5. Adjusting: the *so what?* "How we would adjust something to us — or us to it as a result of it."
6. Managing: how all of the above are working together for the purpose of . . .
7. Purposing: the overall intention behind the message. Is it being carried through intact from addresser to addressee? What, if any, are the distortions along the channel blocking intention?

In strict scientific prose, functions 1 and 2 predominate; in poetry, 3, 4, and 5 play much larger roles. How are these functions aiding, checking, collaborating with each other in the channel? How are the first five managed (6)? In what ways could adjustments be made to better carry forward 7? How is quintessential meaning carried by and through its context? These are the questions that should be asked in designing beginning reading programs and in the most sophisticated literary analysis.

Now to the method itself. Its premise is that the exploration of sound-letter and simple sentence relations for themselves can be combined with the study of meaning. "Teaching a language effectively consists of inventing, arranging, presenting, and testing" sentences in situations. The use of words in clear verifiable statements has to be geared to the beginning reader's capacity. It is found, however, that second language training, though faster, works best if the order of the beginning reader's entry into reading is followed. The features of the Richards method are:

(1) *Sequencing*. Experimentation with seven languages and the "Language Through Pictures" experiment convinced Richards of an ideal order in which sentences in situation (sen-sit) should be arranged. This order is subject to four conditions: the ambiguity of each sen-sit is minimal; each sen-sit prepares for the next one; each sen-sit is confirmed by those that follow; disturbance of the new sen-sit by those taught before is kept to a minimum. Sequencing allows the child or newcomer to have an easy progress and

at the same time to realize that the answer that he seeks may be found in what he has already absorbed. Under the strictest sequencing even error can be valuable if the learner can see where he went wrong and how he can get back on track. A sequence of sen-sits becomes a qualitative matter of relationships among parts *within* the sequence. It is not a quantitative matter of memorizing a number of letters, words or phrases. To give one example, a chief feature in the sequencing should be contrast in space and in time:

		above.
I am here.		I am
I am there.		I am
		below.

I was there.	I am here.	I will be there.
He was there.	He is here.	He will be there.

These initial oppositions can be simply enacted and demonstrated to and by the new learners. Opposition and comparison are two of the chief intellectual tools at our disposal in thinking ("human reason, human capacity for paralleling") and they should be built into the earliest stages of the language training progam.

(2) *Letter and word intake*. The components of the sequence must be introduced progressively. If one begins with, say, ten letters rather than the full complement of twenty-six, the child's opportunity for easy entry into this difficult task is greatly increased. In the Language for Learning program, a thirteen minute film encodes six sentences after presenting them orally and displaying their meaning with simple stick-figure drawings. The learner hears and repeats the sentences, grasps their meaning, and observes a hand writing them letter by letter on the screen. The letters used are *a d e h i m n r s t*. Twenty-two related sentences are introduced with these letters only. In the next film the pace slackens, only seven of the ten letters are introduced, *e d r* being added later. Since there are letters which we are likely to confuse (*p* and *q; p* and *b; b* and *d; u* and *n*), care is taken to postpone the introduction of "rival" letters. Again, the principle of opposition is employed:

This is a *man*.	This is a hand.
This is a *hat*.	This is a head.

"This is a" remains the constant, a pointing formula. It is undistracting because it is always the same, and attention may be given to the four familiar nouns. Furthermore, comparison may be presented visually: *man* keeps level — *hat* has initial and terminal peaks   ; the middle of the words, *a,* remains the same. Later, *b* and *d* may be contrasted by showing the word *bed,* which does in fact have the shape of a bed.

(3) *Depiction and channel interplay.* Television and film, Richards believes, are the answer to world illiteracy. But we should not be mechanical in the use of machines. Too often the use of mixed media to aid language training proceeds along the line of the "clue for intelligent guesses" (Chall's phrase). What a picture can do is "to enable a hypothesis to validate or invalidate itself from nothing more than careful observation or comparison." Channel interplay is one of Richards's novel theoretical tools. Three perceptual channels are used in concert: the eye attempting to see marks on paper; the ear attempting to sense the sounds; the vocal organs attempting to repeat the sounds. Writing develops the fourth channel. Channels are taught to check and control one another. When three or four channels are operating, as when a child is manipulating a computerized teaching machine, one channel may help another that is lagging, and the child who corrects himself and thus advances enjoys the confidence that results from self-corrigibility. Bentham said that push-pin could give us much pleasure as poetry; Richards believes beginning reading can be as much fun as pinball.

The following channels are operating in beginning reading:[14]

(a) how a child hears sounds "interplaying" with how he would say them;
(b) how a child sees the marks on paper "interplaying" with how he would make them;
(c) what he thinks they mean "interplaying" with what he can do about it.

"All his life meaning has been for him something he can do about *it:* about the situation which supports and prospers the meaning." When he was learning speech, the child found the elements of (c)

14. These examples are taken from a speech delivered by Richards at the Brookline Reading Institute, 1 March 1969.

to be in closest mutual control of one another. In learning to read, "Meaning" and "what he can do about it" are vitally operative, and should provide the method with its guiding principle.

(4) *Similarity programming.* Another novel instrument is Richards's use of similarity programming which is meant to contrast with contiguity programming. In the latter the problem for the learner is a filling in of the missing piece of information:

$$a \quad b \quad c \quad ? \quad e \quad f \quad g$$

In similarity programming, on the other hand, the problem consists of supplying an analogous part to an incomplete whole:

$$a \quad : \quad c \quad :: \quad e \quad : \quad ?$$

Both contiguity and similarity programming work together. But similarity is preferred because it encourages in the learner a wider search for guiding parallels in sameness and difference, "identity of structure ordering diversities of material." It leads a student to ask himself, "what is the problem?" Contiguity programming on the other hand tends toward blind automatic memory, much of which may be irrelevant and time-wasting — and discouraging. Both approaches can be used together and are far preferable to the memorization of rules of grammar and phrases.

(5) *Machines.* In his *Design for Escape,* subtitled *World Education Through Modern Media,* Richards leads us to ponder that our only escape now may be the instruments that, thus far, have tended to corrupt us. The most capable channels for teaching are film, tape, records, picture-text, and television, and from the early 1930's Richards's methods have kept pace with the swift development of modern media and machines down to computers. In 1964 and 1965 Richards and Christine Gibson collaborated on research into reading failure sponsored by the U.S. Office of Education. Their report, "Development of Experimental Audio-Visual Devices and Materials," concludes that television could be made to fill the gap in early language training for many underprivileged children and at the same time be used to augment present reading programs. Part of this report contains a detailed study of the use of teaching machines in the Harvard-Arlington mobile laboratory

for helping fourth-grade underachievers. "Some have thought that radical enough *experimentation* with new offerings for new audiences — in Africa and elsewhere — might be the way to TV's *second chance,* everywhere," he writes in *Design for Escape,* concluding with Shelley's prediction:

> And lovely apparitions, — dim at first
> Then radiant, as the mind, arising bright
> From the embrace of beauty . . . casts on them
> The gathered rays which are reality —
> Shall visit us, the progeny immortal
> Of Painting, Sculpture, and rapt Poesy,
> And arts, though unimagined, yet to be:
> The wandering voices and the shadows these
> Of all that man becomes . . .

"Should we not place, among these unimagined arts, Cinema and TV . . . ?"[15]

(6) *Translation.* For beginning or more advanced readers, Richards recommends the exercise of translation, particularly within the same language: English into English (or into Basic English). The original text is not meant to be disparaged by this operation. Rather, by being obliged to seek out possible alternatives along lines of "experimental change" and "comparison," one makes of the translation a genuine elucidating of the original. In the translating process one may observe the various types of control under which the choice of options is made, the deeper principles guiding these choices, and the details in the process of discriminating. Basic English is a favored medium because of its simplicity, the clarity of its design, its well-defined choices.[16] Richards himself has translated Homer's *Iliad,* the Book of Job, five dialogues of Plato, including the *Republic,* and passages from many other literary and technical texts into Basic English or slightly expanded versions of it. Such pieces have been useful in

15. *Design for Escape: World Education Through Modern Media* (New York: Harcourt Brace, 1968), pp. 23, 30.
16. For an interesting point of view on the reductionism of Basic, see Fredric Jameson, *The Prison-House of Language: A Critical Account of Structuralism and Russian Formalism* (Princeton, N.J.: Princeton University Press, 1972), p. 32.

providing newcomers to English with first-rate literature, admittedly in much-simplified form. "Drafting a Basic version, or even studying one, does at least give us an exceptional opportunity to ask ourselves persistently not only what such a passage . . . is saying but how far what it says is true."[17] Is true — in Richards's language training as in his criticism as a whole we come face to face with self-criticism. The texts and the techniques we employ to mine them help us evaluate ourselves even as we probe and silently pass judgment upon them. In so many of the methods he describes, the teacher and the student are to be found in the same person since, upon broad humanistic lines, the process and the goal is self-corrigibility.

17. I. A. Richards and Christine M. Gibson, *Learning Basic English: A Practical Handbook for English-Speaking People* (New York: Norton, 1945), p. 96. As an experiment I shall translate our key passage from Coleridge, cited above, into Basic. This passage points to the advantages of language that can be rewon again and again, with increasing power, advantages that are always only partially realized:

the advantages which language . . . with incomparably greater ease and certainty than any other means,	the powers which words have to work with . . . with far more free play and fixed value than any other ways,
presents to the instructor of impressing modes of intellectual energy so constantly, so imperceptibly,	gives to the teacher for placing deeply in mind designs for thinking with both substance and structure, nearly always, strongly but smoothly,
and as it were by such elements and atoms,	with increasing effect and even by small parts and properties,
as to secure in due time the formation of a second nature . . .	as after the right time to lead to the building of a new nature, a second self . . .
we shall learn to value earnestly and with a practical seriousness	we will know very well why we should value with seriousness and a clean sense of direction
a mean, already prepared for us by nature and society,	a middle way, even now present by our nature, by our history, our education, and our society,
of teaching the young mind to think well and wisely	of teaching the young mind to work by conscious purpose and with highest quality and goodness

by the same unremembered process and with the same never forgotten results,

by the same ways now lost to memory, but with the same effects still operating in the mind,

as those by which it is taught to speak and converse.

as those by which that person had his first experience with language itself.